Invisible Factories

SUNY Series in the Anthropology of Work
June C. Nash, Editor

Invisible Factories:

The Informal Economy and Industrial Development in Spain

LAUREN BENTON

State University of New York Press

Published by
State University of New York Press, Albany

Printed in the United States of America

For information, address State University of New York
Press, State University Plaza, Albany, N.Y., 12246

Library of Congress Cataloging-in-Publication Data

Benton, Lauren A.
      Invisible factories: the informal economy and industrial
   development in Spain / Lauren A. Benton.
            p.   cm. — (SUNY series in the anthropology of work)
      Bibliography: p.
      Includes index.
      ISBN 0-7914-0223-1 — ISBN 0-7914-0224-X (pbk.)
      1. Informal sector (Economics)—Spain.   2. Spain—Industries.
I. Title.   II. Series.
HD2346.S7B46   1990
338.0946—dc20   89-4543
                                                                      CIP

10   9   8   7   6   5   4   3   2   1

For my parents,
Charlotte Russ Benton and George Stock Benton

Contents

Tables

Acknowledgments

Friends, colleagues, government officials, and even strangers in Spain seemed to join in a friendly conspiracy to help me with this book. I had the good fortune to meet Manuel Castells in Madrid in the early stages of the project and benefitted throughout from his encouragement and advice. At the Ministry of Economy, Miguel Muñiz and Anselmo Calleja invited me to collaborate on several government research projects on the informal economy and allowed me to draw freely from the data. I learned a great deal from working with them and with Diego Ramos, José Ramón Lorente, Santos Ruesga, Rosa Conde, and Felipe Saez. In Madrid, Antonio Estevan guided my entry into the electronics industry and generously shared his data with me; in Alicante, José María Bernabé and Josep-Antoni Ybarra took time out from their own important work on the informal economy to help me locate materials and informants.

The success of the field study for this work depended, of course, on the generous cooperation of the many people I interviewed. I am grateful to the employees and entrepreneurs who interrupted their work to answer the questions of a curious foreigner, most of the time with graciousness and enthusiasm. Batiste Pérez, Gaspar Agulló, and other labor leaders I interviewed patiently and cheerfully endured repeated visits. Miguel Angel Pascual, then president of the Neighborhood Association of the Pozo del Tío Raimundo, in Madrid, was always eager to share with me his firsthand knowledge of neighborhood, city, and party politics.

Many people on the other side of the Atlantic also deserve thanks. I owe a special debt to Alejandro Portes, who introduced me to the topic, supported all my efforts, and allowed me to make my own mistakes. Without the insights and encouragement of Charles Sabel, I might never have looked beyond the obvious. Sidney Mintz read an early draft with great care and, along with Richard Kagan, Katherine Verdery, and many other faculty members and students in the Departments of History and Anthropology at Johns Hopkins

University and the Department of Urban Studies and Planning at MIT, contributed comments, criticism, and moral support. I thank these friends and colleagues, who of course are responsible for none of the book's shortcomings.

Thanks but no blame also must go to the institutions and programs that funded the research: the International Doctoral Research Fellowship Program for Western Europe of the Social Science Research Council and the American Council of Learned Societies; the Fulbright Foundation and the Joint Committee on Cultural and Educational Exchange between Spain and the United States; and the Wenner Gren Foundation for Anthropological Research. Preliminary research in Spain was supported by the Council for European Studies.

Portions of several chapters are reprinted, with permission of the publishers, from some of my articles. They are: "Decentralized Industry and the Limits to State Planning," in *Urban Anthropology*, Vol. 17, No. 4, 1989; "Gender Roles and Industrial Development," in *World Development*, Vol. 17, No. 2, 1989; "Industrial Subcontracting and the Informal Sector: Restructuring in the Madrid Electronics Industry," in *The Informal Economy: Comparative Studies in Advanced and Developing Countries*, edited by Alejandro Portes, Manuel Castells, and Lauren Benton, Baltimore: Johns Hopkins University Press, 1989; and "La Informalización de la Industria Española: Trabajo No Reglamentado y Desarrollo Industrial," in *Papeles de Economía Española*, No. 26, 1986. The Ministry of Economy in Spain kindly extended permission to reprint sections from my report *Trabajo a Domicilio en España*, published in Madrid in 1986; I am the report's sole author.

My parents, my friends in Cambridge and New York, and my best friend, Eduardo Garcia Urbin, are fully responsible for the distractions that made working on the book often impossible and, ultimately, possible. I will try to repay them in kind.

Introduction

On a residential back street of the Spanish city of Elda, the sounds of midmorning include the hum and whir of industrial machinery coming, it seems, from behind every other door. In house parlors, second-story apartments, garages, and store fronts, men and women are bent over cutting tables, sewing machines, and the heavy equipment used for mounting shoes on wooden lasts. In one garage, shoes slide along a small production line; the air in the tight, poorly ventilated place is thick with fumes of glue. Vans appear and disappear on the otherwise quiet street, as they pick up piecework to deliver to homeworkers or return with completed batches. There are no whistles, no lunch wagons, no workers in the traditional blue overalls, and no placards announcing the names of firms. The familiar sights of an industrial center are entirely missing, and yet industrial work is everywhere.

On the outskirts of Madrid, 400 kilometers away, the tiny town of Paracuellos del Jarama is perched on a bluff above the Jarama River. Several hundred small firms occupy the riverbank below. The land in the makeshift industrial park is zoned only for agricultural uses, and the roads are unpaved and difficult to traverse in wet weather. At the top of a steep track winding up the bluff, a firm of seven people—five of them working "off-the-books"—is producing electronics components in a ramshackle building filled with secondhand and homemade machinery.

Such scenes are not typical of the images we associate with modern industry. Yet the enterprises are not vestiges of artisan production from an earlier area. Not far from the residential-industrial side street of Elda, one can find large, modern factories whose doors have closed. Most of the workers in the busy garage-workshops used to be employed in such factories, and they are still producing parts of high-fashion shoes for export to Europe and the United States. Outside Madrid, the new firms dotting the landscape have little in common with cottage industry, although

1

many of them are poorly endowed subcontractors. The small, seven-man workshop that is precariously placed on the slopes of the bluff in Paracuellos del Jarama is making medium-quality printed circuits for some of the country's largest electronics producers.

Both scenes are evidence of productive decentralization, a process that has proceeded at a particularly rapid pace in Spain in the past decade but also clearly has counterparts in many other parts of the world. An explosion of subcontracting, an increase in the numbers and varieties of home-based producers, a proliferation of small-scale firms, and a surge in off-shore production—these trends have been documented in settings as different from one another as urban Ohio and rural Sri Lanka. The decentralization of industrial tasks is, of course, itself hardly new. Even the earliest examples of factory production relied on industrial outworkers to perform some jobs, and the type and amount of subcontracting have always varied by industry, as well as within particular industries over time. But the recent trend of restructuring has some novel features. In the contemporary industrial landscape, the shadow of the large, centralized factory is often now simply missing. Industrial outwork, always an option that large firms could use to minimize risk in uncertain markets and reduce the costs of seasonal adjustments, is now the dominant feature of many production processes. The scaffold of the industrial structure has changed its shape, and the organization of industrial labor, together with its meaning to participants, has altered in the process.

Present for the first time, too, is a large, ambitious state that has pacted in the postwar era with business to regulate the cyclical swings of capitalist growth and with labor to oversee the terms and conditions of industrial employment. Decentralization in the 1970s and 1980s injects a new, unpredictable element into the state's calculations about how to foment and monitor industrial growth. Policies that were developed during the decades of postwar economic expansion in the advanced economies no longer seem viable, while in developing countries, a tradition of centralized, state-led development schemes seems outmoded. National interest-group leaders find, too, that they can no longer look to familiar guideposts for their actions. Particularly for industrial labor leaders, the new environment calls for novel forms of organizing that cannot build easily on workers' past experiences of protest nor rely on traditional bargaining positions. In short, we are witnessing not only a new chapter in bargaining over the distribution of the costs and benefits of industrialization, but a realignment of the alliances underlying the broad regulatory context for industrial growth.[1]

We have new ground to break in studying this shift because productive decentralization in industry was not predicted in standard economic theories. Marx and the classical economists he criticized shared a similar vantage point in history, and both looked back to observe the increasing scale of production and its progressive centralization as features inherent in the very nature of capitalist growth. One tradition of economic thought thereafter continued to echo Adam Smith's prediction of ever-greater specialization in the division of labor within the factory; another tradition, founded by Marx, portrayed the factory system as the culmination of capital's quest to separate the means of production from workers and appropriate their skills.[2]

Inherent in both perspectives was a tendency to view industrialization as a predictable process guided by the built-in logic of capitalist growth. For mainstream economists, this understanding was tied to a vision of "classic" industrialization that was based loosely on the historical experiences of England and the United States. Developing economies would grow by emulating the rise of mass production in the advanced countries, where growth would, in turn, be preserved by extending the principles of factory organization to every corner of the economy. For Marxist scholars, capitalist expansion was a relentless process that reflected the necessary search for wider markets, new arenas for investment, and an ample supply of free labor. Neither perspective could account for the resilience and vitality of alternative forms of production, except to suggest that they acted to fulfill certain systemic "needs" or discontinuities that arose in transplanting the principles of classic capitalist industrialization from one country, or from one sector, to another.[3]

The experience of recent industrial restructuring compels us to view industrialization as a far more complex and open-ended process than either of these approaches implied. In advanced economies, the crisis of large-scale industry and the impressive record of small firm growth have called for a profound questioning of the role of mass production—and mass markets—in future capitalist expansion. In developing countries, the combination of rapid industrial growth and slow labor absorption in large, state-regulated industry has invoked a search for alternative theories of development that can account for such a significant departure from patterns of growth predicted on either the left or the right.

The shared goal of these efforts to reevaluate long-prevalent myths about industrialization is to understand decentralized and unregulated forms of production as elements central to modern capitalism rather than as backward or anomalous behavior. Until recently, however, the common ground of different streams of study of industrial change was difficult to locate. In development circles, the tendency had long been to search for theories to account for the exclusion of vast numbers of producers from the modern industrializing sector. A dualist model was first used to characterize rural subsistence areas as repositories of surplus labor that would be absorbed gradually into modern industry. Yet, as Third World urban centers swelled, job creation in the modern sector clearly could not keep pace with the influx of workers from the so-called traditional economy. Existing theories could account for the permanence of large, poor populations in Third World cities only by suggesting that they were dedicated simply to "surviving" while queuing for entry into modern firms.[4]

The preservation, and even recreation, of backward subsistence areas meanwhile suggested an uneven spread of capitalist markets and signaled the imperfect penetration of the capitalist mode of production. One attempt to explain such phenomena—and to account for slow development in the Third World in general—was provided by early versions of dependency theory. This perspective portrayed backward areas as superexploited; surplus value was siphoned from remote zones to the cities of the developing world and finally back to the metropoles of the capitalist core. True growth took place only when the advanced economies were distracted from imperialist intentions by political or economic crises.[5]

Yet, as with the view of modernization it criticized, dependency theory perpetuated an image of the working poor as a "marginal" population that was excluded from the modern, capitalist economy and superexploited in largely unskilled and undesirable occupations. It was left to empirical studies in the 1970s to document the surprising dynamism of many "marginal" activities and to show that participants often viewed their occupations as stable and relatively rewarding, not merely as a means to survive while waiting for access to blue-collar status and positions. The studies also revealed that many of the seemingly marginal economic activities of the poor were, in fact, directly tied to modern production and distribution processes. Even the street vendors and garbage pickers of Third World cities turned out to be integrated into elaborate commercial and production networks when researchers probed the connections of suppliers, buyers, and casual labor bosses to established, and sometimes very large, firms.[6]

The concept of the "informal sector" was introduced to describe those economic practices that often appeared to fall outside the realm of modern production processes but were, in fact, distinguished mainly by the *lack of state regulation*. The activities were found not to be uniformly traditional, either in their origins or in the technology they employed. Their growth clearly does not just depend on changes in the survival strategies of the "surplus" population but also responds directly to producers' efforts to incorporate unregulated labor in modern industrial processes, often with the explicit aim of reducing labor costs or diffusing worker opposition.[7]

These insights arrived simultaneously with discoveries of the widespread nature of productive decentralization in the advanced economies. Economists at first tended to portray the trend as merely a new wrinkle in an existing dualist structure. According to this view, larger firms with skilled workforces dominated a panoply of smaller firms and relied on their ability to recruit and organize a less skilled, less protected, and more fluid segment of the labor market (comprising largely women, minorities, and migrants). The segmented structure of the labor market, in other words, paralleled a dualist structure in industrial organization whereby large firms could concentrate on mass production and relegate production for highly volatile markets to smaller, dependent enterprises.[8]

But in the same way that development theorists introduced the concept of the informal sector as a critique of dualist notions about the separateness and lack of dynamism of "traditional" activities, observers in the advanced economies found that the newly created small firms were not necessarily subordinate to the interests of large capital. Rather than simply siphoning cheap labor and its benefits to larger enterprises, the sector of small firms could itself spur industrial growth by independently generating technological change, product innovation, and original, highly flexible, systems of production and distribution. This was possible in part because the dismantling of large factories—originally sought by employers in order to cut costs and diffuse worker opposition—also promised to release some workers from the strict hierarchy and stifling controls of the factory. While sweatshop labor might make a comeback in some places, elsewhere workers would regain control over their own skills, reuniting mental and physical capacities in a way that would lend their work new meaning while also enhancing the climate for innovation.[9]

Separate streams of scholarly debate, then, began to converge in a view of industrial restructuring as an ongoing and open-ended process that was being driven as much from below as from above. This, at least, was what I perceived at the time I began my study of industrial restructuring in Spain. Although the separate sets of literature continued to treat productive decentralization in the advanced economies and the growth of the informal sector in the developing world as two distinct phenomena, both trends were clearly part of a larger process. Certainly both trends were in part responses to pressures in the 1970s to reduce costs and increase flexibility in the face of the economic crisis. The growing contradiction between the requirements of large-scale production for mass markets and the explosive growth of new, more fragmented, and more variable markets was also clearly a systemwide change that would reinforce incentives for industrial restructuring in all parts of the world economy.[10]

Yet it was also apparent that the different political and social conditions that surrounded restructuring in its various settings would produce a wide range of experiences, and some strikingly different outcomes, of industrial reorganization. The responses of workers to restructuring certainly would not be uniform. Even in places where labor had a history of strong mobilization in opposition to earlier attempts to divide the industrial workforce, there would be room for more conciliatory postures and even active promotion of the changes by workers who perceived some benefits from recasting traditional roles within the industrial hierarchy. For the state, too, uncertainties abounded. A panoply of new, small, and scattered units of production, and a new class of entrepreneurs often operating on the borderline of illegality, would not fit easily into the familiar categories of political constituents and national bargaining groups.

If sweatshops and economic backwardness would result from industrial restructuring in one place, while technological innovation and the revival of craft might emerge in another, one challenge was clearly to understand the factors responsible for shaping different patterns of industrial change. Underlying this approach is the conviction that no superior logic dictates how the profile of industry must evolve. The process will always be contingent on local political, social, and cultural forces that deserve to be placed at the center of economic analysis. [11]

The problem thus invites a truly interdisciplinary approach to development economics, both in the research methodologies employed and in the multifaceted analysis required to understand the complex interaction of social, political, and cultural trends. Particularly because a significant proportion of decentralized production involves unregulated, or informal, labor, fieldwork and participant observation are essential in tracing changes in the organization of production within particular industries. And because many phases of production have been shifted outside the factories to settings where very different sets of social relations structure relations of production, analysis has to be extended to the cultural patterns and political attitudes that shape participants' choices about work and "regulate" production in the absence of state controls.

The style of analysis I chose for this study, then, assigns workers and worker-entrepreneurs a prominent place, while also relating their actions to the posture of state officials and the strategies of corporate managers. What workers do—what they strive for and how they react to the changing economic and political climate—affects not just the texture of their own lives but also the very direction and speed of industrial development. The "anthropology of work" becomes, in this approach, far more than the detailing of workplace conflicts or the ethnography of industrial tasks. The microfoundations of the politics of industrial restructuring shape tomorrow's constraints on economic policy and draw the lines for future conflicts between capital and labor.

The dynamics of the restructuring process will also help to guide the changing relationship of particular regions and nations within the global economy. I chose to examine the recent evolution of industry in Spain precisely because the challenges in this case fall somewhere between those in advanced countries dealing with mature manufacturing sectors and conditions in developing countries seeking to nurture infant industries. Spain's experience is relevant to the plight of a middle group of countries caught between dependency and development. Their stake in the outcome of productive decentralization is particularly high, as I argue in Chapter 1. They are charged with the task of restructuring industry to allow export-led growth to proceed; productive decentralization plays a role in both short- and long-term strategies to achieve such restructuring.

Spain's experience is interesting not only because it throws light on the dilemmas faced by this middle group of countries, but also because it promises to enhance our theoretical understanding of the way political shifts and industrial change are linked. The Spanish transition to democracy coincided with an economic crisis that caused the informal economy to expand dramatically. Chapter 2 traces the historical path that led Spain from rapid growth and a highly regulated labor market in the 1960s, to crisis and political uncertainty in the mid-1970s, and to high unemployment and rapid industrial restructuring in the 1980s. The ties between the political transition and the new face of the Spanish economy are addressed again in later chapters.

Part II analyzes two contrasting cases of "spontaneous restructuring" in industry through rapid growth of the informal sector. The electronics industry in Madrid is moving haltingly toward a pattern which incorporates some high-tech cottage industry. The Alicante shoe industry, in contrast, is relying on sweatshop labor to maintain its competitiveness in world markets. The technological requirements of production in the two industries explain some of the differences we find; but social, cultural, and political conditions have helped to produce the strikingly different patterns of industrial change.

I turn to an analysis of this context of industrial restructuring in Part III. Chapter 5 focuses more closely on the impact of the social setting of industrial outwork on its contribution to industrial restructuring. It examines, in particular, industrial homework, its conditions, and its changing role in Spanish industry. I suggest that family and community play a crucial part in exerting control over the production process in the absence of direct supervision by employers and the state. Gender is the missing element needed to explain the widely different trajectories of workers' careers in formal and informal employment. Chapter 6 examines the question of how politics has shaped industrial restructuring in Spain. I look in particular at how workers' experiences in the labor conflicts of the Spanish political transition helped to guide their responses to "informalization." After thus exploring the political preconditions for dynamic growth in decentralized industry, I return in Part IV to a broader assessment of the political and economic effects of productive decentralization and the implications for an understanding of the distinctive pattern of capitalist growth observed in semiperipheral countries.

We have only recently begun to grasp the complex and open-ended nature of industrial change. Ideological controversies about the benefits of industrial growth, stalled debates about the terminology used, and artificial divisions among scholarly disciplines—all have helped to prevent us from viewing industrialization as a *social* process whose outcome is not predetermined. Just as people make and experience class structures, they experiences and help to fashion the industrial structures in which they work. The quality of individual experiences, I hope to show, matters very much to the direction taken by the larger economic and political systems that constrain our opportunities and frame our efforts.

PART I

1 *Industrial Restructuring and the Informal Economy*

Two seemingly contradictory goals stand behind studies in the political economy of development. The first is to develop an understanding of global patterns of economic change; the second, to explain the peculiar logic of individual experiences of development. The two objectives sometimes pit disciplines and methodologies against one another—economists versus anthropologists, for example, or model-building versus ethnography. But neither type of analysis can be effectively pursued without attention to the other; the experiences of individual countries and regions directly affect the larger structure at the same time that they are shaped by global forces beyond their influence or control.

Anthropologists made this point when they raised the "local response" objection to rigid interpretations of a schema of the world economy as one divided into a core, semiperiphery, and periphery.[1] Numerous case studies showed the way local cultural patterns and political struggles both affected the relationship of particular regions to the world economy and helped to determine its trajectory. Most of these studies focused on the place of peasant societies within the world system or the role of ethnicity in the class configurations which structured outside alliances.[2] Much less attention has been devoted to local differentiation in patterns of industrial development and their implications for the world systems perspective.

The gap in research is explained in part by the slowness with which ethnographic studies of economic processes in developing countries discarded a preference for rural settings. The bias reflected an implicit assumption that peasant societies were closest in character to the so-called primitive cultures with which ethographers had honed their skills. More important, scholars in many disciplines still labored under the impression that industrialization—in contrast, they supposed, to rural economic change—is accurately prefigured in earlier experiences of industrial growth and that its contours are more closely determined by technological imperatives.

13

Yet many of the same kinds of processes that shape rural economies and their insertion in the global economy also influence industrial development and its relation to larger economic structures. Relations of production in industry are also *social* relations; they reverberate with, and help to create, cultural meanings, at the same time that these are recast as ideas about power and politics. Patterns of industrial development vary according to the way conflicts are defined and experienced on the shopfloor as well as in the wider arena of national politics and international markets.[3]

A strong bias toward studying rural change in Spain has long postponed analysis of industrial development as a social and political process.[4] But the social relations and conflicts surrounding production directly affect Spain's evolving position in the international economic order. Analyzing how this relationship unfolds is central to understanding possible scenarios of industrial growth in other national economies facing similar challenges in international markets.

Industrial Growth in the Semiperiphery

The rise of a group of nations to occupy a distinct middle ground between the advanced countries and the rest of the developing world is a relatively recent phenomenon. Before the 1960s, one could correctly characterize most Third World economies as predominantly agricultural. By the end of that decade, a handful of advanced developing countries had emerged; most of their workers were employed in dynamic industrial sectors, and their industrial growth rates had surpassed those of both the advanced economies and the majority of less developed countries (LDCs). Imports of manufactured goods from the middle group of countries to advanced markets had increased fivefold during the 1960s, and industrialization in most cases had brought significant internal changes, including rapidly increasing Gross Domestic Product (GDP) per capita.

Different definitions place between eight and 25 countries in this middle category.[5] They have been dubbed newly industrializing countries (NICs) in development circles, although industrialization is hardly new in some of the cases commonly included, such as Argentina or Spain. An alternative name for the middle category is one that is taken from the world systems perspective. In theory, the perspective bases a definition of the "semiperiphery" not just on the middle group's position in trade but also on similarities in internal political structure. Semiperipheral countries in the modern economy may share strong states and a tendency toward establishing authoritarian regimes. They may also show particularly fragmented elite class structures, which, at times, contribute to regime instability. While world systems theorists look for such common patterns of class structure and class alliances, they often adopt operational definitions of the semiperiphery that are based on the same or similar macroeconomic criteria as those used by development economists to identify the NICs.[6]

Regardless of the name used for the middle group of countries, their recent, rapid economic growth has clearly posed an important challenge to previously widely accepted views of development. On the one hand, sustained industrialization in developing countries contradicts many of the tenets of dependency theory. The initial unsatisfactory response of dependency theorists to the phenomenon was to suggest that the rapid industrial growth did not constitute "true development" because it was carried out under the aegis of foreign capital and would result in increasing inequality.[7] On the other hand, the semiperiphery's record of growth cannot be attributed to conditions which neoclassical economists would hold to be necessary and sufficient for economic "takeoff." Competitive advantage cannot explain sustained growth in manufacturing exports in many cases, particularly because wages in the semiperiphery have tended to rise faster than in either the advanced economies or the LDCs.

The very success of semiperipheral countries in exporting manufactures has generated some new obstacles to continued development. These obstacles can hardly be ignored by political leaders in the semiperiphery. Their countries have often traded vulnerability to fluctuations in world prices of raw materials and agricultural goods for greater sensitivity to shifts in the world demand for manufactures. At the same time, lower-cost producers from LDCs offer increasing competition in the market for standardized and low-quality consumer goods. Pressures to maintain competitiveness tend to perpetuate dependency on outside sources of capital and technology, which are needed to fuel industrialization and industrial restructuring. Finally, protectionism on the part of governments in the advanced economies endangers continued growth in even the most successful export categories.

The state may take actions to overcome some of these obstacles and perpetuate "export-led" growth. One approach is to employ authoritarian measures to keep wages at internationally competitive levels. The viability of this strategy depends, of course, on internal political conditions and external political alliances. Even where repression of workers' movements is possible and appears to benefit industrial capital in the short run, it may also generate further obstacles to sustained growth, including the threat of future political instability. Economists recommend a range of more specific policy measures designed to encourage exports of manufactures (for example, subsidies to exporters of nontraditional goods or relaxation of restrictions on needed imports).[8] But these policies are also not uniformly effective. Although state intervention has indeed played a crucial role in promoting export-oriented industrialization, successful intervention depends on the quality and stability of political alliances, and not merely on the package of measures adopted.[9]

While the state cannot be expected to find a prescribed solution to increasing international competition and rising factor costs, producers may adopt their own strategies for cutting costs and enhancing flexibility. One response by employers has been to seek to avoid the costs associated with state regulation of the labor market. Access to the sphere of the economy not regulated by the state—the informal sector—offers producers a way of reducing both operating costs and the costs associated with adjusting the size and skill composition of the labor force. Informal labor is distinguished by the lack of state supervision in the formation and enforcement of contracts between workers and employers; in most of the semiperipheral countries, this means that workers in the informal sector do not receive social security, retirement, or health benefits and are not able to call on the state to enforce union pay scales, severance pay requirements, or even safety regulations.[10]

To be sure, recruiting unprotected labor in order to cut costs is not an entirely new strategy. Incorporation of unregulated labor into the production process through such mechanisms as subcontracting and homework is a common feature of capitalist industrialization everywhere; in developing economies, these and other kinds of unregulated labor comprise an informal economy that is often in fact larger than the formal sector.[11] But where most previous studies of the informal sector in developing countries have characterized it as a relatively stable, often backward segment of the economy comprising everything from subsistence agriculture to high-paid urban services, our interest is in the portion of the unregulated economy—a significant portion, I would argue—which expands and contracts directly in response to changes in the structure of modern industry and which, in fact, is an integral part of that structure. In many semiperipheral economies, the informal sector is both a stable component of the economy and a recent phenomenon which responds to the new challenges facing such countries since the 1970s.

This new expansion of the informal sector surely affects the implementation of traditional forms of industrial policy by the state: Will the trend undermine such policies by giving producers an independent, if imperfect, solution to their problems? Will workers' movements, emerging with strength in many semiperipheral nations as part of a larger political struggle over the distribution of the benefits of growth and the scope for human rights, be significantly weakened by the shifting of employment underground? Informalization creates an entirely new, and little understood, dynamic of growth in highly decentralized structures: Will the greater flexibility of decentralized and "informal" industry aid semiperipheral countries to redirect production of manufactures to higher-cost, higher-fashion, and more restricted markets? Or is informalization a regressive trend simply leading to deteriorating working conditions and reduced incentives for innovations?

These questions remain unanswered by evidence of a wide variety of patterns of informalization in advanced and semiperipheral countries. The experiences range from steady gains in world markets for manufactures based on the dynamism of small firms to stagnating exports, sluggish investments in industry, and a growing subordinate stratum of poorly remunerated informal jobs. The overarching question is what conditions lead productive decentralization in these opposing directions.

The Informal Sector: Source of Cheap Labor or Catalyst of Dynamic Growth?

A key case illustrating the potentially positive effects of productive decentralization on industrial development is that of Italian industry in the 1970s. Italy can hardly be classified as a semiperipheral country, although one scholar places it "on the periphery of the core" (Lange 1985). But Italy's experience is, for many reasons, instructive.

Early works on the rise of the informal sector in Italy interpreted the phenomenon mainly as an outgrowth of industrialists' responses to escalating labor conflicts in the late 1960s, which culminated in the *autunno caldo* of 1969. In order to avoid further confrontations with organized labor and to bypass the higher costs of keeping a unionized workforce, Italian firms decentralized production by allocating work to subcontractors, including informal enterprises (Bagnasco 1977). Toward the decade's end, however, a quite different interpretation began to supplant this one. The revision was based on the observation that, in particular sectors and regions of Italy where decentralization had been marked, the overall economic results had been positive. In Emilia Romagna and in other regions of central Italy, industrial exports had risen steadily as a share of total Italian exports between 1963 and 1980. In general, the regional economy had suffered very little from the global recession of the mid-1970s, and economic performance had been considerably above that of other areas (Brusco 1982).

Observers argued that the flexibility of the fragmented and semi-informal industrial structure had permitted more rapid adjustment to shifts in both the content and strength of demand. This flexibility, it was argued, consisted not only in the facility with which informal firms could expand and contract the workforce as levels of output changed, but also in the capacity of the small firms to adapt the organization of production and the use of technology to changes in style (Brusco 1982). The results of this system of production were positive for Italian industry as a whole: The manufacture of high-quality consumer goods placed Italian industry in a strong position vis-a-vis other exporters of manufactures to advanced-country markets. The impact on some individual firms was also found to be beneficial. Although many small enterprises continued to work as subcontractors, they were able to benefit from their control of production techniques to emerge from a position of dependence within the industrial structure (Sabel 1982).

The claims of enthusiastic scholars did not stop here. It was also argued that conditions and wages in small and even informal workshops were in many cases the same or better than in larger, unionized factories. This was due to the strong demand for skilled workers, the wider scope for these workers to utilize their skills, and the greater degree of worker control over the pace and organization of production. The hierarchy of the large Fordist firm, or mass production factory, was replaced by relations of production based primarily on social relations encompassing both workers and management (Brusco 1982; Sabel 1982; Capecchi 1989).

Several factors appear to explain the emergence of this pattern of industrial growth in Italy. The first is the spatial context of industrial restructuring, in particular the concentration of key industries in different subregions of central Italy. Firms in the shoe, ceramics, and machine tool industries, to name just a few, are clustered according to production type in various towns of the central region. The high degree of concentration has helped small firms to join to overcome some of the obvious difficulties associated with their small size and their position in a fragmented industrial structure. Associations of small firms have formed in some areas to collectivize tasks such as bookkeeping, or to facilitate small firms' direct access to the export market. The proximity of small producers in the same industry, moreover, is seen to stimulate the diffusion of new technologies and to foster cooperation among skilled workers and entrepreneurs who are already connected through social networks outside the workplace (Sabel 1982).

A second major variable cited to account for the dynamism of decentralized industry is the political context in which the new microenterprises operate. A strong tradition of worker cooperatives is suggested as a precondition for the economic vitality of informal enterprises (Saba 1981). This political orientation amounts to one manifestation of a deeper commitment to collaboration among workers that becomes crystallized in the "high-trust" organization of production in the small firm. A related condition favoring the peculiar pattern of industrial growth in Italy has been the unusually high degree of political cooperation among small businessmen, workers, and local government in the Communist-led municipalities of central Italy. The considerable scope for autonomy of local and regional governments in evolving their own, locally based industrial policies clearly helps to account for the success of local efforts to improve the plight of industrial outworkers (Sabel 1982; Capecchi 1989).

Finally, two conditions related to the economic context of

productive decentralization were clearly extremely important in guiding the outcome of this process. First, the initial trend toward decentralization of the production process in Italy began in the context of still rapidly expanding global demand. This meant that the newly created small firms faced very favorable conditions both in replicating existing products at lower cost and in searching for innovative products. Second, it seems crucial that there was simultaneously a critical mass of skilled workers, often already experienced in the techniques of mass production through employment in large factories, and an overall shortage of skilled labor (Brusco 1982). Workers thus were often able to choose between employment in established factories or self-employment and participation in new enterprises. They benefitted both by being able to use earnings from formal industry to develop outside ventures and by having a fallback in regular employment if such ventures failed.

In summary, the factors that appear to be responsible for the dynamism of the informal sector in the Italian case are the spatial clustering of new, small firms; the existence of a lively tradition of worker cooperativism; local government autonomy; the good relations between local officials, small businessmen, and workers; market expansion; the nature of workers' past experiences in industrial employment; and a relative overall shortage of skilled industrial labor. The presence of such a mix of conditions must be highly unusual. The Italian experience can thus hardly constitute a "model" for advanced developing countries that face some of the same challenges.

Nevertheless, the case remains useful as a starting place for analyzing the effects of productive decentralization in other settings. It reminds us, first of all, that the informal sector in industry is not necessarily backward. Nor is informalization uniformly negative in its impact on working conditions. Second, the Italian experience underscores the link between the nature of relations of production in the informal sector and the potential for industrial outworkers to improve their position vis-a-vis decentralizing producers. Even though the political and social conditions under which productive decentralization took place in Italy are so peculiar, the case establishes clearly that productive decentralization at least opens up an *opportunity* for greater control over the production process by workers. Finally, the Italian experience suggests that the relationship between fragmented, informal workshops and established, formal factories may determine the overall effect of productive decentralization on industrial growth. If newly created, small firms are able to overcome their subordination to established producers, they may move the entire structure toward innovations in design and technology that permit rapid adjustments to new trends in world markets. It is not surprising that the dynamism of the new production structure in Italy, and the variations on this pattern which can be found in a handful of other places in the advanced economies, has given rise to claims that a new pattern of capitalist growth—dubbed *flexible specialization*—may be emerging in the wake of a broader trend toward decentralized production. Piore and Sabel (1984) have argued that the appearance of networks of specialized firms that can respond flexibly to market shifts marks a "second industrial divide" and an end to the era of mass production.

However, studies of the informal sector in other countries have followed a different approach and have produced a quite different, and more pessimistic, view of the role of the informal sector in industrial development. Although entrepreneurial flair, modern production techniques, and rapid labor absorption also may characterize the informal sector, it is more common in developing countries to find that subcontracting, homework, and other forms of outwork serve mainly to siphon cheap labor into modern production processes controlled by large national and even international capital. Rapid expansion of the informal sector in recessionary periods may reflect workers' efforts to "get by" under harsher economic conditions more than their ability to generate an alternative dynamic of industrial growth.

Consider the example of the southern cone countries of Latin America, where the informal sector increased rapidly after the late 1970s. The imposition of bureaucratic-authoritarian regimes in these countries in the mid-1970s led to the "opening" of their economies and the adoption of policies designed to favor export-oriented industrialization. With real wages continuing to fall rapidly and worker opposition stifled, conditions should have proven ideal for a boom in manufacturing exports. But a dramatic increase in nontraditional exports in the late 1970s was short-lived. If the burgeoning informal sector played a role in this short boom, that contribution was no longer in evidence in the next decade. Rather than attracting skilled workers and fomenting innovation, the informal sector served mainly as a refuge for workers unable either to emigrate or to find jobs in the formal economy. (Portes and Benton 1984; Fortuna and Prates 1989; cf., Benería and Roldán 1988).

The experiences of the southern cone countries and, indeed, of most Latin American countries, do not contradict findings of more dynamic patterns of industrial restructuring in the advanced economies. Rather, the contrasting cases underline the importance of those factors which support the transformation toward "flexible specialization" in some places. In the southern cone, for example, informalization took place after the crisis of the mid-1970s and not during the earlier period of expanding world demand. Further, the very success of the bureaucratic-authoritarian regimes in reducing real wages meant that industrial employers faced reduced incentives either to introduce innovations in established factories or to search for novel contributions from auxiliary producers. Industrial workers, meanwhile, having received ample benefits and protection from the state in the past, did not view informal labor as a desirable or acceptable replacement for coveted stable jobs. Nor were producers encouraged either by local or national governments to form cooperatives or other worker associations to improve their position. In short, the peculiar constellation of expanding demand, cooperativism, local government autonomy, institutional support for informal-sector ventures, and a strong position for skilled labor was absent as a backdrop to industrial restructuring.

Still, we cannot yet be satisfied with the level of analysis produced so far in existing, scattered studies. A clear set of hypotheses is needed to link together those factors which may lead productive decentralization in different directions. We have introduced one hypothesis, namely that the benefits of productive decentralization to industrial development in the semiperiphery depend directly on the ability of industrial outworkers to overcome a strictly subordinate relationship to producers at the top of the production ladder. The analysis of the Italian experience introduces the further hypothesis that the position of industrial outworkers in the structural hierarchy of industrial firms depends in turn on their capacity and willingness to abandon the organizational tenets of factory production—autocratic control over workers, deskilling, and the atomization of tasks—and replace these with forms of production which enable them to capitalize on the peculiar *strengths* of their small size, skill composition, and the relative absence of state regulation. This capacity depends, finally, on the nature of workers' past experiences in industrial employment (specifically, their participation in organized protests) and their willingness to alter the relations of production; and, more broadly, on the nature of social relations surrounding production, including patterns of authority within the family and the character of political alliances which may constrain workers' actions.

The case studies presented in this work cannot, by themselves, prove or disprove the above hypotheses nor substantiate completely the view that politics is preeminent in guiding industrial develop-ment. I use these hypotheses as a loose framework of analysis, however, and hope to show that close attention to the themes they highlight can yield a comprehensive understanding of informalization in one setting. By extension, the findings may also bring into sharper focus the obstacles to continued industrial growth elsewhere in the capitalist semiperiphery.

As I stated in the introduction, my interest in the informal sector does not disguise any a priori vision of the informal sector's functions in the economy; in fact, I look explicitly at the ways in which the role of unregulated labor changes as restructuring in industry takes place and at the way the role also may vary across industries and regions, even within the same country. Nor do I follow some analysts of the crisis of mass production in supposing that the move away from centralized factories implies a resolution of the contradictions of capitalist industrialization; alternative forms of "regulation" in the labor process entail new and heavy burdens for some workers. The goal is not, in other words, to establish a typology of formal-informal relations or to pass judgment on a trend in industry which history is likely to carry forward, however we explain it. Instead, the social and political conditions we often think of merely as colorful background to larger, systemic shifts come to the fore and assert their power to redirect industrial development and reshape the world economy.

2 Unregulated Labor in Democratic Spain

The situation of Spain in the 1970s and 1980s summarizes, in many respects, that of all the newly or rapidly industrializing countries. No longer able to complete with low-cost producers and severely affected by the crisis of the mid-1970s, Spain was fighting to have its industry secure a more competitive position in upscale markets and more technologically advanced industries. In some sectors, the state forced noncompetitive firms to close and reduced state support to all but the most promising ventures; in other areas, industrial restructuring took place spontaneously, albeit with the quiet complicity of the state, through the expansion of the informal sector. The effect of this phenomenon—itself in part a product of recent political change in Spain—ultimately depends on the evolution of political alliances at the national and local levels and on the politics of production within informal industry itself.

The Spanish case is of special interest, moreover, because it combines certain features of the Italian and Latin American examples outlined in the previous chapter. On the one hand, the composition of industry in Spain and the country's relationship to its trading partners appear to favor the pattern of development pursued in Italy. In particular, Spain's recent entry into the European Economic Community (EEC) puts it in a privileged position to challenge Italy's dominance in light manufacturing imports to other EEC countries. Superficially at least, Spanish light industry resembles its Italian counterpart closely: Producers in various industries are clustered in a handful of cities and towns in several more economically advanced Spanish provinces, and these industries in particular appear to have experienced dramatic decentralization over the last decade. Some of these manufactures, such as shoes, toys, hand tools, light metal products, and synthetic textiles, have already had considerable success in exporting to advanced-country markets and figure among the leading NIC producers in their respective categories.

25

At the same time, Spain clearly faces certain barriers to the long-term success of export-led industrialization which it shares with the advanced economies of Latin America. The timing of radical restructuring—it coincided with the economic crisis—placed strong pressure on Spanish industry to cut costs but left little maneuvering room for exploring new styles of production. Moreover, the Spanish economy is simultaneously emerging from a long period with a highly regulated industrial sector. Labor has occasionally become reactionary in its attempt to salvage state benefits and protection for workers, while large and small capitalists zealously advocate deregulation; the state's ability to promote a third alternative through industrial planning rests on its precarious moral authority, made more tenuous by the obvious continuities of many state institutions in democratic Spain with the authoritarian government of the past. The state's actions are also constricted by strong international pressures to implement austerity programs.

During the nearly 40 years of rule by the dictator Francisco Franco, Spanish economic planning was a highly centralized affair. Liberalizing measures opened the economy to international investors and allowed more play for competition in domestic markets only at the end of the 1950s. Labor unions organized clandestinely for years and became especially militant in the 1960s, but they were recognized as national bargaining agents only in the late 1970s, when the transition to democracy was consolidated under the first of a series of pacts signed by representatives of labor, business organizations, and the government. The narrow scope for public discussion of economic policy matters under Franco gave way quickly to a controlled debate over a few issues central to the tripartite negotiations surrounding successive pacts.

The politics of the posttransition period has been dominated by the Socialist Workers' Party (Partido Socialista Obrero Español, or PSOE). The Socialists swept into power in the elections of 1982, after the dissolution of the Union of the Democratic Center (Unión Centro Democrático, or UCD), whose leader, Adolfo Suárez, had presided carefully and conservatively over key moments of the transition, first as the provisional leader hand-picked by King Juan Carlos, then as the head of the first democratically elected government. The PSOE, under Felipe González and a cadre of other young, charismatic leaders, was positioned from the start as a moderate reformist party, and its broad appeal was confirmed when the Socialists garnered an even larger majority in the 1986 elections. More technocrats than ideologues, the Socialists were committed to a program of fiscal austerity combined with further liberalizing measures, an agenda that even the party leadership has had trouble defending as socialist in its inspiration or goals. Still, the twin triumphs acclaimed by the PSOE are the successful negotiation of Spain's entry into the EEC and the resurgence of strong economic growth in the late 1980s. The Socialists would also claim credit for preventing the reemergence of a sharp left-right polarization in Spain, but it is more accurate to say that they astutely occupied a large political center that was firmly committed to stability in the postauthoritarian period.

Spain's economic record has indeed been stunning in recent years. In 1987, the country registered the highest growth rate in the European Common Market and the highest in its own history since before the onset of the economic crisis in 1974. The latest Spanish boom is explained by many conjunctural factors, not the least of which is accelerated foreign investment in the wake of EEC integration and on the eve of the opening of EEC labor markets in 1992. But the troubles of the Spanish economy—and the political tensions surrounding them—did not disappear. The focus of much public debate and considerable hand-wringing on the part of government leaders was the persistence of alarmingly high rates of unemployment. Even with the return of strong economic growth after 1986, the joblessness rate continued to hover around 20%.

In the context of political transition and economic bust and boom, the process of productive decentralization has had unique importance. An enormous expansion of the informal sector was evident after the mid-1970s, and particularly after 1979. Observers at first characterized the informal sector as a degraded substratum of the economic system, a source of cheap labor performed by workers deprived of legal rights and superexploited under substandard conditions. The resurgence of organized labor during the transition, the pressures generated by the economic crisis, and, above all, the rigidity of the Spanish labor code—these factors were considered the primary motives for informalization. But such explanations left important questions about the political origins of the trend and its potential long-term effects on industrial growth unanswered. They did not account, either, for the persistence of a large unregulated sector in the late 1980s, when *la crisis* gave way so suddenly and dramatically to *el boom.*

The Rise of the Informal Sector in Spain

Placing the development of Spain's unregulated economy in historical perspective requires distinguishing among at least three phases of Spanish economic development since the Civil War. During the first two decades of the Franco regime, the officially-sanctioned conditions of labor were such that a sharp boundary between formal and informal sectors in industry is difficult to distinguish. During the 1960s, a second period, of unprecedented economic growth, gave rise to some of the preconditions for the subsequent expansion of the unregulated economy. But it was not until the following decade, when severe economic downturn coincided with the political transition to democracy, that we can begin to speak of a large informal sector in Spain or, more precisely, of a process of informalization and restructuring in Spanish industry.

The overwhelmingly formal character of Spanish industry in the first of these periods reflected the overall weakness of the economy and the paternalistic attitude of the Franco regime toward regulation of the labor market. Growth of domestic demand throughout this period was far too slow to stimulate manufacturing production; at the same time, the autarkic policies of the regime undermined the growth of exports. By the mid-1950s, the Spanish economy had only managed to recover its prewar strength. Per capita income reached its prewar level only in 1954; at the end of the 1950s, roughly 40% of the low total value of exports still consisted of agricultural goods, the same percentage as in 1929.

The strict control of wages, made possible by the suppression of organized labor, was an integral part of the regime's economic policies throughout this period. Real wages actually declined between 1940 and 1955 (Lieberman 1982). In part to mitigate worker opposition, and in part because the measures fit well with the corporatist ideology of the regime, the state designed a paternalistic, protective labor code. The coincidence of these two factors—the comparatively very low wages of Spanish workers and the state's policy of extensive regulation of the labor market—help explain the relative unimportance of the informal sector to industry during this period. With real official wages stagnant or falling, firms had little incentive to seek unprotected labor outside the formal economy. Furthermore, although state regulation of work constituted one of the ideological underpinnings of the regime, the institutional rigidity of the labor market during this period should not be exaggerated. Many forms of casual labor that would later contrast markedly with the more regulated conditions of labor in formal industry were at this time accepted as norms. Examples are the temporary labor of construction workers or the homework done by both men and women in light industry. The open and legal character of these types of employment makes it misleading to characterize them as belonging to an informal sector in Spanish industry.

The period of rapid economic growth of the following decade offers a more complex panorama. Spain's economic boom of the 1960s has received less attention than the "Brazilian miracle" of the same period, but its scale and significance are in many ways comparable. In the space of one and one-half decades—from the introduction of liberalizing economic policies in 1958 to the onset of the economic crisis in 1974—a stagnating and largely agricultural Spanish economy was transformed into a major producer of a narrow but important range of capital and consumer goods. Average annual increases of both the gross domestic product and industrial productivity in this period surpassed similar growth rates in the European Common Market and in the United States. Economic expansion brought about significant changes in the composition of the labor force and in national income: By 1972, industry had replaced agriculture as the largest employer, and per capita income had registered a threefold increase over the previous decade.

The impoverished condition of the Spanish economy at its start must be considered in evaluating the impact of the boom. Even by the end of the 1960s, Spain's per capita income was still the third lowest in Europe, and Spanish industrial productivity, despite its spectacular rise, remained at less than one-half the average of that of the European Common Market (Lieberman 1982). Nevertheless, industrial growth between 1959 and 1975 was responsible for a significant change in Spain's international position. Exports of manufactured goods grew as a share of total exports from 22.6% in 1961 to 36.7% in 1973; the increase was even more dramatic in

exports of machinery and transport equipment, which together
accounted for 3.6% of the value of exports in 1961 and 17.5% in
1971 (UN International Trade Statistics). By the mid-1970s, Spain
could be characterized as a leading newly industrializing country,
whose exports to member countries of the Organization of Economic
Cooperation and Development (OECD) were particularly competitive with those of other NICs in capital goods and transport
equipment, but also in footwear, chemicals, light metal manufacturing, and various other industries (see A. Edwards 1979).

The sheer pace of economic growth in this period obviously
acted as a brake on the expansion and consolidation of an informal
sector in industry. As long as the prospects for continued economic
growth appeared favorable, firms hired new workers in spite of the
costs entailed in creating new posts. In fact, the opportunities for
expansion encouraged the *formalization* of rural industry and its
establishment independent of its symbiotic relationship with
agriculture.

One significant exception to this pattern was the transformation
of the urban labor market brought about with the influx of workers
from rural areas. The majority of the 1.8 million Spaniards estimated
to have left the countryside between 1960 and 1973 settled in
Spanish cities (Wright 1977). A large proportion of migrants found
work outside Spain, especially in more advanced Western European
countries, and they contributed to growth at home by sustaining a
sizable, steady stream of remittances. The distances travelled by both
sets of migrants prevented their return to rural areas as a temporary
refuge from economic difficulties. Nearly 45% of new migrants in
Barcelona between 1961 and 1975, for example, were Andalusians,
and the figure was 75% for Madrid (Bier 1980). The new and cheap
labor force entered Spain's urban labor market as casual workers,
mainly in construction work, in services, and in an array of activities
surrounding the organization and provision of the extensive
settlements they created. The wages and conditions of these workers
did contrast with those in industries where the advent of collective
bargaining had already prompted significant wage revisions in the
early 1960s.

However, not until toward the end of the decade and the
beginning of the 1970s did a sharp division between regulated and
unregulated labor begin to emerge. One key for this change was the

consolidation of workers' opposition to the regime. Increased labor strife meant continual upward pressure on wages, halted only briefly during the freeze on wages in 1967 and 1968. The introduction of collective bargaining, but particularly the gradual escalation of plant-level participation, also forced greater compliance with labor regulations in large firms. At the same time, the state's interest in keeping down wages—to maintain the faltering economic momentum—and in quieting worker opposition encouraged the extension of worker benefits. Unemployment benefits instituted in 1959 were gradually expanded, and the fragmented social security system was centralized. In 1972, the state began a quiet campaign to adjust employers' contributions to social security and to bring them into line with actual wage costs.

To Spanish business, which was still awaiting fulfillment of the government's pledge in the first stabilization plan to curb restrictions on the labor market, the rising indirect costs and the new regulations were ominous signs. Already certain procedures for getting around state regulations were in common practice. Employers encouraged and sometimes compelled workers to take on extra hours so that new employees would not have to be hired, or they reported salaries lower than those actually paid to workers.

Spanish scholars writing on the rapid expansion of the informal sector beginning in the late 1970s have placed considerable emphasis on the maintenance of institutional rigidity in the labor market and the rising indirect costs of labor as principal causal factors. The informal sector, they argue, grew rapidly mainly because it offered firms a refuge from these costs and constraints (Gómez 1982; Vázquez and Trigo 1982; Casals and Vidal 1985). Employers' social security costs did rise rapidly during the 1970s, as did fiscal pressure on firms. Although these costs were still lower than in other European OECD countries, they were comparatively high as a percentage of the GDP (Trigo and Vázquez 1983). At the same time, direct labor costs showed substantial increases through the mid-1970s; yearly increments in real wages between 1971 and 1976 averaged 7%. The combination of rapidly rising wages and increased indirect costs clearly had the greatest impact on firms in labor-intensive industries, and affected already fragmented, highly competitive industries disproportionalely.

A further incentive for the "informalization" of industry was the reemergence of strong labor unions during the transition. The strikes during 1975 and 1976 warned of the potential consolidation of a labor movement capable not only of pressing for higher wages but also of asserting control over the organization and regulation of production. By 1978, when the role of labor unions and collective bargaining was officially recognized, more than one-half of salaried workers in industry were union members.[1] The further fragmentation of industry and the resurgence of informal labor offered an escape from confrontations with unions and a strategy for diluting the force of the movement over time (Gómez 1983).

This explanation of the rise of the informal sector in Spain as a response to institutional and political pressures resembles the early interpretation of Italian informalization as a reaction to the strength of Italian labor unions. However, the content of workers' demands and the timing of the strike wave were quite different, with important consequences. The workers' movement on the one hand was broadly political, with the permanent dismantling of the Franco regime as its overall objective, and on the other hand was motivated by quite specific economic goals, mainly the substantial revision of salaries. Despite the leadership and participation of the Spanish left, the movement did not share the political orientation of unrest elsewhere in Europe during 1968 and 1969; workers did not propose radically altering their relationship to capital but were responding instead to a backlog of basic reforms that had been postponed or ignored during the authoritarian regime (see Chapter 6).

A second difference, of course, was that whereas the proliferation of small, underground firms in Italy took place in an expansionary period, Spanish informalization corresponded with a period of weakened demand and general economic crisis. The dimensions of the crisis in Spain were in fact greater, and its duration longer, than in other European countries. One has only to survey the dramatic fall of the major economic indicators in 1975 to appreciate the initial impact of the crisis. The annual growth rate of the GDP dropped from an average of 6.35% between 1967 and 1974 to less than 1.1% in 1975, and the growth rate of investments in fixed capital plummeted in the same year (see table 2.1). Still worse, Spain did not experience the modest recovery that occurred elsewhere in Europe between 1976 and 1978, and the economy was ill-prepared for the shock of a second petroleum crisis in 1979.

Table 2.1 Index of Four Economic Indicators, 1973–1983
(Base of 100 = Average 1967–1974)

Year	Unemployment Rate (2.08)*	Annual Growth of GDP (6.35)*	Annual Growth Fixed-Capital Investments (6.52)*	Current Acct. Balance of Bayments ($286m)*
1973	129.6	133.9	219.3	110.2
1974	152.1	85.0	102.8	63.4
1975	193.9	17.3	−59.8	59.0
1976	235.2	45.7	−30.7	47.9
1977	271.6	40.9	−18.4	95.0
1978	355.6	45.7	−69.0	131.4
1979	434.3	17.3	3.1	121.7
1980	565.8	20.5	21.5	39.6
1981	702.1	3.1	30.7	41.3
1982	793.8	25.2	21.5	48.7
1983	867.2	31.5	−36.8	81.2

* Value of base of 100.
Source: Banco de Bilbao (1983:131,234).

Independent of the political uncertainty surrounding the transition, the state contributed to the pressures for informalization, in part unwittingly. Successive governments continued to apply a strong anti-inflationary economic policy. Yet given the low growth of productivity, inflation was needed to offset the steady rise of wages. Massive plant closures were "inevitable" by the late 1970s (Lieberman 1982). Between 1975 and 1983, the number of salaried jobs declined by 12.2%, the biggest decrease in the European OECD; industrial salaried jobs dropped in the same period by 19.5%. The level of estimated unemployment rose from slightly more than 5% in 1976 to 22% in 1984. The new army of workers losing jobs in the formal sector, together with the large numbers coming into the labor market for the first time, represented a willing labor force for the unregulated economy.

The severity of the crisis itself, rather than the institutional pressures already in place, might thus represent the fundamental cause of informal sector growth in Spain (see Sanchis 1983; Celada, López, and Parra 1985; Miquélez 1982; Moltó 1982). According to this view, it is impossible to arrive at an abstract evaluation of the level of indirect costs and the degree of institutional rigidity that firms found tolerable. Entrepreneurs' perceptions of these costs clearly depend on other economic and political considerations, and on sociological factors, including their attitudes toward labor and toward the authority of the state (Sanchis 1984). Undeniably employers perceived institutional rigidity and rising labor costs as excessive after the mid-1970s precisely because these existed in the context of severe economic recession and political instability.

This more sophisticated understanding of the factors contributing to informal sector growth is made more complex by the effort to explain recent trends in the Spanish economy. While annual increases in GDP rose to 3% in 1986 and to 5.3% in 1987, the unemployment rate stayed unacceptably high. Job creation in these two years was also up, by 2.3% in 1986 and by an impressive 4.5% in 1987. But these gains were offset by a steady rise in the economically active population, as young people continue to pour into the market for jobs and increasing numbers of women also seek entry. Some of the new jobs being created are undoubtedly positions that have "emerged," in the improved economic climate, from the underground economy. But the proportion of workers who are likely to engage in unregulated activities has not decreased. Nor does it appear that continued reforms to make the labor code more flexible have succeeded in convincing employers to put all their workers on the books. The constancy of the informal sector phenomenon suggests it may be a *structural*, not merely a conjunctural, feature of the economy in democratic Spain.

The Character of the Informal Sector in Spain

The process of informalization in the Spanish economy is, in fact, distinguished both quantitatively and qualitatively from earlier forms of casual employment. Estimates of the size of the informal sector in Spain have been based essentially on three different types of evidence: (1) approximations of the supply of workers for the unregulated economy; (2) statistics on the demand for money in the national economy; and (3) the testimony of observers or self-reporting by participants in the informal sector. A fourth indicator used less often is the growth of output in sectors where the size of the formal sector has been shrinking while productivity has remained about constant. Despite the shortcomings of each of these approaches, the results help to confirm more impressionistic evidence that the informal sector has expanded rapidly since the late 1970s and this it is not a marginal part of the economy but rather accounts for a sizable portion of the GDP and employs a significant segment of the population.

National employment statistics provide some evidence that the labor supply for the unregulated economy grew dramatically between the mid-1970s and the mid-1980s. The percentage of the population that was economically active actually showed a slight decline between 1975 and 1981, an exceptional trend among OECD countries. As unemployment rose swiftly, the proportion of unemployed workers collecting insurance payments from the state also dropped steadily, from 65% in 1980 to less than 40% in the first half of 1984, further swelling the ranks of potential participants in unregulated activities. Finally, the numbers of "self-employed" workers outside the agricultural sector increased significantly at the same time that salaried employment was dropping. In construction, for example, self-employed workers increased by 25.5% between 1980 and 1984, while salaried jobs declined by 30.9%.

Based on certain assumptions about the willingness of some groups of workers to accept informal jobs, Ruesga (1984) calculated that the potential labor supply for the informal sector in 1979 was equal to slightly more than one-fourth the size of the officially recorded economically active population (EAP). Using different criteria, he estimated that the *minimum* level of actual employment in this sector was around 10% of the EAP. Such estimates are somewhat arbitrary because they not only rely on incomplete information about the employment preferences of different segments of the population but also cannot be verified. The latter problem is shared by other global estimates of the informal sector in Spain based on comparisons of the actual demand for money in the national economy with the demand generated by registered economic activities. This method, which has been used in the United States and elsewhere to estimate the informal sector, requires the analysis of historical series of data, and the absence of accurate figures in this form has posed an important obstacle to the method's application in Spain. Nevertheless, two attempts have been made: Applying the Gutman method, Moltó estimated that the unregulated economy increased from a base of 0 in 1973 to .9% of the GDP in 1979 and to 1.8% in the following year (Moltó 1980). Using a different method, Lafuente (1980) found that in 1978, the informal sector represented 22.9% of the GDP. Together the estimates at least confirm the view of the informal sector as a large and expanding part of the economy.

In an attempt to arrive at an accurate measure of the informal sector, the Spanish government sponsored a national survey in 1985 to detect off-the-books labor.[2] Despite the inherent limitations of a method requiring self-reporting, the survey turned up some significant results. As Table 2.2 shows, the survey found that only about two-thirds (67.5%) of the working population in the last quarter of 1985 was complying with social security regulations; one-fourth (25.1%) could be classified as unregulated labor. For certain categories of workers, the proportion employed informally was much higher. For example, 33.1% of self-employed workers, and 42.6% of female workers, reported that they were working off-the-books. Older and younger workers were found to be more likely to participate in unregulated employment than middle-aged workers. And greater participation in the informal sector was evident among those without

Table 2.2 Informal Sector Workers as a Percentage of the Work Force and by Professional Category

Sector of Employment	Professional Category		
	Salaried Workers	Self-Employed Workers	Total Employment[1]
Informal Sector[2]	18.8	33.1	25.1
Formal Sector	81.2	66.9	67.5
Other[3]	—	—	7.4
Total Employment[1]	100.0	100.0	100.0

1. Workers who reported having worked in the survey week together with those who worked an average of at least 13 hours per week during the previous three weeks.
2. Defined in relation to social security coverage. Category includes: Employed but not registered with social security (70.2%); employed and registered but not making payments (12.7%); employed while receiving unemployment compensation (4.3%); and other types of irregularities (12.9%).
3. Data from these cases missing, not classified, or excluded from study.
Source: Juan Muro et al. *Análisis de las condiciones de vida y trabajo en España.* Ministerio de Economía y Hacienda, 1988.

family responsibilities; single workers were twice as likely as married respondents to engage in unregulated work.

The national survey showed that significant proportions of workers in agriculture and services, particularly in the hotel and retail sectors, were employed off-the-books. The incidence of casual labor was greatest in agriculture, where the proportion reached 42.1%. It was next highest in commerce, hostelry, and repair services (38.9%) and in other services (28.1%). The incidence of informality was hardly negligible in industry, however, Nearly one-fifth of construction workers were reported as working off-the-books, and rates of informality in other sectors ranged from less than 10% in heavy industries to more than one-fourth in miscellaneous manufacturing industries.

Indeed, considerable evidence shows that many jobs were shifted to the informal sector through a reorganization of production within industry. For example, a high proportion of self-employed workers detected in the national survey had worked previously in formal, salaried jobs. Furthermore, informal sector workers with past employment had usually held positions in the same sector. The clear implication is that officially recorded job loss in a given sector translated directly into more underground employment in the same sector.

The findings of the national survey are consistent with other analyses of informal sector growth in various light industries, where interviews with informed observers yield estimates that the informal sector accounts for between 15% and 40% of production (see, e.g., Casals and Vidal 1985; Vázquez and Trigo 1982). Casals and Vidal (1985) in their study of the textile industry in Sabadell, Catalonia, found that declared productive capacity decreased substantially between 1970 and 1981 but that no corresponding decline in production took place. Increases in productivity do not explain this discrepancy; the machinery declared to be in use also dropped by one-third, while the labor force declined by only 12% during the same period. The figures suggest that the machinery eliminated from established industry must have continued to function outside the "official" sector. Productivity in the unregulated sector also must have been even higher than it is in established firms.

Quantitative estimates suggest a simultaneous increase in the supply of labor for jobs in the unregulated sector and a rapid expansion in the volume of activity in the informal economy. Qualitative analyses permit us to go a step further and assert a direct relationship between industrial restructuring and the creation of a work force for the informal sector. The distinction between the demand for certain kinds of labor and the formation of an adequate labor supply tends to disappear in the analysis of informalization as a process of change within industry. The break-up of established firms has often led directly to the creation of informal enterprises. These are as much a product of workers' responses to industrial change as an outcome of the cost-cutting strategies of firms faced with high indirect labor costs and economic crisis. Jobs in the informal sector are this "born restructured" (Celada, López, and Parra 1985); that is, they form part of a new set of relationships among firms in industry at the moment they are created.

The clearest illustration of the direct connection between restructuring formal industry and emerging informal enterprises is the creation of the latter in the wake of plant closures (Miguélez 1982; Casals and Vidal 1985). When established factories close, production is often reorganized in small, underground workshops, in many cases with the same machinery and some of the same workers. These firms may produce the same product as the original factory or they may specialize in particular phases of the production process. This pattern of informalization is most evident in industries where vertical economies of scale are minimal. Production can be easily broken up into separate phases and the handling of intermediate goods does not present significant extra costs. On the contrary, economies of scale may occur *within* particular phases of production, where the concentration of workers with similar skills permits more efficient utilization of machinery.

A similar fragmentation of the production process may also occur, however, in industries where the technical requirements of production are quite different. In the construction industry, for example, production has been reorganized along similar lines in the wake of the crisis. Through the early 1970s, large construction jobs usually required crews of hundreds of workers, almost all of whom were employees of the original contractor. In the past decade, this system has been supplanted by one involving much greater reliance on small firms specializing in one or another phase of production. Contractors hire only a small crew of supervisors and technical "troubleshooters"; the rest of the work is subcontracted to small firms, many of which hire workers on an informal basis and pay them piecework rates rather than an hourly wage.[3]

Some evidence also exists to suggest that the fragmentation of production extends to other industries which, in contrast to construction and assembly manufacturing, are not labor-intensive. One study of industrial firms on the outskirts of Madrid revealed that a high percentage of small firms founded since the onset of the crisis were metal manufacturers and woodworking shops. The rest represented such diverse industries as printing, food processing, and the manufacture of chemicals and plastics (Celada, López, and Parra 1985). A study by the Valencian regional government showed that in the toy industry, not only are the more labor-intensive phases of production (for example, the sewing of dolls' clothes, painting dolls, and light assembly) increasingly being put out to homeworkers, but capital-intensive phases such as plastic molding and various types of metalwork are also being subcontracted to new small producers as the older established firms give way to smaller, decentralized ventures specializing in marketing and design (Consellería D'Industria 1984).

Together with the findings from the national survey, the case studies support the view that informalization in Spanish industry is best understood as an integral part of a more generalized industrial restructuring. The convergence of the economic crisis and the political transition helped to accelerate this trend, which gained momentum particularly after 1979. The findings raise important questions about the probable effects of this phenomenon on industrial growth and on industrial relations of production. Does the continued growth of small and informal enterprises reflect the special dynamism of small-scale industrial development, or does it simply arise from the defensive strategies of industrialists in the face of persistent adverse political and economic conditions? Will the process result in a general degradation of labor conditions and a return to autocratic control over the labor process, or can it generate entirely new relations of production and greater worker autonomy in ordering the production process?

According to the hypotheses outlined in the previous chapter, answering the first of these questions requires determining the relative dependence or independence of informal enterprises. Two variables are of fundamental importance: the relationship of the firms to others in the industry and to the market, and the firms' technological sophistication and capacity. At one end of the range of possibilities is the firm with complete dependence on other enterprises for work orders, for specifications of the work to be done, and for the provision of the necessary machinery. In this extreme position of dependence, the informal firm functions as little more than a system of pooling casual labor. At the other extreme is the enterprise producing either finished foods of its own design, which it markets directly, or intermediate goods, which it sells to various clients. In the latter case, we would expect relative autonomy and technological sophistication to be mutually reinforcing: producing for a range of clients often entails greater variation in the design of the product; greater control over production and design, in turn, promotes innovation and attracts a wider clientele.

A similar range of possibilities exists for labor conditions in informal economic activities. Self-employment may allow for greater control over the labor process; it may also simply serve to disguise forms of wage labor in which the worker assumes the costs and risks of an employer. Similarly, informal associations among workers may lead to greater collaboration in the organization of production and to profit-sharing arrangements, or they may involve greater exploitation and the simple reproduction of the shop-floor organization of the established factory. While previous studies of the informal sector in Spain have tended to agree that informalization has resulted in the degradation of labor conditions in industry, they have not examined closely the varying degree of worker voluntarism in different industries, the factors limiting the scope for worker initiative, or the basis for regulating the labor process in the absence of legal controls and union supervision.

The next two chapters present two case studies of informalization in Spanish industry and attempt to evaluate both the prospects for growth and the nature of working conditions in newly emerging, small firms. The cases chosen for study—the shoe industry in Alicante and the Madrid electronics industry—are both geographically highly concentrated industries located in areas of Spain where industrialization is relatively recent and especially rapid. The choice of these two regions protects us from the familiar bias of economic studies in Spain that focus exclusively on either the highly developed northeast or the poorer, more agricultural economy of the south. It would be perhaps obvious to look for the emergence of flexible specialization in Catalonia or the Basque region. In the former, a long tradition of entrepreneurship and relatively active regional industrial planning provide some favorable conditions for dynamic industrial restructuring; in the latter, strong regional loyalties and the widely publicized success of the Mondragón cooperatives suggest a fertile social environment for new experiments in industrial organization.[4] By the same token, it would be easy to predict less dynamism in the informal sector in Andalusia, where casual labor has long served workers' needs to complement income from seasonal agricultural work, without providing an impetus to strong industrial growth.[5] By focusing on changes in the "third Spain"—regions where industrialization is both new and vibrant—we open the analysis to true alternatives in the unfolding of industrial restructuring and in the role that informal industry will play.

The two industries were selected also because of their contrasts. While one represents a quintessentially labor-intensive industry that is heavily oriented toward the export market, the other comprises more varied and more sophisticated production processes, and is just beginning its bid to increase exports. Technological requirements in each industry are very different, yet both sectors are central to Spain's objectives of maintaining industrial competitiveness and fomenting the growth of exports for nontraditional and upscale markets.

The industries present examples, moreover, of two different geographical settings for productive decentralization in Spain. The first corresponds roughly to the pattern discovered in central Italy: The production of certain commodities is concentrated in a cluster of towns, and decentralization entails the expansion of unregulated industry into the surrounding rural and semirural areas. In the second setting, the large metropolitan area, informal labor appears commonly in services and in the growing numbers of industrial firms on the urban periphery. These contrasting physical settings correspond to very different social and political contexts for production and are associated, not surprisingly, with diverging patterns of industrial change.

PART II

3 High-Tech Cottage Industry? Productive Decentralization in Madrid's Electronics Industry

I argued in Chapter 1 that the transformation of the informal sector from a degraded industrial substratum to a forum for innovation and development depends upon the social relations of production in the workplace. Cooperation and control over production enable new subcontractors to exchange their dependence on larger enterprises for relative autonomy in product design and access to a wider market. This chapter traces the process of productive decentralization in Madrid's electronics industry and evaluates the progress toward independent specialization achieved by small, newly formed subcontractors. The small enterprises comprising the industry's "auxiliary" branch perform tasks that used to be carried out within large electronics firms. Their capacity for providing high-quality goods and services is crucial to the continued expansion of the industry.

The right conditions for dynamic decentralized growth seem to be present in the industry. In the production of professional (not consumer) electronics, innovative design and astute marketing can compensate for rising wages; in Madrid, the presence of a skilled workforce makes such solutions seem possible. The importance of the electronics industry to national goals of improving home-based technology and encouraging nontraditional exports also suggests that liberal government support should be forthcoming. Finally, the industry has experienced strong demand in the domestic market and has plenty of room to improve in the export arena. The questions is, has decentralization so far contributed to the industry's impressive growth? And what promises, or problems, does the trend imply for future development?

The Setting: Madrid as an Industrial Center

The pattern of decentralization in Madrid's electronics industry has been shaped, in part, by the local economic environment and the history of industrialization in the region. Madrid's appearance as a major industrial center in Spain is relatively recent. While growth of Catalan textiles and Basque heavy industry led industrial development in the nineteenth century and the early part of this century, Madrid remained primarily a center for public administration and services. Until the late nineteenth century, industrial development in the area was limited to the production of goods to supply the expanding local market, along with the nascent paper and publishing industries, and the activities associated with the construction of the railroad. Between 1880 and 1930, Madrid industry remained mainly oriented toward provising a range of finished goods for local consumption. The city also consolidated its role as the most important financial center in the country. The global crisis of the 1930s, coupled with the devastation of the Spanish Civil War, halted the tentative progress toward diversified industrialization in the region.

The political and economic role of Madrid underwent an important change with the victory of Franco's forces in the Civil War. The new regime favored not only political centralization but also an enhanced economic position for the capital. Created in 1941, the *Instituto Nacional de Industria* (INI) invested heavily in the Madrid region throughout the 1940s and 1950s. In keeping with the regime's overall strategy of fomenting the development of basic industries, investment in Madrid went mainly toward the financing of large concerns producing intermediate and capital goods, especially transport equipment, electrical machinery, and chemicals. The growth of these industries stimulated the development of auxiliary industries and indirectly fed local demand for goods and services. That demand was also kept buoyant by the continued concentration of administrative posts in the capital and by public spending on large construction projects. The 1950s saw the first great wave of in-migration to the city, a process that further reinforced local demand for construction materials and for a wide array of finished goods.

This phase of modest growth was followed by a period of extremely rapid industrial development. Between 1955 and 1975, the value of production in Madrid industry increased fivefold, outpacing growth even in the services. Industrial development in the region was particularly marked during the boom decade of the 1960s. Within

Spain, the rate of growth of industry in Madrid was surpassed only in Valencia. By the decade's end, the region had become the second largest industrial center in the country, after Catalonia. Although services continued to dominate the Madrid economy and to account for roughly one-fifth of the national value-added in this sector, Madrid industry also assumed national importance. In 1975, on the eve of Spain's economic crisis and the transition to democracy, the region accounted for one-fifth of national production in the paper and printing industries, 15% in metalworking and in the garment industry, 13% in chemical production, and 11% in the manufacture of construction materials (Comunidad de Madrid 1984).

Two related trends appear to characterize Madrid's rapid industrial growth. Although manufacturing continued to specialize in finished goods and to depend heavily on outside inputs, products were increasingly destined for areas outside the region. A diverse range of consumer goods industries, from clothing to pharmaceutical products, thus "arrived" on the national market, becoming competitive with traditionally stronger producers of these goods in other areas of Spain. Second, a small but important group of nontraditional industries took advantage of the groundwork laid by state and foreign investments in the previous decades and grew rapidly during the boom of the 1960s. This group included machinery, transport, and electronics or electrical manufactures. This last industry was moving rapidly toward becoming the leading sector in the region (Celada, López, and Parra 1985).

The spurt in growth of nontraditional industries in Madrid and the continued importance of light manufacturing of consumer goods produced a peculiar industrial structure. The average size of Madrid firms was larger than in the rest of Spain, a fact that reflected both the state's support for large-scale enterprises and the high proportion of foreign investment in Spain—roughly one-fourth of the total—concentrated in the region. Much of industrial employment was centered in the large firms; in 1973, 45% of industrial jobs were in firms with more than 250 workers. Yet small firms were much more numerous and continued to dominate industry. Of the firms surveyed, 90% had fewer than 26 employees in 1973, and 98% held fewer than 250 workers (Comunidad de Madrid 1984).

Mainly because of its privileged position as the financial and political center of the country, Madrid was in a better position than

the more traditional industrial regions to bear the shock of the
economic crisis. Indeed, the full effects of the crisis were delayed until
the late 1970s. The large share of the services in the economy, where
labor demand proved most buoyant, mitigated the overall impact on
employment. The same factor helped to keep small industry afloat by
maintaining local demand for finished goods. Even though
withdrawal of international capital and decline in the growth of
public investment were inevitable, the considerable stake of both
large national and international capital in Madrid industry also meant
that disinvestment was neither abrupt nor devastating in its effects.

Madrid's advantageous position during the crisis is reflected in
the fact that unemployment in the capital remained consistently
lower than in Catalonia or the Basque region throughout the decade
following the economically disastrous year of 1974. Nevertheless, the
changes set into motion by the economic downturn did alter Madrid's
economy and its industrial structure; the effects of the crisis on
employment, although not as dramatic as in some other regions, have
not been negligible. In the decade between 1974 and 1984, Madrid
lost approximately 200,000 jobs. Industrial employment dropped by
about 17%, compared to a decrease of 4.7% in the service sector, and
a spectacular 41% drop in construction, an industry that had been the
mainstay of migrant workers in the previous decades. Other
important industries also showed serious decline: Employment loss is
estimated at 60,000 jobs in Madrid's large metalworking industry and
at 20,000 in the city's textile industry (Comunidad de Madrid 1984).

In addition to cutting back jobs, industry also responded to
the downturn by decentralizing production, both functionally and
spatially. The restructuring is most in evidence in the construction
industry, where the large firms have reduced their permanent work
forces dramatically and now subcontract most production to small
firms and groups of *autónomos* (self-employed workers). The large
firms thus avoid having to pay indemnities for laying off workers and
are able to shift the burden of paying social security to small
subcontractors and to the workers themselves. Not surprisingly, this
shift has been accompanied by an increase in the number of informal
jobs in the industry, which directly replace regular jobs.[1]

A similar process is evident in Madrid's garment industry. A
study of 16 important garment manufacturers in Madrid showed that
all had decentralized certain phases of production. In this industry,

decentralization appears to have followed two different patterns, with modernized, high-fashion firms putting out those product lines and phases of production that are most vulnerable to shifts in fashion, and less technically advanced firms tending to subcontract low-quality tasks, responding to fluctuations in the volume of demand (Grasa and Carricajo 1985). According to union officials, the process has resulted in an increase in the number of small firms in the area and a substantial rise in homework for the more labor-intensive tasks.

Further evidence of generalized industrial restructuring is the spatial decentralization of Madrid industry. While industrial firms during the 1960s were concentrated in the city of Madrid and in a "first ring" of industrial towns on its outskirts, a "second ring" of former bedroom communities and agricultural towns has increasingly become an important destination for industrial firms. In some cases, this shift has accompanied a boom in the population of outlying municipalities, which nevertheless tend to be plagued by higher unemployment rates than in the capital itself. The new settings for industry often lack an appropriate infrastructure and occupy land that is still zoned for residential or agricultural uses (Celada, López, and Parra 1985; Comunidad de Madrid 1984). Decentralization has also spread production even further afield. In a variety of industries, firms have shifted some phases of production to rural areas outside Madrid where labor costs tend to be lower. I learned of one Madrid metalwork shop, for example, that was forced to close when its main client, a major electronics company, cancelled its contract and shifted orders to a tiny family firm in Toledo. At least one Madrid shoe factory transfers its piecework as far as Alicante, and it is quite common for shoe producers to transport work to the mostly rural province of La Mancha.

Newer activities have reinforced this trend by adopting a decentralized pattern from the start. The production of software and services for the computer industry, for example, has seen explosive growth in the Madrid area over the last several years. The new firms tend to shift rapidly from urban to suburban locations, or else they opt from the start for outlying areas close to the headquarters of major clients and at the same time within easy reach of large institutional customers in the capital. This pattern is, in turn, part of a larger process of decentralization in the computer industry whereby production of hardware is being shifted to coastal Mediterranean areas while management, financial services, and software production concentrates in Madrid (Estevan 1988).

Spatial decentralization of industry in the Madrid area in part represents a continuation of earlier decentralizing tendencies and reflects the expansion of some existing firms in need of larger facilities. But the trend is also linked to recent restructuring. Many new, small firms produce intermediate goods for larger, decentralizing firms. The latter also seek to cut fixed costs by moving to lower-priced land on the city's periphery where they may also benefit by recruiting cheaper labor from peripheral towns with higher levels of unemployment than in the capital.

Is there any evidence that this process of productive decentralization in Madrid industry could lead to a revitalization of industry in the region? Labor-intensive industries, where the process is most in evidence, appear to be unlikely places to look for innovative trends generated by informalization. In the construction industry, the new "self-employment" is best understood as a form of disguised wage labor, in which workers involuntarily accept the risks and burdens of independence. The large firms in the industry have, if anything, consolidated their dominant position. In garment production and in other light manufacturing industries, there is some evidence that decentralization has encouraged the formation of high-quality specialty workshops (Grasa and Carricajo 1985). But the ability to lower costs through a strategy combining spatial decentralization and subcontracting to sweatshops or homeworkers helps to forestall pressures to revamp production or marketing techniques in such industries.

The effects of decentralization in more capital-intensive industries in the region appear more complex. A study of spatial decentralization in the Madrid region produced some interesting findings about the independence, technological capacity, and market position of new small firms in a wide variety of industrial sectors (Celada, López, and Parra 1985). Researchers working for the Madrid regional government completed a census of small firms in Paracuellos del Jarama, a zone of industrial "squatters" to the northeast of Madrid, and conducted a survey of small enterprises in Fuenlabrada, a somewhat better-established industrial town to the south. Of the nearly 300 firms surveyed, 44% produced finished goods, and only 18% of these worked exclusively from designs supplied by commercial agents or other firms. A slightly larger proportion arrived at the design through consultation with the client. Not surprisingly, producers of intermediate goods showed a greater degree of dependence on other firms for specification; 59% received these directly from their clients. However, a significant proportion (24%) produced intermediate goods of their own design, and another 17% negotiated product design with their clients.

It is also unclear whether these small firms occupy a subordinate position in the market. The vast majority of producers of intermediate goods (73.6%) had three or more clients, while another 11% marketed their goods directly through wholesale or retail outlets. Only 7% were dependent on a single client. The authors' conclusions that the firms they studied should be characterized as subordinate partners in an industrial putting-out system appears questionable in light of these findings. At the same time, it is clear that not all the firms are independent producers of specialized goods. As the authors of the study point out, the smallest and most precarious firms display the greatest extremes of subordination and autonomy, and of technological primitiveness and sophistication.

A logical next step is to examine the dynamics of change within particular industries. Decentralization in the electronics industry provides a useful contrast to restructuring in more labor-intensive industries. The industry has, moreover, emerged as Madrid's leading employer. The case is particularly relevant to understanding the prospects for growth in those semi-industrialized countries which have fallen behind both the advanced economies and other NICs in developing high-technology industries.

Decentralization in Madrid's Electronics Industry

The development of Madrid's electronics industry reflects the close involvement of large international and national capital in the region's economy. Understanding the origins of the industry is essential to analyzing the causes and effects of decentralization over the past decade. My account of the industry's early development is based on the work of Antonio Estevan, whose extensive research on small and medium electronics firms also served as the starting place for fieldwork on the new, small subcontractors generated through decentralization.[2]

Madrid's electronics industry developed out of a telecommunications industry started in the 1920s, when the Spanish government awarded the rights to develop the national telephone system to International Telegraph and Telephone (ITT). That company subsequently founded Standard Eléctrica, S.A., to produce the needed equipment. When, as a direct result of the Civil War, ITT lost control of the national telephone company, *Companía Telefonica Nacional de España* (CTNE), the two companies maintained a virtual monopoly of supply (Standard) and demand (CTNE) for electronic equipment over the following 15 years. The INI entered the industry in the 1940s, although it remained a marginal force compared with the two giants.

This situation began to change only toward the end of the 1960s, when CTNE decided to break Standard's monopoly of production in telecommunications. This strategy was not intended as a direct attack on Standard; by this time, CTNE also held a 20% interest in the company. CTNE this created two large firms in Madrid, bought a third Madrid company from INI, and opened a cable factory in Zaragoza. Standard benefitted from the rapid economic growth of the 1960s and expanded by buying Marconi from INI in 1969, creating another large firm, Citesa, and increasing the size of its own work force.

Other firms also began to be formed during this period, and the industry widened to include television, medical electronics, defense applications, and other subfields. Madrid continued to be the undisputed center of the industry. Between 1960 and 1974, about 20 medium- to large-sized firms were established in Madrid, and by the mid-1970s the electronics industry was the largest producer and one of the largest employers in the Madrid area. In 1976, about 30,000 people were employed in professional electronics in Madrid, compared to about 25,000 in sectors such as printing and automation, and 40,000 in textiles. As with enterprises in other capital-intensive, state-backed industries in Madrid, firms in the electronics industry tended to be large, with an average of about 500 workers. The production process was generally highly centralized, with distinct phases of production carried out in separate sections within the firms.

The sale and style of production clearly reflected firms' extensive ties to multinational companies and to the Spanish state.

But this characteristic also made the industry extremely vulnerable in the face of constricted public investment and the withdrawal of international capital accompanying the economic crisis. Other factors also converged to place considerable pressure on large firms. The steady rise of wages, prompted by the increasing militancy of Madrid industrial workers in the mid-1970s, made loss of jobs in the large firms inevitable. In addition, the development of microchip technology meant that large assembly work forces were becoming obsolete. This change alone would have forced some cutbacks even in the absence of other debilitating factors. The most spectacular job loss in the industry resulted from the reconversion of Standard in 1982 and the slow reduction of its work force from a high of 25,000 to fewer than 20,000 (see Chapter 7). Other large firms also reduced their work forces, producing a loss of about 6,000 jobs over the last decade, or about 20% of the work force that existed in the mid-1970s. Some subsectors, such as defense and medical electronics, were hit particularly hard by the stagnation of public investment during this period.

However, despite its vulnerability, Madrid's electronics industry appears to have come through the crisis with a considerably better record than that of other major industries. Job loss in the large firms appears to have stabilized, and overall employment in the industry has risen slightly, an exceptional trend in most Spanish industry and certainly in Madrid, where, as we noted above, industrial employment suffered a severe drop between 1974 and 1984. Electronics remains the leading producer in the region, and it has been estimated that the industry, including all its various subsectors, employs around 40,000 workers.

Madrid has also held its own as the leading center for electronics production in the country. We should emphasize that this role depends on Madrid's dominance of professional electronics, the sector comprising telecommunications, defense, computers, medical equipment, and other professional electronics applications. The smaller subsectors of consumer electronics and electronic components are heavily concentrated in Barcelona and its surrounding area. Madrid holds an estimated 40% of firms and accounts for more than 50% of employment in the Spanish electronics industry as a whole; in professional electronics, Madrid's share of employment and production is closer to 70% of the total in this subsector (Estevan 1986).

The main exception to this pattern is in computer equipment; as we noted earlier, computer producers have tended to locate their plants away from Madrid, on the Mediterranean coast (Barcelona, Valencia, and Malaga). However, these are large, mostly isolated plants; no other region has developed a network of professional electronics firms that can rival that of Madrid. From now on, when we talk about Madrid electronics, we will be referring to professional electronics producers.

The health and continued expansion of this industry have much to do with the recent creation of numerous new and small- to medium-sized firms. These differ substantially from the firms that dominated the industry a decade ago. Very few—probably fewer than 20%—have direct ties to international capital or to CTNE, INI, or other large sources of national capital. They tend instead to be self-financed ventures, begun by working professionals who spotted new opportunities in specialized markets not controlled by the large companies. Estevan estimates that at least 60 such firms started up between 1974 and 1984, and these consolidated their positions rapidly (Estevan 1984). Of the 45 small and medium firms Estevan studied for the Madrid regional government in 1984, more than one-half had been founded after 1978; most were firms with between 10 and 50 workers and were headed by engineers or others with professional degrees.

The new enterprises also depart from the traditional model of firms in the industry because they have opted for highly decentralized structures. Most subcontract the main phases of production and assembly, reserving for themselves the more technical phases such as design, installation, testing, and maintenance. In order to remain competitive, older and more established firms have also joined this trend. For both new and older firms, decentralization has proved extremely advantageous. Start-up costs and barriers to entry into new product lines are significantly lowered because firms do not need to invest in machinery to perform all phases of production. Particularly when more labor-intensive phases of production, such as assembly, are subcontracted, indirect labor costs are also reduced. Finally, decentralization permits firms to concentrate their efforts on research and design, as well as on devising new marketing strategies.

Although the emergence of the new, decentralized firms may have helped establish the potential for dynamic growth in the electronics industry, significant obstacles to the industry's competitiveness with other international producers remain. Exports have increased substantially, but they still form a relatively small share of the market, particularly for small firms with less experience in foreign markets and a weaker marketing infrastructure. In general, the industry finds itself, according to Estevan, "unable to match the pace of technological development among leading producers of the United States, Japan, West Germany, Great Britain, and other advanced countries specializing in the most dynamic products, and also unable to compete in price with the producers of Southeast Asia." (Estevan 1984, 95). Yet, exports clearly must expand if the industry is to thrive; the domestic market is limited, both in the volume and the range of goods that comprise it.

Several features of the industry must change in order for its competitive position to improve substantially. Innovation is obviously one key to growth. So far, most recent original developments have consisted of minor improvements aimed at replacing imported products in the national market. The structure of the new firms may facilitate further innovation and experimentation. In particular, the close involvement of technical personnel in production and the increased expenditure on research and development made possible in the decentralized firms are hopeful signs. However, other obstacles remain, including the tight market for credit, which is particularly troublesome to small producers, and the lack of an already established reputation for Spanish electronics in the international market.

In addition, it is important to ascertain whether the newly decentralized structure may not itself pose some obstacles to continued growth in the industry. The existence of a group of small subcontractors capable of providing high-quality goods and services to electronics firms could prove to be an important asset. I have already mentioned that one advantage of such a system is that it helps to free producers to concentrate their efforts on design and marketing. In addition, it would facilitate improvements of quality and refinements in style all the way down the line. A highly developed system of subcontracting would offer two quite different, but equally attractive, benefits to producers. They would be able to expedite production by choosing from an array of standardized components produced by the auxiliary industry, and they could rely on the greater flexibility of small firms to produce small series of high-quality goods adapted to the needs of particular clients or markets. If subcontractors do not display these features, then decentralization may represent little more than a strategy for shifting costs and risks to smaller firms, which merely reproduce the same tasks more cheaply, with the same or a lower level of quality.

In part because the auxiliary industry in electronics is so new and in part because its activities overlap with those of other industries, very little information has been available abut this lowest level of production. Estevan found that the 45 small- and medium-sized entrepreneurs he interviewed could name a total of 160 workshops they employed to carry out different specialized phases of production. His study did not determine whether most of these firms served mainly the electronics industry or were enterprises that had long been established as subcontractors or even as independent producers in other industries. It was also not known whether the firms were, in fact, moving toward either of the goals outlined above. Although producers rarely voiced dissatisfaction with the quality of work obtained through subcontracting, they pinpointed several problems, particularly the lack of technological sophistication in the auxiliary industry and the dearth of high-quality standardized components and subcomponents in the Spanish market. Producers' accounts revealed little about the conditions of employment in the small firms and the obstacles the latter might face in trying to improve their performance.

Small Subcontractors in the Electronics Industry

To answer these and other questions, I studied the histories and progress of 25 subcontractors in the Madrid area. Although the dearth of information about these firms made a representative sample impossible, I used the information gathered by Estevan and in my own preliminary interviews to select a varied group of small producers for study. I relied on several criteria in making the selection. First, the sample was constructed to include both firms that appeared to have few clients and firms that clearly had many. Second, it was designed to contain firms working for large electronics producers, as well as enterprises apparently serving only small clients. Third, I selected firms in five of the seven areas most frequently subcontracted by electronics producers, maintaining a roughly even balance between subsectors whose production processes are intrinsically tied to electronics and others in which firms could also conceivably serve clients from other industries. The firms were grouped as follows: metalwork (7); painting and silkscreening (6); assembly of subcomponents (5); printed circuits (4); and transformers (3).

Between April and June 1985 I conducted semistructured interviews with the owner-entrepreneur in each firm and, where possible, also held informal conversations with workers and spent time observing production within the enterprises. The interviews gathered basic data about each firm, including its age, legal status, and the size and composition of its work force. I also solicited more qualitative accounts of the firm's development, the owner's work history, the firm's relationships with clients (and with any subcontractors), and its future prospects. Additional questions focused on the internal organization of production in the firm, relations among workers (or between workers and employers), and the entrepreneurs' general political outlook, particularly his view of government support for, and interaction with, small businesses. I kept a printed questionnaire with me while conducting the interviews, although most conversations were informal: Questioning did not follow a set order and varied in its detail according to the circumstances of the particular firm and the openness of the informant. Many of the interviews took place while I stood or walked with informants on the shop-floor. Observation of work on the shop-floor complemented the information from owners and helped to corroborate some of their statements.

In evaluating my findings, one must first understand something about the nature of the production process in electronics. The process accommodates decentralization extremely well. A number of distinct phases of production can be carried out at separate times and in separate locations without disturbing the rhythm or overall organization of production. The first several phases of any production process—engineering design and the constructing and testing of prototypes—as well as the final two phases—testing and installation—tend still to be carried out in the firm originating the product idea. The intermediate phases, which are most often subcontracted, can be divided roughly into two types of activity: the fabrication of parts and subcomponents, and the assembly of circuitry, subcomponents, and complete apparatuses.

The following five processes are those which are subcontracted most frequently:

1. **Printed circuits.** All electronics firms have these components prepared by specialized firms. The standard process involves the creation of "boards" or "cards" that have circuitry patterns first photo-silkscreened, then chemically etched, into the surface. The cards are also drilled with holes to accommodate the subcomponents that will later be soldered onto the surface. Because the pattern of circuitry varies for each series produced, standardization is not a realistic goal in this subsector. Quality can vary substantially, however, and several production processes exist for more compact, more sophisticated circuit boards that few Spanish firms make.

2. **Metalwork.** Virtually all electronics products carry some sort of metal casing, and this is an area of production that almost all new firms subcontract to avoid the necessary investment in machinery. A growing demand is found both for standardized metalwork and for small, highly varied series. Only a small handful of firms in Spain produces standardized products sold by catalogue; at the time of this study, Madrid had only one such firm. For both standardized and customized jobs, numerical control machines are extremely desirable, although the costs are prohibitive in most small firms, which continue to use older machinery and to rely on workers' skills to provide the required precision. Despite the fact that several thousand metalworkers in Madrid are officially unemployed, an excess of demand for skilled workers is found in this area; metalworkers accustomed to less precise types of work generally do not have the skills needed in production for the electronics industry.

3. **Painting and silkscreening.** After metal parts are prepared they are chemically treated and painted. The company logo or other information is then applied by silkscreen. Again, these processes were formerly performed inside electronics firms, and they are now usually subcontracted to specialized workshops. Multiple subcontracting results when metalworking firms agree to do the painting and then put it out to other small producers. The painting techniques do not differ much from those used in other types of metal painting, although greater attention to different types of

chemical treatments, paints, and techniques of application is needed for the higher-quality work demanded by many electronics producers. Clients place a high value on painters' ability to judge the combination of treatments most appropriate for different jobs. Some notion of design principles is also useful to painters and particularly to silkscreeners, who are sometimes called upon to create or modify existing designs.

4. **Transformers.** These components range from the very small transformers used in consumer electronic goods to the very large parts used in electrical plants. The basic production process is the same and consists of wrapping wire around bobbins and encasing these in metal. The preparation of small transformers is done with a simple machine, not unlike a sewing machine, and can be done by homeworkers. Considerable competition exists in the market for the simpler transformers, many of which are from firms in Barcelona because of the concentration of consumer electronics firms found there. Madrid transformer producers find that they must seek to specialize further, offer additional products and services, and keep wage costs low to remain competitive.

5. **Assembly of subcomponents, circuitry, and cables.** With the development of the microchip, the labor requirements for the assembly phase of production have been substantially reduced. However, the task of placing subcomponents on circuit boards (and that of soldering these by hand in small firms without automatic soldering equipment) is relatively unskilled and labor-intensive. Subcontracting assembly work is fairly common as a result and lends itself to the use of unregulated or semiregulated labor. In his study, Estevan detected several groups of *autónomos* who do assembly work. Homeworkers also may be hired on a temporary or piecework basis to do assembly work. Several nonprofit organizations in the Madrid area employ handicapped workers. Not surprisingly, established firms find that demand is erratic and low-cost competition plentiful; as with producers of transformers, they must search for other activities to supplement earnings or offer clients a wider range or more specialized types of assembly work.

Because the nature of production is so different in these subsectors, the conditions of employment and the relations with clients are unique in each case. Nevertheless, the similarities among the subcontractors are more striking than their differences. Only one of the firms was founded before 1970 and nearly two-thirds were started after 1978, mainly to fill the demand for subcontracting from the newly formed, small- and medium-sized electronics producers. The firms are small; only three of them have more than 25 workers.[3] They are scattered on the periphery of Madrid, with the largest concentrations in the eastern industrial section of the city, to the northeast along the Madrid-Barcelona highway (where electronics producers are also concentrated), and to the south in industrial areas such as Fuenlabrada and Arganda del Rey.

Determining to what degree these firms have been, or will be, successful in becoming independent producers capable of innovative contributions to the electronics industry requires examining the way labor is organized within the firms and the nature of relationships of subcontractors with their clients. The following subsections discuss each of these questions in turn. Some obstacles to continued development in the auxiliary industry will become apparent in my analysis and will be explored in Chapter 6, which examines the political context of industrial restructuring in Madrid.

Internal Relations of Production

One of the most striking features of the auxiliary firms is that most of them were founded under similar circumstances and by individuals with similar work histories. In the majority of the cases, the firms' founders are skilled workers who left jobs in larger firms to strike out on their own. In some cases, they were driven to do so because firms had closed. For example, one worker-entrepreneur had held successive jobs in three firms, all of which had closed; he had accepted machinery instead of a cash indemnity from his last employer and used it to establish his own business. But the majority of those interviewed had voluntarily left other, stable jobs to start their own businesses. They cite as reasons for doing so their desire for independence, their disapproval of the way their former employers managed their operations, and the desire to "create something"— capital, jobs, a particular type of product, or a legacy to pass on to their children. Only a few said that they regretted having started their own firms, and most described the experience with evident pride. Even the worker cited above who turned to self-employment after successive lay-offs described the change positively and reported that his "big mistake was not to have done it sooner."

Many of the firms started out an informal enterprises. Skilled workers frequently began by accepting work on a casual basis while still holding other jobs in order to save the necessary capital to become fully independent. A number of others began working under extremely rudimentary conditions, producing in their own homes or in small sheds, or even paying to use machinery set up in other workshops. Particularly during this initial stage, worker-entrepreneurs commonly relied on family labor, which had the double advantage of being less expensive (sometimes unpaid) and also highly flexible. In addition, the workers themselves usually worked for a long time before being *dado de alta* ("put on-the-books") as self-employed workers or establishing their firms as legal entities.

The process by which the firms were formed has certain important implications for the way the labor process within them is now organized. First, although none of the firms is still clandestine, many preserve certain characteristics of the initial, informal stage. It is not unusual for skilled workers to earn more than they would working for larger firms, but they generally also have to work harder; contract regulations about overtime and vacations are often replaced with informal agreements between workers and owners that allow for greater flexibility in work schedules. One entrepreneur argues that such practices are not only essential to the small firm but also better for the worker, who may earn more and receive part of his pay in cash bonuses not included in his officially reported salary:

> In a small firm a worker can earn more because he can negotiate more. For example, say I have more work today because I have to deliver an order to a client tomorrow . . . . I can ask a worker to stay and we'll negotiate what he's going to receive. Legally maybe it shouldn't be done, but it's better. Instead of having two unhappy workers at 40,000 pesetas a month, you get one satisfied worker at 80,000 a month.

In some firms, owners also admit to hiring extra workers on an unofficial, temporary basis during busy periods. This type of casual labor is, of course, greater in firms that face more volatile demand and rely more heavily on unskilled labor. For example, one firm specializing in the assembly of subcomponents had six extra workers on the day I visited, in addition to its regular work force of 13. The temporary workers were being paid with cash and on a daily basis to help prepare backlogged orders.

Some firms continue to use family labor, although this is not necessarily off-the-books labor. Three are family enterprises run by children of the companies' founders. In other firms, family labor is used precisely because it is especially flexible. For example, in three of the small painting workshops, close relatives of the owners work as they are needed, doing lighter productive as well as administrative tasks; in one case, young children help out on weekends and during peak production periods. Although using family labor clearly helps lower costs, this objective is not the only one employers consider in hiring close relatives. Some owners hope to prime family members for skilled work or positions of responsibility within the firms; in other cases, firms provide opportunities to family members who cannot find other jobs. One worker-entrepreneur who employs his son to assist with silkscreening put the youth to work because he "didn't like to study, and he couldn't find any other job."

In most of the small firms, the atmosphere is more relaxed than it would be in large factories. Workers talk among themselves while they work, and they may leave their posts for short breaks without disrupting the production process. Employers seldom penalize tardy workers and they often set more convenient hours to accommodate commuters. Because the owners are themselves skilled workers who either participate in production or play some direct role in its supervision, they are often on the shop-floor talking with employees or working alongside them. It is not uncommon for a worker-entrepreneur to stop and show an employee how to perform or improve his performance of a particular task. Both workers and entrepreneurs seemed to prefer the relaxed atmosphere; when asked about the differences with the new firm and the larger one where he had worked previously, one partner in a small workshop responded:

> Here everything is much better. There you had to fill out little cards to record what you had done every minute of the day. Here you don't. There we started work at 8 and you had to punch your card. Here we start at 8:30 because that's the hour we all decided is best to miss the morning rush hour. Somebody has a birthday and we all go have a drink together . . . . Let's just say the atmosphere's informal, relaxed.

One is tempted to romanticize the small firm's more intimate atmosphere and to exaggerate its positive effects on productivity. Some advantages are indeed very apparent. In particular, the small setting allows workers to help each other with difficult tasks more easily as well as to give each other advice on the best way to adjust to different jobs. Greater attention can be given to the individual talents and preferences of workers for particular jobs, and this in and of itself helps boost productivity and improve quality. However, important problems of organization and management still exist in the small firms, and the "high-trust" atmosphere does not solve them in every case.

Some limitations of the small firms can be blamed on entrepreneurs' lack of managerial experience. As former employees, most have no formal training and little direct experience in running a business. The very structure of production in the firms also makes learning business skills more difficult. Precisely because the owners of small firms are skilled workers knowledgeable about the production process, they face serious dilemmas in trying to free more of their own time to attend to marketing, product development, and administrative tasks. Some of the small entrepreneurs have tried to cope with this problem by relying on family members or other trusted individuals to supervise production in their absence. The supervisory function of close kin was made strikingly clear when the wife of an owner interrupted an interview to report that a worker had not returned from lunch and that production had stopped.

Owners who do not have kin or business partners to act as supervisors work under considerable strain. One owner of a painting workshop opted to scale down production by one-half, paying the heavy indemnities to lay-off workers, because he was unable to supervise two shifts effectively; even after the reductions, he was searching for ways to maintain the quality and pace of production in his absence and was considering hiring someone to monitor workers' activities—but only if he could find "*una persona de confianza*" (someone trusted).

Even when trusted supervisors are available, production may suffer from the prolonged absence of worker-entrepreneurs, who often are the most skilled in performing certain tasks. A partner in a printed circuits factor reports that he is able to spend time outside the firm only because he has "handpicked" highly skilled workers who "can work without supervision . . . deal with clients, and make decisions." Delegating supervisory responsibilities may backfire, however; the "high-trust" atmosphere that develops through the daily contact of workers and entrepreneurs-acting-as-workers may be replaced by worker antagonism toward a supervisor whose authority is delegated rather than based on a thorough command of the production process.

Innovative solutions to this problem have been found by some firms in the reorganization of productive tasks and the further breakdown of the traditional separation between workers and management. Such solutions have come more easily to firms that were founded by several skilled workers who had known each other previously as employees in other firms. In these enterprises, the same debilitating pressure on one individual to handle all aspects of managing the firm is not found. In several cases I observed, workers began rotating positions of responsibility in areas such as production supervision, sales, and financial management to determine which workers were most suited to, and happiest with, particular tasks. If such duties are distributed widely, all worker-entrepreneurs may still retain a hand in the production process. In one metalworking firm, for example, the worker in charge of sales was also responsible for programming jobs on the firm's numerical control machine, a task that left him free most of the time to talk with clients and attend to paperwork.

A somewhat different solution to the problem is to reorganize productive tasks in such a way that workers necessarily become their own supervisors. Giving workers more control over the production process draws them into the circle of high trust in the firm and changes the social form that supervision takes. Rather than having one person oversee the activities of many, owners interact with workers as colleagues and collaborators. The clearest example of such a strategy was found in a metalworking firm in which individual workers are assigned responsibility for an entire job, from start to finish, in contrast to the more usual division of labor by specialized task. According to the two partners who own the firm, the disadvantages of such a system—in particular, lower productivity because workers have to change jobs often and inevitably perform some tasks better than others—are outweighed by its advantages. Checking up on an individual worker or job means talking with only one employee because no one else can be held responsible for delays or problems with quality. Workers apparently respond well to this system, in part because it makes the work more challenging and continually forces them to upgrade their skills in a broad range of activities. On one afternoon when I observed work in the firm while both owners were absent, employees worked steadily but without haste, rotating from one machine to another and pausing to give each other assistance or advice.

A more direct way to distribute responsibility evenly among workers is, of course, to form a cooperative. Three of the firms I studied were cooperatives, but only two of these had been started by workers who believed that sharing responsibilities was essential to the firms' success. Both have experimented—in one case, highly successfully—with a management system based on bimonthly meetings to vote on major decisions. The third firm is an example of what union leaders refer to as a "false cooperative"; it was formed by workers to save their jobs when they were threatened by the closure of a privately owned firm.

Forming a cooperative is not always an ideal solution to problems of management and control within the small firms. Some entrepreneurs are resistant to sharing ownership and decisionmaking after they have alone made the initial sacrifices to establish their businesses. Several of the firms studied abandoned early efforts to form cooperatives because of repeated failure to reach consensus among members. In one case, the current owner claims that shared decisionmaking stood in the way of the firm's growth:

> In this [business] you have to be looking constantly at not only the national but also the international markets to see what [machinery] is available. In a cooperative, when the moment comes to buy new machinery, your vote counts the same as that of the guy who sweeps the floor, and *he* doesn't want to invest even after you explain that if you don't do it, the firm won't survive.

The fact remains, however, that in many cases cooperative efforts would help solve some of the major problems experienced by subcontractors. Given this possibility, it is surprising that more of the loose associations observed among skilled workers are not formalized as cooperatives. Later in this chapter, and again in Chapter 6, I examine some of the reasons a surge in cooperativism has not taken place.

Technology and Marketing

Subcontractors clearly use various forms of unregulated labor to cut labor costs, and their ability to do so is undoubtedly one factor accounting for their success in attracting clients. But it is probably not the most important factor. The small subcontractors believe that their clientele places greater emphasis on high standards of quality and precision in production. This claim is confirmed by most clients, and it is reinforced by the finding that those subcontractors that have been able to establish a reputation for quality have no difficulties finding work. Entrepreneurs questioned about their marketing strategies say that they have none; clients come to the firms with work and the subcontractors sometimes have to turn jobs down. "After I got my first client," one small producer of printed circuits reports, "I never had to go looking. The clients just came to me."

It is less clear to what extent the work done by small subcontractors could objectively be considered high in quality. One client, a production manager at an electronics firm linked to a large multinational company, complained that subcontractors in Madrid are ignorant of international standards and cannot be relied upon to produce work of even quality. He noted that some of the problems stem from the lack of support from other elements of Spanish industry; for example, high-quality materials for many jobs are simply not sold locally, and, in any case, precise specifications needed to compare locally bought materials to international standards are not routinely available. The subcontractors themselves report these shortcomings. But other problems arise from a lack of quality control. As an example of the substandard work sometimes done by subcontractors, the same buyer cited a job done for his firm in which the shades of paint on different parts of a piece of equipment did not match. The job had to be redone in-house. "It's not that the owner himself wasn't skilled. But his workers are not as highly qualified, and they don't work carefully."

Clients seek to avoid problems with quality by learning as much as they can about the reputations of firms as well as about their internal structure and equipment. They prefer working closely with a small number of skilled subcontractors whose work has proved satisfactory in the past. In each area of production, a core of firms well known as medium- to high-quality producers is found. Clients may solicit bids on a given project, but they usually do so only with a limited number of proven suppliers, and final decisions are not always based on price but also consider the firms' known strengths and weaknesses. In some cases, the entrepreneurs' individual expertise and ability to contribute ideas to the design of a given product enter into clients' decisions. For example, one buyer noted that he preferred to have metalwork done by a firm with a numerical control machine, because this ensured standardized quality; another client said he chose a particular painting workshop over others with similar equipment because the owners of the workshop not only knew how to do certain processes but also routinely made independent decisions about when they should be done.

Some small firms, once they have established a reputation for high-quality work and reliability, can afford to choose among prospective clients. Interestingly, while beginning firms hope to work for large companies in order to garner prestige, already successful producers often prefer smaller clients. This finding suggests that the small scale of enterprises neither poses an obstacle to relative success nor represents merely a transitional phase of growth. The structure of small firms is more appropriate to meet the demand for diversified, short series. Owners also value the potential for contributing to the design of specifications through close contact with clients. A partner in a small, highly successful metalworking firm makes this point:

> For me, it's a thousand times better to work for a small firm. With the big ones, you're not supposed to make any changes. For example, a while ago we had an order from [Company X] to make some boxes for cables. The man who was working on them here realized that in the design the hole for the cables was misplaced. So he moved it. When they found out, you can't imagine how upset they were. We had to change [the boxes] all over again—that is, make them *wrong*. No, I want to be able to talk with the man who gives me work and explain to him how it has to be done and then show him.

Newly formed firms usually cannot afford to turn clients away. How can they establish a reputation that ensures they will find sufficient work? Such firms can connect with the market initially in two ways. First, small enterprises can begin by doing jobs for other subcontractors. This strategy is particularly common among painting and silkscreening workshops, or specialized metalwork shops, which are subcontracted by metalworkers. The latter earn a premium simply for acting as middlemen between clients and the smaller workshops. A similar arrangement is made by some producers of printed circuits, who establish small workshops to assemble subcomponents on the circuit boards they produce. Some clients actually prefer such a system, because it means they have to maintain contact with only one supplier and do not have to expend the time and energy necessary to oversee work done in all the firms. The main advantage to the sub-subcontractors is that they are assured a steady supply of work without having to submit themselves to close scrutiny by clients. The small workshops can thereby build a reputation based on the list of clients for whom they work indirectly. Indeed, this system yields striking examples of small, semi-informal, or undercapitalized forms that produce or prepare components for large, prestigious corporations. One example is an all-purpose metalworking, painting, and silkscreening workshop in which a single skilled worker and several assistants prepare components for multinational computer companies. The jobs are distributed through a larger metalworking firm. Another small workshop receives about one-half its orders from an adjacent metalworking firm; the catalogue the smaller firms shows to prospective clients includes pictures and descriptions of jobs done for prestigious firms with whom they have never had any direct contact.

A second marketing strategy for newly formed firms is to solicit clients directly for an opportunity to "show what they can do." Most producers trying a new subcontractor will begin by giving them relatively unimportant or low-quality jobs, gradually increasing the difficulty if the firms prove themselves to be capable and reliable about meeting production deadlines. The recent growth in the number of small electronics producers in the area means that an expanding demand for subcontracted work exists. New firms can also compete for low-quality work for larger firms by offering lower prices, sometimes based on lower wage and overhead costs permitted by semiregulated practices. The clearest example of a firm pursuing such a strategy is a small factory producing printed circuits. Started by a former employee of one of the leading firms in this subsector and located in a peripheral, nonindustrially zoned area on Madrid's outskirts, this firm began several years ago to produce low-quality printed circuits using homemade equipment (for example, chemical baths in hand-held buckets). The work force and the number of clients have expanded gradually, and the firm now employs seven workers—five of whom work off-the-books—to produce printed circuits for about 15 regular clients, including two of the largest electronics producers in Spain. The owner notes that the key to the firm's progress has been the cooperation of clients who gradually made greater demands on the firm but "never gave us anything we couldn't handle."

Firms that contact clients directly and those that work mainly for other subcontractors do not always make steady progress toward widening their clientele. Their ability to do so depends both on their solution to the problems of internal structure and management and on their continual improvement of the firms' technical capacity. The latter requires either substantial profits that can be reinvested in machinery or access to credit. Both requirements present new firms with a dilemma. They must enter the market with competitive prices, but doing so reduces margins for profit and postpones necessary modernization. Access to credit is, at the same time, restricted until owners can demonstrate that their firms are established, viable concerns. The catch-22 is that an owner cannot make such a claim until he has a regular clientele that can, in turn, only be attracted and held when the firm has adequate equipment to guarantee prompt production of at least medium-quality goods.

Access to credit is, in fact, a problem that plagues most firms in the auxiliary industry. Particularly in subsectors in which substantial capital investments are necessary to purchase and upgrade machinery— for example, in printed circuitry and metalwork—entrepreneurs complain bitterly of the cost and difficulties of obtaining credit. These same problems also affect firms in less capital-intensive areas which are attempting to specialize. For example, several firms in the assembly or production of transformers were seeking to develop new, specialized products they could market directly. One small firm that had formerly done mainly assembly work had already designed and produced a personal computer prototype. Entrepreneurs in these firms complained of both the lack of credit to support such ventures and the dearth of information that would help them make appropriate decisions about product development and marketing.

In addition to providing an alternative means for controlling work, the cooperation of workers within firms may also lead to spreading the financial burden of credit and reinvestment. Workers not only contribute their skills to a firm but also their capital and/or collateral for obtaining loans. One metalworking cooperative I studied, for example, was able to buy a numerical control machine, a step that had radically improved the competitive position of the firm by ensuring more even-quality work and greater productivity. The move also meant assuming a large debt and temporarily curtailing the growth of workers' earnings. Such a decision could only be taken because the firm is a cooperative whose members are skilled workers with similar positions in its productive and administrative structure.

As a result of decentralization, a system of cross-subcontracting is clearly emerging in Madrid's electronics industry. Small auxiliary firms do not depend heavily on only a few producers but are able to deal independently with a wide range of clients based on their ability to produce high-quality goods. However, while a handful of firms in each area of production has attained this status, a substratum of less well-established firms still struggles either to consolidate direct ties with clients or to escape altogether from the more competitive and less remunerative areas of the auxiliary market. These new ventures must now also compete with better-established firms, which have not only more secure markets but also more capital. Whether the decentralized structure of the industry continues to move in the direction of flexible cross-subcontracting among independent producers depends to a large extent on whether the struggling smaller firms will be able either to improve standards fast enough to compete with other subcontractors or to diverge into areas where they will not meet such competition head on. The failure of such strategies would prolong the dependence on other subcontractors and reinforce pressures to maintain low wages.

Conclusion

Decentralization in electronics has given rise to a strikingly different pattern from that which has thus far been observed in other Spanish industries. In most previous studies, as well as in the research on the Spanish shoe industry presented in the next chapter, the informal sector is characterized as a relatively stable and degraded substratum of the industrial structure. Small firms form in the wake of plant closures, and working conditions tend to be far worse than those in established industry.

These features of decentralization in other industries suggest that strict comparisons with restructuring in the electronics industry are not appropriate. None of the firms studied was actually clandestine, even though some used casual labor. However, the small firms examined in the electronics industry were generated by a similar process of decentralization, undertaken during the same period and prompted by similar motives. Many of the firms were indeed informal during the early stages of this process and certainly owe some of their initial success to the lower wage costs made possible through self-exploitation of worker-entrepreneurs and the use of family and causal labor.

The factors that distinguish this case are the evolution of the informal sector beyond this stage and the potential benefits of the new structure to the industry's development as a whole. Many of the small firms did not long remain in a subordinate position within the industry, and they have been able to base their success on steady improvements in quality, a trend that has made possible continued decentralization and greater concentration on research and design among electronics producers. The workers' situation within the firms also does not appear troubling. Skilled workers earn roughly the same or more than they would get in similar jobs in larger factories, and worker-entrepreneurs are generally enthusiastic about their greater independence. The firms are meanwhile contributing to the future development of the industry by training young workers; more than one-half of the work force in the auxiliary industry sample comprises workers younger than age 30, many of whom are apprentices.

The peculiar characteristics of the industry can account for some of these features. With the exception of assembly work, the productive tasks that have been decentralized have been relatively complex and capital-intensive, and they have required mainly skilled labor. The industry as a whole, meanwhile, has experienced mild expansion, and, as a result, the demand for skilled labor has remained strong. This means that skilled workers are less likely to be tolerant of substandard conditions in small firms. It also means that most new firms have themselves faced growing demand at the crucial initial stage in their development, and that in some cases the transition from semi-informal, struggling enterprise to well-respected small firm was extremely rapid.

Yet these factors alone would still not account completely for the performance of firms in the auxiliary industry. The main protagonists in their development have been skilled workers, many of whom voluntarily left other industrial jobs to start new firms. They tend to be men in their thirties and forties, with little entrepreneurial experience but with strong convictions about the virtues of making it on one's own. Some skilled workers have, moreover, been willing to experiment with new forms of associations that enable them to escape some of the difficulties of internal management and technical capacity encountered because of their relative newness and small size.

However, we have also seen evidence that many other enterprises continue to struggle to overcome such problems. Difficulties in resolving internal management problems derive mainly from the excessive isolation of worker-entrepreneurs, both within their firms and in relation to other producers. Externally generated obstacles, such as unfavorable terms for credit to small firms, also plague most of the microenterprises. The two sets of problems—as well as their possible solutions—are closely related. In the most successful firms, replacing autocratic systems of control with production styles based more on cooperation among skilled workers has gone hand in hand with improving the quality of production and resolving problems of capitalization. In later chapters I explore the reasons such solutions have not been more widely adopted.

4 Sweating for Export: "Underground" Labor in the Spanish Shoe Industry

Of all the so-called traditional industries, Spain's shoe industry was perhaps in the best position to emerge from the period of restructuring with renewed vitality. It held a strong position in international markets prior to the economic downturn, and the specific characteristics of the industry favor dynamic decentralized growth. It is geographically very concentrated and already highly fragmented, has a large skilled labor force, and boasts a tradition of risk-taking and entrepreneurship by workers. Industry participants are acutely aware of the challenge before them: to begin to act more like Italian producers, who have based their competitiveness on leadership in fashion, and to become aggressive sellers rather than passive suppliers to European and American markets.

This chapter evaluates whether spontaneous restructuring of Spain's shoe industry is supporting such goals. The first part of the chapter outlines the industry's development up to 1975. The second part is based mainly on interviews with 25 informants from the shoe industry, including factory owners, informal entrepreneurs, workers, labor leaders, employer representatives, and government officials. It describes entrepreneurs' strategies in the face of the economic crisis and political transition and analyzes the effects of informalization on their attitudes and on their firms' prospects for continued growth. Finally, I examine the plight of small firms that have been generated by spontaneous restructuring and contrast their situation with that of subcontractors analyzed in the previous chapter.

The Vinalopó Valley and the Rise of the Spanish Shoe Industry

Alicante, the center of shoe production in Spain, is the southernmost province of the Valencian region, which comprises one

73

of the newly created *autonomías* (autonomous regions with semi-independent governments, created under the democracy). The Valencian region skirts the Mediterranean between Catalonia and Murcia. Its economy has been characterized by swift industrial development dating from the 1960s. During that decade, the growth of industrial employment in Valencia outpaced that of all other Spanish regions.

The pattern of industrialization in Valencia also differed from those of other areas in Spain. First, with a few important exceptions—the Ford plant outside the city of Valencia and the Sagunto steel works, for example—industrial growth has involved mainly the expansion of sectors producing light consumer goods. Examples of successful light manufacturing industries are furniture, ceramic tiles, toys, textiles (particularly blankets and rugs), shoes, and light metal manufactures. Second, a high proportion of production in these industries has been oriented toward export markets. In the latter half of the 1970s, about one-third of all industrial production in Valencia was for export, accounting for one-fifth of the exports from Spain's entire economy (Mas, Mafé, and Rico 1982). In 1979, three-quarters of exports from the Valencia region consisted of consumer goods (Bru 1982).

A further peculiar trait of industrial development in Valencia is that it began as an internally generated process led by small, mostly family-run firms. The structure of the leading industries continues to be heavily weighted toward small- and medium-sized firms. Production is, moreover, geographically highly concentrated. The shoe industry is centered in a handful of towns in the Vinalopó Valley, in the province of Alicante; ceramic tile producers are heavily concentrated in several towns in Castellón Province; textiles are produced mainly in and around the town of Alcoy, in Alicante; and the toy industry is also centered in several towns in that province. As in central Italy, special types of production within each of these industries are also concentrated in particular towns. For example, Onil is the center of doll production, while firms devoted to other kinds of toy production are clustered in Ibi and Denia; Crevillente specializes in the manufacture of rugs, while Alcoy is the center of production of blankets; the town of Elche produces most of the shoe industry's sports shoes, while Elda's specialty is fashion shoes and Villena is known for children's shoes. Exporting firms are also highly concentrated in particular areas. A small group of towns accounts for roughly three-fourths of exports in the shoe, tile, and toy industry.[1]

To these distinguishing features of what has been dubbed the "Valencian path" to development should also be added the peculiar relationship of industrialization with agriculture in the regions of most rapid industrial growth. Throughout Spain, rural areas underwent a dramatic transformation during the boom decade of the 1960s. Emigration, increased productivity in agriculture, and local economic changes (such as the growth of tourism) altered the fundamental social, cultural, and economic bases of Spanish rural society.[2] In Valencia, industrialization was made possible in part by a peculiar symbiotic relationship with agriculture, the unique character of which has been important in shaping both the pattern of industrial growth that has emerged and the region's response to economic crisis over the last decade.

Industrial growth in Valencia had its roots in the reaction of farmers and rural laborers to the precarious and unstable conditions endemic to agriculture in the region. A portion of the area's agricultural economy was based on the cultivation of two cash crops, rice and citrus fruits; another portion depended on poor subsistence farming and localized, less successful attempts at cash-crop farming, such as the cultivation of grapes for wine in the southern districts of Alicante. Rural workers were forced by the seasonal nature of labor, particularly in citrus production, to find other sources of income. Small farmers were also driven to other pursuits by the insecurity wrought by a variable and often excessively dry climate. The beginnings of light manufacturing in Valencia can thus be traced to local efforts by peasants and rural laborers to supplement income from agriculture. As both domestic and foreign demand for industrial goods expanded, these activities developed, sometimes very rapidly, into important national and international industries.

The evolution of the shoe industry in the Vinalopó Valley conformed neatly to the Valencian pattern of development. Named for the small and usually dry river that winds through it, the Vinalopó Valley in Alicante, where the shoe industry is centered, is incapable of supporting a self-subsisting rural economy and is unsuitable for successful cash-crop production. Growth of a promising wine industry was curtailed at the end of the nineteenth century after the spread of a disease affecting the vines ended a profitable export trade with

France. The small average size of land holdings had already forced peasants to turn to various other activities to supplement their income from farming. The most important of these activities was the use of plant materials to manufacture goods for local sale and export to other regions. In the latter half of the nineteenth century, artisans using the local *esparto* grass began to produce *alpargatas*, simple cloth shoes with woven soles. These were produced mainly in Elche, already a commercial center of some importance only 20 kilometers from the active port of Alicante. Alpargata manufacturing led to the creation of an artisan shoe industry in the Upper Vinalopó Valley, particularly in and around the town of Elda.

Both industries experienced rapid growth in the first three decades of the twentieth century. A crucial stimulus to growth was the emergence of an export market for shoes during World War I. The market for *alpargatas* also expanded as a result of the introduction of rubber soles around 1920. Neither industry was hit as hard as were other manufactures by the contraction of international demand at the end of World War I. Between 1915 and 1935, shoe production in Elda increased by 300%; in Elche, output rose by 273% during the same years (Forner 1982). This trend was accompanied by the spread of production to a number of small towns in the surrounding area, most notably Petrel, Villena, and Monovar.

Despite the rapid growth that characterized this period, the technological level of the shoe and *alpargata* industries continued to be quite low. Small firms were dominant, and many were in reality home workshops run by artisans who labored as subcontractors for larger firms or for independent entrepreneurs. The level of investments in machinery was low, and productivity depended on the preservation of a long working day. The production process was dominated by the *zapatero*, or master shoemaker, who carried out all the major production tasks by hand, except for the sewing of the uppers, usually done by female assistants. The *zapateros* were experienced craftsmen. Their work required not only considerable skill but also physical force to mount the sewn shoes onto the wooden lasts and meticulous care to prepare the leather soles to be sewn onto the uppers. Workers and entrepreneurs now in their thirties and forties still remember vividly the *zapateros,* clad in long leather aprons and bent over their benches, working long hours to turn out only a handful of finished pairs.

Although the shoe industry still appeared quite traditional in many respects, changes during this early phase of development prefigured modernization. The industry's expansion in the 1920s brought about the formation of an industrial proletariat in the two largest shoe-producing towns. Elda had some 11,000 workers in the shoe industry by the end of the decade, while in Elche about 12,000 workers were employed in the production of *alpargatas*. By the 1930s, a small industrial bourgeoisie was also emerging in the two towns, particularly in Elda, where the creation of the Bank of Elda marked the first attempts at local self-financing (Forner 1982).

Growth in the industry suffered, as it did in other Spanish industry, in the aftermath of the Civil War. But the 1940s and 1950s did see the rise of some large, family-owned enterprises and the gradual transformation of the production process. The large firms introduced more women into the work force and incorporated many homeworkers, both male and female, directly into the factories (Bernabé 1976). In the 1950s, piecework wages gradually replaced the system of paying all but homeworkers by the day. Piecework was initially introduced by factory owners who began to offer premiums based on the quantity and quality of production in order to attract the most skilled workers. Employers found that the system also facilitated the change to a more detailed division of labor in the factory and the gradual phasing out of the *zapatero*. Despite such changes, production continued to be organized around the activities of a few highly skilled workers who moved freely around the workshops. This arrangement was accompanied by a system of individual bargaining with employers over the terms and conditions of employment. One worker recalls:

> The system was different from the way it is now that mechanization has unified the process. In artisan production, each worker did things in a different way and people were paid differently for the same work. Someone who could turn out better-finished shoes was paid more, and so was someone who produced more. Each person had his own peculiarities, and this made it very difficult to achieve unity among the working class.

The trend away from artisan forms of production rapidly accelerated as a result of the sudden takeoff of the export market in the 1960s. In 1961, exports accounted for only 4% of total production in the shoe industry; by 1971, this proportion had grown to more than 40% (Bernabé 1976). The period of most marked expansion began after 1967 and was helped by the devaluation of the peseta and the liberalization of import restrictions on shoes following the trade agreements of the Kennedy Round.[3] During this takeoff period, the United States represented the most important market for Spanish shoes; in 1972, the United States received nearly 70% of such exports, although this figure subsequently showed gradual decline (Méndez 1982). American importers placed demands on Spanish firms to produce shoes much more rapidly, and in much greater quantities, than they had done in the past. At the same time, foreign buyers demanded higher and more standardized quality, and introduced new techniques and unfamiliar shoe styles. They sometimes directly supervised production.

Spanish firms had to modernize production methods to meet the new requirements. One important change was the introduction of the assembly line. In the older system, workers had to leave their stations to retrieve new batches of shoes on which to work; now metal tracks were installed in most factories and used to slide racks of shoes from one worker to another. A second, simultaneous change was the attempt by several firms to implement a "scientific method" for remunerating workers—a form of Taylorism. This system substituted salaries for piecework wages, although it also tied salaries to worker productivity. Workers were timed to set an average speed for each task, and they were then expected to produce consistently at that rate; their pay was docked if they failed to do so, and they were paid premiums according to the percentages by which they surpassed the average rates.

The dramatic boom in exports and the concomitant modernization of the industry established Spain firmly among leading international producers of footwear. The value of imports of shoes from Spain to OECD countries rose at a faster rate between 1965 and 1973 than imports from any other NIC except Taiwan; and although Taiwan finally surpassed Spain in OECD markets in the mid-1970s, the latter remained a strong second in 1976.[4] The international reputation of Spanish footwear had advanced significantly, a change that was symbolized by the evolution of a local contest among shoe producers at Elda's annual town fair into an international trade fair for marketing Spanish shoes. Employment in the industry had grown accordingly. According to the Ministry of Industry in 1979 an estimated 1,846 firms were producing shoes in Spain and employing more than 56,000 workers; these figures undoubtedly exclude many microenterprises and casual workers. More than one-half of the firms (56%) and workers (53%) were concentrated in the province of Alicante.

Certain features of the industry suggested some fundamental weaknesses. One growing problem stemmed from the absence of outlets for workers to defend their interests. Industry participants were aware that the industry was straddling a fault line and that unseen tensions were preparing it for a dramatic shift. Terms of new contracts were still being "negotiated" in the state-controlled *sindicato vertical* (vertical union), where the interests of employers and the state dominated those of workers. Official wages in the industry were thus extremely low, not only compared to wages for workers in the shoe industry outside Spain but also compared to levels set in other Spanish industries.

To be sure, workers' actual earnings did not reflect official wage rates. During the nearly 15 years of rapid growth in the industry, demand for skilled workers was strong, and employers had to offer competitive wages to workers, usually by adjusting the piecework rate so that workers' earnings were significantly above levels stipulated in the industry's official contract. Although the discrepancy probably contributed at an early stage to mitigating worker opposition to the nonrepresentative contract negotiations, the gap between official and real earnings increasingly became a focus of controversy. In replacing piecework with the "scientific method" of calculating workers' earnings, employers found that they could force actual wages lower, and they could cite the official contract terms as justification for doing so. One labor leader recounts the impact of this change:

> Back when the contracts were signed by the Francoist union—the fascist syndicate—we knew that the contracts existed, but nobody participated and nobody even knew when the negotiations took place or when the contracts were signed. We lived under the law of supply and demand . . . each with his own little personal contract. But one day someone sa[id] that the contract [was] going to be applied. This meant that salaries were going to go down by some 200% because, with no worker intervention or pressure, the industry had one of the worst

contracts in Spain . . . the first attempt to apply it was what
made the alert sound . . . and marked the start of the workers'
movement.

By the mid-1970s, the rising strength of the workers' movement
posed a serious treat to the status quo. An underground movement
led by workers in the shoe industry (discussed in Chapter 6) had
already succeeded in infiltrating the vertical union and was now also
agitating for direct worker representation and the creation of
independent unions. It appeared extremely likely that workers would
soon gain the power to negotiate their own contracts with employers
and that the result would be substantial increases in wages and
benefits to workers. For an industry whose recent success in the
export market had been based in part on relatively low wages paid to
skilled workers, these projected events appeared quite threatening.

A further troubling characteristic of the shoe industry at this
juncture was that, despite its impressive record of sales, it had not yet
established a solid footing in international markets. Particularly in its
early stages, the export boom was characterized by strong sales to the
United States and somewhat weaker ties to European markets. In
contrast to their European counterparts, U. S. buyers tended to foster
close ties to individual producers, whom they then supplied with
designs and large orders. In some cases, Spanish producers came to
depend on a single foreign buyer for all orders, thereby risking sudden
and serious setbacks if importers shifted to other producers within
Spain or to firms outside the country.

Clearly, the most important motives for clients' interest in
buying from Spain were cost advantage and the ability to control
production closely. The collective skill of workers in the shoe-
producing region was also an important factor, but it could not
overshadow cost considerations; only a small percentage of
production was in very high-quality shoes where workers' skills could
represent a decisive factor in preventing the transfer of orders to
lower-cost producers elsewhere. The essential element that would
have ensured continued interest even in the face of rising costs was an
independent identity for Spanish fashion, and this element was
entirely missing. Perhaps if a gradual adjustment of wages to much
higher levels had accompanied growth in the industry, producers
would have adopted more aggressive strategies to assert their

independence from importers; but as long as tight restrictions on collective bargaining were in place, firms could make substantial profits simply by following importers' specifications and, at the same time, avoiding costly investments in market research, distribution, and design.

The Shoe Industry and the Economic Crisis

Several factors converged in the late 1970s to end the euphoric period of expansion in the shoe industry. Faltering demand in international markets and accelerated competition from low-cost producers such as Brazil, Taiwan, and Korea brought about slower growth of exports and, finally, a net decrease in exports in 1979. Many factories that had produced mainly for export responded to the downward trend in the export market by turning to the domestic market, where competition now intensified at a time when domestic demand was also very weak.

At the same time, the end of the Franco era promised radical change in a political structure that had been very successful in holding down official wages in the industry. The workers' movement was gaining momentum throughout Spain and was particularly strong in the shoe industry. In 1976 and 1977, a broad-based movement to achieve direct worker representation in industry negotiations culminated in a national strike, directed by workers in Alicante. The strike paralyzed the industry for two weeks. Together, the raises obtained by workers after the 1977 strike and in contract negotiations repeated six months later were substantial. Workers also won many other concessions, including expanded vacations, and improved pay and conditions for female workers. The vertical union was finally dissolved in 1976 and the representative unions were legalized the following year (see Chapter 6).

Determining which of the above factors—the decline in exports or the resurgence of the labor movement—was more important in motivating entrepreneurs to adopt informalization as a fundamental strategy during the late 1970s is extremely difficult. Employers interviewed belittle the importance of the labor movement, pointing out that actual wages in the industry were already considerably above those stipulated in the contracts. They emphasize the importance of the shock of a declining export market and note that a shift by many firms to more aggressive marketing in the domestic market further exacerbated problems for most producers. However, employers do agree that the movement led by workers during 1976 and 1977 effectively ended what they had regarded as a tradition of close personal relations and trust between workers and employers, particularly in the small firms that dominate the industry. Some employers report that they felt betrayed by workers whom they had thought were bound to them by a sense of personal loyalty. Such perceptions of broken trust no doubt contributed to employers' decisions to dismantle their firms and to create new businesses which would differ both in structure and in atmosphere to those of the older, paternalistic system.

Labor leaders themselves disagree as to whether the rise of organized unions prompted employers to seek to fragment the production process. Some current labor leaders suggest that this event in fact helped to stabilize the industry because employers could finally ensure worker cooperation if they were willing to come to terms with the unions. However, other leaders, particularly some of the main protagonists of the 1977 strike, claim that informalization was often a direct response to the workers' movement. They point out that employers were entirely unused to the type of worker intervention in the labor process that was advocated in the 1977 movement and suggest that, even if factory owners did not turn to informal labor as a direct response to rising costs of labor, they did so to stave off what they regarded as a direct attack on their prerogative to control the terms, conditions, and organization of work.

Some further evidence that informalization has served in part as a strategy for solving problems of control in the workplace is the largely unsuccessful bid by employers to establish Taylorism as an industry norm. They wished to do so, first, because introducing the system usually results in a net decrease in wages. Employers acknowledge that, although they often promise to maintain the level of earnings with piecework, once the point system is installed, they can reduce earnings by gradually altering the productivity levels set as normal. Second, the newer system offers employers enhanced control over workers' productivity and behavior. While piecework systems may be satisfactory to employers where well-ordered, paternalistic labor relations are in place, they can be threatening when workers begin to organize and negotiate collectively because workers and owners must come to an agreement on the rate to be paid for each different style of shoes. The bargaining procedure unites workers against factory owners and seems to invite workers' direct participation in ordering the production process. An important advantage of the point system, in contrast, is that is ensures that bargaining will remain highly individualistic. One factory owner described in detail how he had struck individual bargains with various "difficult" workers. In one case, after observing that a worker failed consistently to perform her task at the set rate, the owner brought her into the office and asked whether she had some personal problems that were keeping her from working hard. She said she hated factory work, and that it was her ambition to work in an office: "So I made a deal with her. I told her that if she worked up to the set rate from then on, I'd agree not to dock her pay for the hours she owed me and would also promise to put her in the office the very first time we had a clerical opening. From then on, she worked at the correct speed." Other, similar examples are common.[5]

Not surprisingly, workers have consistently opposed the introduction of the new system, and employers and union leaders agree that Taylorist methods would have been implemented in more firms had it not been for such opposition. Many firms tried to install the point system between 1975 and 1980 as a response to the crisis, but their success was uneven. A 1984 survey of 89 firms in shoe-producing centers in Alicante showed that roughly 40% of the firms used a point system at least part of the time, while about one-half continued to use piecework, sometimes substituting other systems of pay (especially during low production periods, when many firms reduce wages to the industry's official minimum). Decentralization obviously offered an attractive alternative to battling to install the unpopular point system (Ybarra and Manteca 1986).

Whatever the precise importance of one or another of these causal factors, the industry clearly began to undergo a process of rapid, spontaneous restructuring in the late 1970s. The government, the unions, and the employers' association are in broad agreement about the timing and impressive dimensions of the trend. Although measuring informal sector growth directly is difficult, if not impossible, even official industry statistics confirm abundant impressionistic evidence. Between 1979 and 1982, official employment in the industry decreased by about one-third, from 56,261 to

37,907. During the same period, the number of registered firms dropped by 26%, from 1,846 to 1,368. Production, meanwhile, increased steadily after declining in 1979. Comparing 1983 figures from the Ministry of Industry with those of 1979, we find that for legally employed workers to be responsible for total gains in output, productivity would have to have increased by nearly 80%. There is very little evidence of profound changed in the productive process of established firms that would account for such an increase; in fact, between 1979 and 1981, the amount of electricity officially reported consumed in the industry dropped by 17% and gross fixed-capital formation remained constant (UN Industrial Statistics Yearbook 1983, vol. 1).

The process of informalization that has swept the industry since the late 1970s has been characterized by several trends. First, a wave of plant closures has been paralleled by the proliferation of small, informal shoe factories. In some cases, these are formed directly in the wake of closures and incorporate some of the same workers and machinery. Factory owners sometimes have helped to organize these ventures, leasing machinery to groups of workers and becoming commercial agents whose low-risk, high-profit activities contrast markedly with the plight of producers under the new market conditions. In other cases, workers have formed cooperative ventures to save their jobs and have pooled their savings to buy the firms' machinery. These trends often involve the transfer of the entire productive structure of firms—including the mechanized assembly process—underground. The new informal firms both serve established businesses and compete directly with them: Formal firms and commercial agents may subcontract clandestine factories to produce shoes for them at substantially lower cost than they could manage themselves; at the same time, some of the new firms damage the interests of established producers by underselling them and forcing them to reduce prices, particularly in the domestic market, where informal factories can reach the market more easily with low- and medium-quality shoes.

A second, closely related process of restructuring has been the decentralization of more labor-intensive tasks. Whereas during the years of expansion large firms in the industry tended to have sections producing all the various phases of production, this condition became untenable after the mid-1970s. One result has been the expansion of homework, particularly for the sewing of uppers and the various tasks related to this process and, to a lesser degree, in the final stages of production needed for finishing the shoes. Both these areas of production were dominated by women within the factory, and employers have been able to rely to some extent on natural turnover—traditionally higher among women than men—to reduce the number of workers employed in these phases within the factories. New firms, including new informal enterprises, also have reduced these sections (especially the *aparado*) to a bare minimum, adding to the demand for homeworkers.

Homeworkers, in smaller numbers, had always been employed to perform these tasks. Yet two entirely new features in the decentralized structure of firms also exist. The first is the putting out of other tasks that had normally been done inside firms. A notable example is the subcontracting of leather cutting by some factories. This phase of production is traditionally male-dominated, in contrast to the sewing of uppers, and does not lend itself easily to outwork because the materials that have to be given to workers are so costly. Yet it has become increasingly common for this phase of production also to be subcontracted to industrial outworkers. A second change has been the growth in the number of informal cutting and sewing workshops. These provide firms with the same advantages as homeworkers—lower costs and greater flexibility—but also simplify the tasks of distributing and collecting materials, and of negotiating over the cost of different jobs. Again, these specialized, informal workshops serve both established firms and new, restructured factories.

A final process of change that has accompanied spontaneous restructuring has been spatial decentralization. Within Alicante, Ybarra (1982) found that investment in the shoe industry in semirural areas surrounding the major shoe-producing towns has outpaced the growth of investment within those municipalities. But registered job creation in rural areas has not kept pace with that in more traditional shoe-producing areas, suggesting that much of the labor in outlying areas is clandestine. Employers and union officials interviewed also confirmed that this is the case. Piecework is shipped frequently to small towns in La Mancha; shoe producers in Madrid also distribute work to small towns in La Mancha and even as far away as Alicante.

Until the beginning of the 1980s, the processes of productive decentralization and informalization were regarded with considerable ambivalence by factory owners. Although virtually all producers used some form of casual labor—particularly homeworkers to sew the uppers—they benefitted unevenly from the new forms of informal labor. Established producers who had not closed their firms and who had not been able to reduce their work forces substantially through turnover and attrition were particularly distraught by recent trends. Interviews with 42 employers were conducted for the Ministry of Economy in 1982, and the topic of growing *clandestinaje*, or clandestine labor, was raised by the vast majority of informants before they were asked to comment on this phenomenon. The employers made a clear distinction between types of informal labor that they viewed as traditional and acceptable in the industry (most notably homework), and the new informal factories, which they regarded as presenting unfair competition that would eventually lead them to close.

The informants also made it clear that, if forced to close their businesses, they would continue to be active in the shoe industry, even if to do so meant joining the underground economy. Many employers, however, also claimed to be strongly resisting pressures to join the trend of massive restructuring. One important motive for their reluctance was a sense of obligation to preserve what were fundamentally family businesses. In describing the firms' histories, many spoke of the considerable sacrifices and described closure— which many perceived as imminent—as something that was being forced upon them by recent changes in the industry. Losing firms entailed social and emotional, as well as financial, losses to their families (see Picó 1976).

Yet at the time these interviews were conducted, changes were already underway that would alter employers' outlook. First, a number of measures adopted by the government resulted in actively encouraging firms to close. One such policy offered special discounts to new firms on social security payments for workers. This measure had been introduced in 1981 to stimulate new employment creation, but government officials would later claim that it also was intended to help the underground economy to "emerge" by lowering the economic barriers to legalization (see Chapter 7). One union leader in the shoe industry notes that the month after this measure was introduced, he "spent night and day responding to new plant closures" in Alicante. Employers interviewed in 1982 complained that the measure made staying in business more difficult because they now faced competition from informal producers and "*legal* unfair competition" from new firms paying lower social security rates.

A second event influencing employers' attitudes was the introduction of a reconversion program for the shoe industry in May 1982 (see Chapter 7). Employers had been advocating a broad program of direct assistance to firms that would include postponing social security debts and subsidization of the large indemnities that had to be paid to workers in order to reduce the work force, a particularly high priority in the industry's large firms. Employers were looking, in other words, for a state-sponsored plan for industrial restructuring, the sort of reconversion program that had been offered heavy industry. What they got instead was a bill promising vaguely defined programs of technical and financial assistance for the industry as a whole, with direct subsidization being offered only to firms that could show they had paid social security debts in full through March 1981. In an industry where social security costs accounted for as much as 25% of the entire wage bill and in which delays in payment had become the norm, this requirement excluded the majority of firms. Employers interviewed only a few months after the decree-law was passed characterized the provisions of the bill as ludicrous. Employers I interviewed in 1985 were unanimous in condemning reconversion as a farce and were forthright about its effects on their decisions. As one entrepreneur put it, "When we found out that the government wasn't going to give us legal reconversion, we decided to do it ourselves; that's when the *reconversión salvaje* [untamed or wild reconversion] began in earnest."

The *reconversión salvaje* was, in fact, already underway, but between 1980 and 1985 the process rapidly accelerated. A further, and perhaps decisive, factor in encouraging its spread was the increasing use of a technique that permitted a given firm to "close" and immediately "reopen" merely by changing the firm's name, incurring a tiny loss, and paying the necessary fees to accountants. This bookkeeping technique allows firms to restructure production and reduce their work forces without incurring any of the usual costs; it also permits them to take advantage of the tax breaks and other advantages offered new firms. Social security debts are wiped out in one stroke, and firms become free to reduce their work forces and even to weed out intractable or underproductive workers.

The tactic, which employers and workers refer to simply as "changing names," is perfectly legal. It involves in effect declaring a false bankruptcy, in part through planned nonpayment of social security and other taxes. Factory owners have almost all the fixed assets in the firm "leased" to them by members of their family, so that the book value of firms is well below their actual value and assets are protected when firms declare bankruptcy. The government becomes responsible for indemnities to workers and, in addition, must also pay them unemployment compensation. Workers thus receive a large cash payment and are sometimes hired and paid by the "new" firms, unofficially, until unemployment insurance expires. Workers lose their rights to seniority bonus pay they had accrued in the "old" firms, although extra, under-the-table payments may be worked out individually with those who stand to lose the most by reorganization. Finally, workers also sacrifice permanent contracts when they switch over to the "new" firms. The latter can take advantage of a range of newly established hiring practices, including temporary, two-year contracts to replace the fixed contracts that entitled workers to severance pay.

Some entrepreneurs had already taken advantage of this tactic in the late 1970s to restructure older firms. A widely publicized case was the "name changing" engaged in by Miguel Hernandez, one of the largest shoe producers in the region, with close connections to U. S. firms. Between 1974 and 1984, in a maze of transfers of workers and machinery, about a dozen firms—all owned in part or in whole by one entrepreneur—were created and then closed again after one or two years of operation. The case received considerable attention when, in 1984, workers of the two remaining factories engaged in a sit-down strike to protest the nonpayment of social security benefits by the "phantom" firms. The workers charged that the two firms had been set up merely to produce orders for a third firm, which had laid off all its production workers several years before and retained only its technical staff. In this case, the tactics used had included both name changing and the practice of subcontracting to evade social security payments.

In the 1980s, false plant closings became epidemic in the Alicante region. No figures are available that show how many firms engaged in this practice, but there is a clear consensus among employers, business leaders, workers, and union leaders that changing names has become the *modus vivendi* of shoe-producing firms. One official of the employers' association, The Federación de Industriales del Calzado Español (FICE), estimated that between 1980 and 1985, 50% of firms in the industry "disappeared," most in order to reopen, either as clandestine enterprises or new firms. The latter can operate at as much as a 20% cost advantage over older factories. Employers can be surprisingly frank about their own use of the strategy. For example, the owner of a small factory in Elda that produces women's fashion shoes for a U. S. company described to me the closing of his firm in 1982:

> We closed one day and opened the very next day in the same factory, with the same machinery, and the same workers, minus the ten or so that we laid off. The factory is on a corner, so we changed the address to the other street, and we changed the name . . . . The [American] company knew about it, and we just continued to produce for them . . . . I could "close" tomorrow again, and take only a 300,000 peseta loss. And I *will* close, the first day I see I'm not making money.

Workers and labor leaders complain that there is very little they can do to prevent closings or protect workers from their ill-effects. The unions have limited themselves in most cases to following standard procedures to obtain the maximum benefits for the affected workers. They can also exert pressure on firms informally to make them retain workers and maintain certain conditions when the firms reopen. While many workers criticize the unions for failing to protect them, union officials point out that the workers themselves bend to psychological pressure from employers to go along with the closures. They also sometimes receive substantial economic benefits in the form of cash settlements, severance pay, and unemployment insurance payments. One worker argues that workers have little choice in accepting the closings:

> Here's how it works. The boss says to the workers, "Look, I'm going to close and if you don't go along with me, I'll close anyway and then none of you will work, because I won't rehire you." If you *don't* protest you can start working the very next day . . . . He'll rehire all of you. You'd also get severance pay and

two months' unemployment and, meanwhile, you'll get paid. You'll lose seniority and some rights, but it's better than being out of a job. Now, what do you think, as a worker, my decision would be? What would you do at age 40 or 45? If you lose your job, you also lose your right to a pension. You are totally without protection, so you keep working, whether you want to or not.

Although the principal motivations for firms to "close" are to erase social security debts and to undertake changes in the labor force, factory owners soon discover that the tactic also brings about significant improvements in productivity. Again, both union leaders and factory owners agree that in the newly restructured firms, workers are made to work harder. Two employers whose firms got a name change claimed that productivity had doubled after the change, although the workers in the firms were exactly the same. Both praised the "improved attitude" of workers, who no longer refuse to work overtime or during vacations. Labor leaders agree that increased productivity has been one effect of the wave of pseudo-closures, but they are understandably critical rather than approving of its implications for working conditions. One union official told me that to find evidence of widespread violations of provisions for overtime, "all you have to do is walk through Elda at 7:30 any evening. You'll hear machinery going in the factories as if it were 10 o'clock in the morning. The same is true on holidays. Ten years, or even five years ago, you'd never find that." Union leaders assert—and many employers admit—that the new, more pliant behavior of workers is directly related to the widespread practice of closing firms. Employers are free to choose among workers for the "new" firms and they can also fire "new" workers when their temporary contracts expire; workers know that if they complain about conditions, they risk losing their jobs.

Factory owners are understandably jubilant about the short-term benefits of the *reconversión salvaje*. Indeed, the widespread practice of declaring false bankruptcies has entirely altered the way entrepreneurs perceive closure. The social stigma formerly attached to closing a firm no longer exists; in fact, a certain bravado is evident among producers who have successfully maneuvered through such a proceeding and have, in doing so, outsmarted a system they perceive to be stacked against them.

What effect this pattern of restructuring will have on the

prospects of the industry as a whole is not clear. The *reconversión salvaje* has, perhaps, achieved the restructuring necessary to restore the industry's competitive position. The "new" firms have streamlined production by subcontracting more labor-intensive phases of production, and some firms have invested simultaneously in new machinery to pursue greater specialization in certain types of shoes, as well as the production of a greater variety of styles. Higher productivity in the new firms will also help to counterbalance the effect of steadily increasing wages on Spain's ability to compete with lower-cost producers in other countries.

However, the recent trend in the industry has many troubling aspects. Perhaps the most obvious of these is that the tactic of closing troubled firms has proved so effective for entrepreneurs that it has all but eliminated the need for long-range planning. Factory owners frequently talk about the uncertainty of the market for shoes; but in contrast to earlier years, they now have available a quick response to instability and can afford to continue to react to market shifts rather than trying to anticipate them. Furthermore, incentives to invest in new technologies are somewhat reduced under the present conditions. Although the tactic of having equipment "leased" to owners has secured it against loss in past closures, several entrepreneurs confirmed that they are wary about attracting attention to a firm with a low book value but with new, sophisticated equipment. More importantly, incentives to explore new production methods do not include an urgent interest in increasing productivity. Substantial gains are already ensured by the greater cooperation of workers who are wary of being laid off and by savings on labor costs through increased informal subcontracting and homework.

A further important shortcoming of the restructured firms derives precisely from their continuity with earlier enterprises. As with their predecessors, most of the new firms limit themselves to producing models that are designed for them, either by foreign buyers, or by independent, specially hired Spanish designers. The latter tend to copy, in turn, from Italian fashions that appear to be selling well. Similarly, shoe producers have remained relatively isolated from firms in the auxiliary industry that supply them with lasts, prefabricated soles, and other components that also change with shifts in fashion (Orgiles 1982). Very little in the new system of production encourages greater participation of factory owners in the design process or greater risk-taking to explore new fashion trends. On the contrary, by already permitting greater flexibility and faster responses to changes in fashion, the new decentralized system fosters a certain complacency about the need for further strides toward creating an independent line of Spanish fashion. This view has, in fact, become more or less the official posture in the industry. FICE officers advocate measures to improve the reputation of Spanish shoes in foreign markets but say that Spaniards have been so successful in copying Italian models quickly that greater originality is not needed.

My interviews are conducted at a time when such claims appeared to be substantiated by the record high performance of Spanish shoe exports in 1984. However, the boom in exports was fuelled by a high U. S. dollar, and subsequent trends—a decline of exports in 1986 and slow growth in 1987, a substantial drop in the share of exports to the United States, and a rapid rise in imports—confirm the danger that Spanish producers will continue to be squeezed by Italian fashion leaders on one side and low-cost competitors on the other.[6] The industry's vulnerability is highlighted whenever the United States threatens, as it has done repeatedly, to adopt new restrictions on imports of shoes.

Significantly, Spanish employers themselves seem quite willing to admit that an essential element of their continued success in exports is the fact that the informal sector has been thriving.[7] Does this mean that the possibility of keeping wage costs low through informalization will remain the industry's principal strategy for responding to new international trends? Or can we find emerging within the informal sector innovative strategies that also support qualitative changes and may lead eventually to establishing a system of flexible specialization?

The Plight of Informal Workshops

Homework comprises a sizable portion of the informal sector in the shoe industry, and much evidence confirms that this type of labor has expanded greatly. Homeworkers are, for many reasons, unlikely protagonists of innovative change within the informal sector. They tend to work in isolated settings and to combine homework with other obligations that place rigid constraints on the use of their time and the nature of their associations with other workers. The peculiar social context of homework and the relations of production it fosters are discussed in Chapter 5.

Greater scope for innovation and independence might be expected among small, underground firms producing shoes or specializing in particular phases of production. Some of these firms have been formed in the wake of plant closures, and new cooperative arrangements among skilled workers could produce innovative ways of ordering production. The appearance of greater numbers of specialized workshops also suggests that technological improvement within particular phases of production is a potential result of restructuring. Finally, if the new small firms generated through informalization were also able to reach the market directly—particularly the export market—then the industry's structure would begin to resemble the flexible, fragmented pattern that helped Italian manufactures sustain their position in world markets through the 1970s.

Little evidence exists, however, that informal enterprises are moving away from their close dependence on established firms and from a system of production that is closer to sweatshop labor than to the image of high-trust firms. Although many cooperatives have been formed after plants have closed, these ventures reflect mainly attempts by workers to salvage their jobs. Moreover, the cooperatives face the same institutional barriers to success that were described briefly in the previous chapter.

Some new firms that begin informally, of course, are able to overcome these obstacles. I visited one very successful new firm which had been started in 1980 as a small, informal venture by 11 workers. They had left their previous jobs when their employer had begun decapitalizing his firm, probably in preparation for closing. Although the workers originally intended to establish a cooperative, they found that cooperatives not only faced more formidable obstacles to obtaining credit but were also regarded with suspicion by other producers and clients: "Our accountant warned us, 'Whatever you do, don't set up a cooperative.'" Instead, the workers created a corporation with an elaborate charter outlining a system of profit-sharing and a procedure for collective decisionmaking. The firm "is a cooperative without being a cooperative." It has been extremely successful and now produces shoes both for export and the domestic market under its own label. The firm has two modern assembly lines and about 40 employees, not including an estimated 100 outworkers. In part because the founding partners were themselves closely connected with the union while in their old jobs, the working conditions within the firm are optimal, according to union leaders.

The history of this firm, according to informants and my own observations, is exceptional among enterprises that begin as small, informal concerns. One union leader remarks that he can "count on one hand" the firms that have advanced technologically and can produce high-quality, fashion shoes. The rest may be loosely separated into three categories: factories producing finished shoes for direct sale; firms producing shoes for other factories or commercial agents; and firms specializing in subcontracted work for one or several phases of production, such as cutting leather or sewing uppers. The last two types of firms tend to display poor labor conditions, own relatively little fixed capital, and depend heavily on established producers or commercial agents for both capital and design specifications. Union leaders complain particularly that workers are forced to spend long hours in cramped, poorly ventilated areas where they face a number of occupational hazards, including toxic fumes from the glue used in shoe production. In the first type of firm—that which produces to market its own finished shoes—poor working conditions also exist, while greater independence from other producers is secured at the cost of sustaining an unstable and marginal position in the highly competitive domestic market for low-cost shoes. Consider the following examples, which are drawn from field research and are representative of the three types of firms described:

1. A small factory in Elche producing sports shoes for the domestic market: The supervisor is a young man in his twenties who voluntarily left a factory job six years ago to start this firm with a partner. The two started working at home, making boots by hand, and now have eight workers using second-hand machinery to make sports shoes in a small, poorly ventilated shack. The firm's biggest problem is marketing. The shoes are delivered to wholesalers and distributors, who continually pressure the firm to lower prices by threatening to buy more cheaply from other clandestine firms. Some of the distributors supply shoes to street vendors and have difficulties collecting; one year the factory was

nearly ruined when a distributor failed to pay. The firm has begun producing its own, more diversified designs, but it does not expect its position to improve radically until it is legally established and can issue and process 90-day letters of credit. It deals now only with marginal distributors who will agree to 30-day cash payments.

2. A small factory in Elda producing shoes for export: The factory was started with the help of a commercial agent who provided funds for the machinery and who now is the factory's sole client. The agent supplies the designs and dictates prices for all orders. The factory is located in a closed garage on a residential street in Elda; there are about 12 workers, and the supervisor says frankly, "If we were forced to pay social security, we'd close." He adds that the firm also saves on labor costs by paying lower-than-average piecework rates and working longer days, often up to 12 hours.

3. A workshop in Elda specializing in cutting and sewing uppers for a large export firm that is part American-owned: Different phases of production are carried out in separate rooms and on both floors of a large, dilapidated family house. There are 36 workers, most of whom are *aparadoras* (women who sew uppers). Each of these workers owns her own machine and pays for all maintenance. The firm produces on average 11,000 pairs a week, a fairly high number. The exporter is its only client, and the entrepreneur says he would probably close if for some reason the firm stopped giving him work.[8]

Only the first firm described has a clear strategy for improving styles and methods of production in order to augment its commercial independence. But this firm, as with many others that produce shoes clandestinely, is operating at nearly the lowest end of the market, using simple technologies to copy designs produced by formal firms. The firm's operators have no realistic expectations of ever directly reaching the export market. The other two firms are clearly subservient to larger producers, and their main function is to reproduce standard tasks at a lower cost. This function is accomplished by saving on social security for workers and by paying them a low piecework rate to encourage high rates of production. Little in either setting recalls the sentiments and conditions observed among subcontractors in the electronics industry: the striving for high-quality production, independence, and worker cooperation.

Conclusion

The main feature that the different types of informal firms in the shoe industry have in common is that they produce shoes or parts of shoes *cheaply*. Unlike the small subcontractors in the electronics industry, these producers compete with each other and with other factories mainly by reducing wage costs through nonpayment of social security. Quality and design considerations are secondary. As a result, ties to clients tend to be fewer and less varied and at the same time more unstable. In such a structure, a sudden decline in the demand for shoes would be felt most strongly by the subcontractors, who would register proportionally the largest drops in employment. Thus, although the new structure is in one sense extremely flexible—the supply of labor to established firms can fluctuate easily—it is, in another sense, highly rigid because adjustments to market changes involve shifts in employment rather than qualitative changes in strategy adopted by the firms themselves. Notable features of firms such as the sewing workshops and the small factory for women's shoes described above are the lack of any strategy to alter dependence on established producers during a relatively prosperous period and the quiet acceptance of closure if the market again declines. In this respect, informal firms mirror their counterparts in the formal sector, for whom closure is a ready alternative to short-term losses.

As we also found to be true in the electronics industry, certain characteristics of the industry itself help to explain this outcome. First, it is true that in the shoe industry the variety of productive tasks that can readily be decentralized is limited, and these tasks tend to be relatively labor-intensive and to rely on traditionally simple technologies. Second, one might argue that the simple tasks that are subcontracted, most of them clustered at the beginning of the production process, do not result in final goods which workers could easily market independently. In this sense, they are of necessity structurally dependent on established shoe producers, who logically retain control over the technologically more advanced assembly process.

A further factor of some importance is that, unlike the electronics industry, which has traditionally been dominated by large firms and controlled growth, the shoe industry has already passed through a period of rapid expansion characterized by the proliferation of small, family-run firms which now must adjust to a period of slower growth. Entrepreneurs who made money during the decade and a half of rapid growth can now afford to be conservative, spending on conspicuous consumption and investing in fixed assets outside the industry (see Picó 1976). The optimum strategy in this situation is to take small risks—with a relatively large payoff if the export market continues to go well—but to hedge carefully against a downturn. The productive structure that has been emerging constitutes a rational response to an unstable business climate: streamlined firms betting on already-established fashion trends and restricting further investments in fixed capital.

But technological and economic factors cannot in and of themselves explain either the force and timing of informalization or its outcome. This chapter has examined one dimension of the politics of production in shoe factories and has shown that informalization offered a solution to problems of internal organization and social control that had been plaguing the industry since the first development away from the model of the small, family-run firms. In those early workshops, the hierarchy of authority blended with the hierarchy of skills: Master shoemakers both directed production and carried out the most difficult and physically most demanding tasks. Later, with the introduction of the assembly line and its increasingly detailed division of labor, piecework wages were introduced, benefitting entrepreneurs by assuring worker productivity without high investments of time and money in worker supervision.

When the economic downturn coincided with increased worker militancy, employers intensified efforts to install the "scientific" method of management, which was designed to depress wages at the same time that it would dislodge informal collective bargaining from its central position in the factories. But this tactic neither proved broadly successful nor, in the cases where it was applied, was sufficient to reverse the distressing trends. Initiated as a way of cutting costs, decentralization soon showed itself to have unexpectedly positive implications—from the point of view of employers—for the problem of control within the factories. Within formal firms, workers find their position so weakened that they must heed employers' demands to intensify work and increase the number of hours worked. Collectively, workers can do nothing legally to prevent a firm from closing and laying off whomever they choose. In short, scope for both collective and individual bargaining in the formal sector has been severely curtailed. The urgency of implementing "scientific management" or alternative new systems of control has waned.

At the same time, new informal firms have inherited the problem of keeping productivity high and wage costs low. The solution in most cases is to rely on a combination of earnings incentives and autocratic control by factory or workshop owners. Employers say they are aided by the fact that workers tend to be inflexible about the total amount of earnings, but not about the time and effort spent to arrive at those levels. Piecework wages may be set at a low level and workers forced to work long hours to reach a level of income acceptable to them. Workers have very few avenues for recourse to reinforce their bargaining position in setting the piecework rate. Answering my question about the way rates are set, one informal entrepreneur said, "Usually, they give a little and I give a little. Then I say 'If that's not good enough for you, you can just leave.' It's usually effective. I am like a judge here. I always have final say."

Technical factors, broad economic trends affecting the market for shoes, and the internal logic of relations of production within established firms all help explain the apparent outcome of restructuring: a two-tiered industrial structure, with an informal sector characterized mainly by poor labor conditions and the simple reproduction of tasks formerly carried out by formal firms. In addition, certain features of the social landscape of the Vinalopó Valley contribute to this trend. One important aspect of behavior shaping attitudes about the recent restructuring is the conspicuous consumption engaged in by both workers and entrepreneurs. On one side, employers in the region have a reputation for investing in lavish homes, expensive cars, and summer houses on the outskirts of the shoe-producing towns. This pattern of consumption was made possible largely by the boom in exports that brought quick wealth to many struggling worker-entrepreneurs. Many of them chose to invest in real estate and other fixed assets because they were relatively unsophisticated and inexperienced about other types of investments; many were merely conforming to behavior common to the nouveaux riches. But this pattern of spending was also consistent with the strategy of decapitalizing firms to hedge against downturns in the market and to elude payment of social security and other taxes. Thus, workers express their indignation when confronted with evidence of employers' extravagance, highly visible in these small communities. Two workers explicitly make the connection between employers' conspicuous consumption and the growth of the informal sector:

> You can *see* the profits. They dance before your eyes. Maybe you've seen those mansions, those houses that look like they belong to Arab sheiks. Those come out of clandestine labor, out of the non-payment of social security, out of the extra money that we pay in taxes because those thieves don't pay.

> If you go along the highway [from Elche] to Santa Pola, if you go to the beach, you see the *señores* who are so insolvent before the State Magistrate with huge properties of fantastic luxury, with fences that almost look like they cost more than the houses themselves . . . . Then you find out that the owner [of one of those houses] is the same man who is refusing to give some worker a paid vacation. He's the same one that you take to court and he ends up laying the worker off because [his firm] is "insolvent."

Interestingly, the criticisms made of employers are also leveled at workers. A fairly high standard of living in the region has enabled many, if not most, workers to buy cars and some even to afford second homes in the country—far more modest, of course, than those of businessmen. Workers' consumption habits are just as transparent as those of employers. The latter often charge that workers' greed has contributed to the growth of the informal sector, because workers want to receive the extra payments and unemployment benefits that frequently accompany closure. One employer remarked:

> The workers and the unions say that closing down the firms is immoral, but what about working while receiving unemployment insurance? I call that immoral. I've seen supposedly unemployed workers driving brand new cars. I can't be expected to have sympathy for them—from what I see, they're not suffering much.

Unlike the dispersed industrial zones around Madrid, the communities where shoe production is centered are close-knit and highly self-conscious. Workers and employers observe closely not only each others' behavior in the workplace but also their styles of living, spending habits, and contributions to local community life, including their financial contributions to such important local events as the yearly town *fiestas*.[9] The charges and countercharges generated by close observation of each others' behavior represent only one of the potentially debilitating effects of the clustering of the shoe factories in a handful of towns. Another is the pressure on workers and entrepreneurs alike to copy and conform to certain patterns of behavior. The wave of false closures, for example, resulted from the rapid spread of detailed knowledge among factory owners about the best way to make the procedure work. If at first some employers were merely imitating a successful business maneuver, others were drawn to the practice because of its growing social acceptability. On another, broader level, employers encounter the difficulty of being innovative or daring when, as one small entrepreneur noted, "everyone is watching." The shoe-producing towns, as another employer points out, are still quite provincial despite the international influences brought in by the export trade.

Such observations bring us full circle back to the comparison of the "Valencian path to development" with the model of industrialization based on the Italian case. Whereas in Italy, the geographical concentration of industries undergoing restructuring facilitated the emergence of flexible specialization by enabling small producers to convene and communicate easily, the same feature in Valencian industry may have had negative consequences for decentralized growth. In the shoe industry, the self-contained social environment of the shoe-producing towns has fostered interclass antagonism at least as much as it has bred intraclass communication. Further evidence that the community context has presented obstacles to flexible restructuring emerge in later chapters, where I examine both the nature of social relations within informal industry and the character of political alliances at the local level.

All the evidence supports the conclusion that spontaneous restructuring in the shoe industry differs markedly from the parallel process of decentralization in Madrid's electronics industry. The newly emerging structure features linear relationships among firms rather than the expanding network of cross-subcontracting found in the electronics industry. Labor conditions in subcontracting firms are generally poor, and nonpayment of social security for workers is virtually a requirement for continued competitiveness. As formal enterprises restructure to take advantage of decentralized, lower-cost production, some invest in improvements and innovative changes in their firms, but most firms prefer to rely on easier cost- and wage-cutting tactics. A remarkably stable informal sector represents the industry's "quick fix" in responding to pressures to restructure. The solution protects profits in the short run while postponing costly readjustments that might provide the basis for long-term expansion.

PART III

5 At Home in the Informal Sector: Gender and Industrial Outwork

The social context of production shapes industrial restructuring and affects the outcome of decentralization. Few would dispute such a statement. But when we speak of industry's "social context" or of the "embeddedness" of relations of production in social relations, what do we really mean? Is *all* social discourse equally relevant to the structuring of relations of production in the informal sector? Does decentralization depend, in its unfolding, on so many, and such variable, social factors that generalization about them is impossible?

I have tried to allow the field research to answer these questions. The comparison between decentralization in the electronics industry and informalization in the shoe industry in Part II points to the importance of several sets of social factors (they cannot be labelled exclusively as cultural or political) that guide the process of industrial restructuring. One set of factors comprises those experiences that shape workers' perceptions of industrial labor and collective action: past experiences in the labor movement, encounters with the state, and the influence of social pressures to adhere to established career trajectories. These types of experiences tend to guide workers' choices in responding to decentralizing strategies of industrial firms. Chapter 6 explores this dimension of restructuring in the two industries already analyzed, while Chapter 7 takes a broader look at the evolution and influence of worker-state relations.

Another set of social relationships that helps to determine the direction of decentralized growth is the subject of this chapter: the division of labor and patterns of authority within the household. Despite a growing literature on women's work in industry, the relationship of such social patterns to industrial growth remains obscure. With a few notable exceptions, gender is conspicuously absent as an analytic category in most of the writings on flexible

105

specialization in industry.[1] This is true despite some evidence from the Italian case that female outworkers have not benefitted to the same degree as men in decentralized economies of growth.[2] At the same time, the literature on women's work in industry in developing countries has not moved much beyond documenting substandard conditions for women workers. The tendency is to lament gender inequality without analyzing the changing dynamics of women's employment in industry or the reasons that different patterns emerge in different places.[3]

The division of labor by gender (and by age) in the household is not a constant, across either time or place. Variations in household structure and family relations have enormously important implications for the way decentralized industrial production is carried out, particularly when much of it is performed in the home itself. The nature of the demand for women's labor changes also as decentralization takes place. Although men's and women's opportunities to alter their working conditions and earnings may be unequal, to interpret this inequality as a sign that gender roles in industry are static is incorrect. Under some conditions, inequality may even become sharper as a result of decentralization.

Home-based production shows most clearly the influence of social roles in constructing workers' opportunities within decentralized industry. Patterns of authority within the household and expectations about women's careers both urge their participation in homework and constrain their opportunities. In this chapter, I examine these connections, but also place them in the context of a changing relationship between industrial firms and home-based producers. Fully explaining the differences between the electronics and shoe industries, I argue, depends on understanding not just how units of production perform in relation to one another, but also how their members create and refer to complex social identities.

Homework in Spain

Home-based production has traditionally played a part in production in labor-intensive Spanish industries such as footwear, textiles, and garment manufacturing. But statistics on the number of homeworkers and information about their occupations have not been regularly collected by the Spanish government. Nor have sociological studies followed this topic closely. Before Enric Sanchis published his doctoral dissertation on homework in the Valencian region in 1984, the last sociological treatise on homework dated from 1908. As a result, we cannot directly measure the growth of homework in Spain in recent years. Data from several studies nevertheless show that homework offers the same benefits as other types of informal labor to entrepreneurs who seek to reduce wage costs and increase the flexibility of the work force. The types of workers participating in homework and the very nature of their work also appear to have changed as a result of recent trends.

These points are illustrated in Sanchis's groundbreaking study of homework in the Valencian region (Sanchis, 1984). Sanchis interviewed 269 individuals from a nonrepresentative sample of female homeworkers in light manufacturing industries. According to this study, homework in Valencia is a quintessential informal occupation: Only two of the 269 informants received social security benefits through their jobs, and the rest were not eligible for any employment-related benefits, including pensions. The average homeworker in Sanchis's group was a 40-year-old married woman whose earnings through homework were equivalent to slightly less than the minimum wage.

Even though these workers generally used their wages from homework to supplement other family income, Sanchis also found that their work could hardly be considered marginal either to the workers' own use of time or to families' activities. Homeworkers' jobs in fact resembled employment in the formal sector in the amount of time they absorbed. Nearly three-fourths of the women interviewed engaged in homework during 11 or 12 months out of the year, and about one-half worked the same number of days a week and hours a day as regular, full-time employees. In many cases, other family members regularly helped homeworkers and the setting for work closely resembled that of small family workshops or informal factories.

Sanchis also demonstrates that a change has occurred in the nature of homework as a direct result of recent restructuring in industry. The traditional career pattern of homeworkers in Valencian manufacturing begins in the shoe factories. Women later opt to take up homework after getting married or having children. Yet, increasing numbers of young women are entering directly into homework now, citing their inability to find work informal firms.

Many young workers may no longer enter the formal sector at all during their working lives. Sanchis has claimed that these and other findings of his study show both the growing importance of homework to formal industry and the nontraditional character of this type of work.

To explore the generality of these findings and add other insights, I undertook the analysis of unpublished data from a national survey conducted under the auspices of the Ministry of Economy in 1983. The survey consisted of a short list of questions inserted in a larger questionnaire on other, unrelated topics. The larger survey was administered in three separate phases, each consisting of approximately 4,000 interviews (a total of 12,457). Respondents were asked an initial screening question about whether any members of their household worked at home. If they answered positively, then they were asked a short series of questions about the nature of that work, who engaged in it and for what reasons, and the percentage of family income that was derived from homework. The survey was administered in all the regions of Spain, with the exception of the Canary Islands, Ceuta, and Melilla.[4]

About 3.8%, or 467, of the households surveyed held at least one homeworker.[5] The average homeworker identified by the survey conforms fairly closely to the portrait drawn by Sanchis in his study in the Valencian region. About three-fourths of the homeworkers are women, with an average age of 39. A relatively small percentage (fewer than 7%) falls outside the economically active age range of 16 to 65. Well in excess of one-half the homeworkers (56%) are described as housewives, and in the vast majority of the cases, earnings from homework are low and used to supplement other family income. The wide variety of individuals who work at home is nevertheless striking. About one-fifth of the homeworkers in the study are heads-of-households. Young people also comprise a significant portion of the group: Workers who are age 29 and younger account for well in excess of one-fourth of the homeworkers, and they also tend to assist homeworkers more frequently than do family members from any other age group.[6]

The survey results permit us to classify workers as "stable" or "unstable" participants in homework. The most significant finding is that most homeworkers view the occupation as unstable or temporary. They do so for strikingly different reasons. On the one hand, about one-third of homeworkers could be classified as "unemployed" vis-a-vis the formal labor market. That is, they have left or lost outside jobs and are engaging in homework only until they can find other work again, or they have never worked outside the home and are looking for their first regular jobs. On the other hand, another, slightly larger group comprises individuals who consider homework temporary but do not indicate whether they might also give it up if financial conditions enabled them to return to "inactive" positions in the job market, for example, as students or housewives (see Table 5.1).

Two groups of respondents may be viewed as relatively stable homeworkers compared with the causal or "unemployed" workers described above. A small proportion of homeworkers (4%) are retirees and, although they may be willing to accept work outside the home, it is less likely that they will actively seek it. A second, larger group comprises individuals who clearly are not looking for, or would not accept, jobs outside the home. This group, which accounts for about one-fourth of homeworkers, also includes a diverse range of individuals, from those who view homework as their permanent occupation or profession—tailors and jewelers are two common examples—to those who cite family responsibilities as a reason for working only at home. Characterizing these individuals as stable homeworkers does not imply that they work longer hours or find homework more remunerative; rather, they share a view of employment outside the home as clearly less desirable.

These patterns become more meaningful when we examine the

Table 5.1 Employment Status of Homeworkers

Employment Status	Number	Percentage
Unemployed—Lost outside jobs or looking for first jobs	152	33.4%
Temporary or casual—Work sporadically and/or temporarily	162	36.0%
Inactive—Retired and/or not interested in working outside the home	129	28.4%
Other situations	10	2.2%
Total	455*	100.0%

* Information was incomplete in 12 cases.

stability of homework for different groups of workers. Homework clearly represents an entry-point into the job market and a temporary phase in the working lives of many young people. Temporary homeworkers between the ages of 16 and 29 make up about one-fourth of all homeworkers. Young workers are most likely to engage in activities that would fall in the service sector, particularly tutoring and office work done at home. They also appear in significant numbers as assistants to other homeworkers in a wide range of activities.

Not surprisingly, women are the least likely to be willing to accept employment outside the home. Nearly one-third of housewives say they are not interested in finding other jobs to replace homework. However, a substantial portion of housewives—more than one-fourth—falls into the "unemployed" category, and most of these have already worked in other jobs and hope to return to jobs outside the home.

Finally, heads-of-household occupy an intermediate position between young dependents and housewives. One-third of heads-of-households are "unemployed," most of them because they have lost outside jobs and not because they are looking for work for the first time. This pattern is reflected in the distribution of these categories by gender: A slightly higher percentage of men than women has left or been laid off from other jobs, although the proportion seeking first jobs for both sexes is roughly equal.

One of the most significant results of the national survey is the broad view it offers of the activities engaged in by homeworkers. These findings also provide further insight into the career patterns of homeworkers. The largest category comprises activities related to the garment industry, including sewing, embroidery, knitting, and tasks related to industrial production in the textile industry. These activities together employ nearly one-half the workers in the study. The second largest group consists of various skilled manual jobs outside the garment sector. Some of these are artisan activities traditionally associated with home workshops: for example, ceramics, jewelry making, and wickerwork. But a larger number of workers are distributed among industrial or semi-industrial sectors. While some of these industries, such as doll-making and footwear, are widely known to employ homeworkers for certain phases of production, others have little traditional association with homework. The fabrication or assembly of metal, wood, and plastic products in the home hardly fits the stereotypical image of homework as relatively unskilled work involving light assembly. Electronics work is another skilled or semiskilled occupation included in this category. Together, sewing and other industrial/artisan activities account for roughly three-fourths of all homeworkers. The final group includes jobs in the service sector, particularly tutoring, hairdressing, and office work (see Table 5.2).

As with other forms of unregulated labor, homework clearly serves to lower the costs of production in the formal economy. If the criterion of social security coverage is the main defining feature of regulated employment in homework, nearly 86% of homeworkers are informal workers. Some portion of the 14% of homeworkers who claim to be registered with social security are probably intentionally disguising their irregular status; of the 21 homeworkers who say their do contribute to social security for homework, only one claims to have payments made directly by a firm.

Strikingly, however, the vast majority of respondents did not try to disguise the fact that they do not receive legal benefits for homework. Undoubtedly, this can be explained in part by a widespread view that homework is not expected to meet the same requirements as other types of labor. Particularly because most respondents view homework as a temporary activity and many accept it only as a substitute for "real" work, workers may not even associate legal norms concerning other types of labor with homework.

Table 5.2 Gender of Homeworkers by Type of Activity

Activity	Male	(%)	Female	(%)	Total	(%)
Services	23	(20.3%)	89	(25.9%)	112	(24.5%)
(%)	(20.5%)		(79.5%)		(100.0%)	
Garment/Textile	15	(13.3%)	205	(51.6%)	220	(48.1%)
(%)	(6.8%)		(93.2%)		(100.0%)	
Other Industrial/						
Artisan	75	(66.4%)	50	(14.5%)	125	(27.4%)
(%)	(60.0%)		(40.0%)		(100.0%)	
Total	113	(100.0%)	344	(100.0%)	457*	(100.0%)
(%)	(24.7%)		(75.3%)		(100.0%)	

* Information was incomplete in 10 cases.

A continuum exists in the situations of homeworkers ranging from intense dependence on the formal sector, exemplified by the family workshop producing goods to the specifications of a formal firm, to the relative autonomy displayed by a skilled craftsman who sells his products directly to the public or to individual clients with specialized needs. While the former represents a direct response to industrial restructuring and functions primarily to siphon cheaper labor and its products into the formal sector, the latter situation may indeed offer some individuals greater independence and "true" self-employment. Between these two extremes lies a variety of situations in which dependence on the formal sector is balanced with the flexibility and potential independence afforded by working at home.

The survey data enable us to place homeworkers in one of three main categories: those who work for one firm or several firms; those who work for individuals on order (*por encargo*); and those who sell goods or services directly to the public (see Table 5.3). The majority of homeworkers (60%) report that they work *por encargo*, while more than one-third work directly for firms. The latter workers are proportionally more significant in industrial/artisan activities, where they account for 45% of the homeworkers. A relatively small proportion—close to 5%—of homeworkers offer goods and services for direct sale. These workers are scattered among various industrial/artisan activities—jewelry-making and ceramics are examples—and in some services. This result casts considerable doubt on the notion that homework lends independence to workers. Even if we include artisan-homeworkers who work for individual clients, the percentage of truly independent artisans in the sample is quite small.

Table 5.3 Methods of Marketing Goods and Services Produced by Homeworkers

Marketing Method	Total	Percentage
Sell directly to public	21	4.9%
Work for firm(s) or distributors(s)	153	35.4%
Fill orders for individual clients	257	59.5%
Other	1	0.2%
Total	432*	100.0%

* Information was incomplete in 35 cases.

Although the survey data do not provide a close look at the division of labor in households where homeworkers are assisted by other members of the family, some telling contrasts are found between these households and families with only a single homeworker.[7] First, in multiworker families, the principal homeworker is more likely to be a head-of-household who is out of work. The implication is that heads-of-household use their authority within the family to mobilize and organize the labor of other family members. As principal homeworkers, they are the informal equivalents of shop-floor supervisors. Second, in contrast to other households, the majority of multiworker families receive their work from firms rather than from individual clients. Their households are thus more likely to participate in productive putting-out systems that are a symptom of decentralization. In fact, a significantly larger proportion of these households—40% compared to 25% for families with only one homeworker—engage in industrial or artisan activities, rather than services.

Assistants in the household tend to be close relatives of principal homeworkers. Several patterns of cooperation among family members are clear. First, heads-of-household tend to be assisted most often by their spouses. Housewives, in contrast, most often receive help from their children, especially daughters. Where there are more than two assistants, the third worker tends to be either a very young or very old member of the household. A veritable pecking order appears to be established within the home that leads family members to recruit assistants over whom they have the most immediate authority.

The results of the national study point toward the distinctive features of homework as an activity centered in the household. Workers' motives for engaging in homework are affected by the overall financial needs of the family. The manner in which work is organized within the home is also influenced by the structure of the family and by patterns of authority within it. While these characteristics of homework are clearly delineated in the national survey, the activity must be examined in the context of a particular industry to grasp its relationship to the recent trend of productive decentralization. The following sections take a detailed look at homework in the shoe industry and the plight of a typical individual homeworker.

Restructuring and Homework in the Shoe Industry

According to a study of the early evolution of the shoe industry, clandestine work and unregulated homework were quite common during the 1940s and 1950s, the period that saw the founding of many of the large, mostly family-owned firms. Toward the end of this period and during the following decade, with the takeoff of the shoe industry and the rapid rise of exports, homework may actually have declined in importance as workers were brought into the factories. While expanding production increased labor requirements, the surge in exports also placed pressure on firms to meet larger orders on time and to produce to the specifications provided by importers. Having workers within the firm gave greater control over the pace and quality of their work (Bernabé 1976).

This trend, however, was reversed in the 1970s. In response to the economic and political pressures already described, firms increasingly began to put out portions of the production process to homeworkers, particularly the more labor-intensive phases of production where a tradition of homework was already established. The phases most appropriate for decentralization were those concentrated at the beginning of the production process, especially the cutting (cortado), the stitching of uppers (aparado), and a series of intermediate tasks. Other jobs that could be done outside the factory, generally by less skilled workers, include lining heels, cleaning shoes, and assembling or attaching adornments on shoes.

Homework is now used for all these, as well as other, phases of production. The most common activity of homeworkers, however, continues to be the stitching of uppers. This is a particularly labor-intensive phase of production, costly to maintain in the factory, and relatively simple to distribute to outworkers. Homework in the shoe industry is, in fact, considered by many industry participants as virtually synonymous with this phase of production.

Factory owners interviewed in 1982 and in 1985 were forthright about the benefits to their firms of putting out this and other phases of production to homeworkers. The principal benefit, of course, is the saving of social security costs and of wages that would otherwise have to be paid to in-house workers during slow production periods. Employers are emphatic about the importance of these savings and some even claim that brining all aparado work into the factories would spell disaster for the Spanish shoe industry as a whole. According to one employer, legalizing the status of homeworkers would bring "total chaos for all shoe-producing firms, not just in Alicante but in all of Spain. It would push our prices higher than those of most [other] countries. As it is, they're already headed in that direction."[8]

Besides saving the costs of social security benefits for homeworkers, firms also benefit from a reduction of overhead costs when they utilize homework. Homeworkers ordinarily provide their own machines and pay their own electricity costs. They also pay for and maintain the necessary workspace. Bringing all homeworkers into the firm would thus signify in most cases substantial additional payments toward the purchase, maintenance, and operation of machinery, as well as added investments in plant capacity. One factory owner states this clearly: "To make a thousand pairs, we would need about 40 *aparadoras*. . . . We don't have the space, the electrical capacity, none of it, so we *have* to use homeworkers."

A further incentive for putting out work to homeworkers is the relative flexibility of this type of labor. Homeworkers may be called on to work during peak periods and effectively "laid off" later without severance pay. Firms may also expand production without assuming the risks associated with augmenting the official labor force. Finally, homeworkers may be asked to do special tasks that are necessary only for certain models of shoes or used only during certain seasons. Again, factory owners are frank about these advantages:

> [W]hen there's no work to be put out, well, you just say, "Look, there isn't any, wait a month," and a month later when you have more work you take it to them, and that's that. If they worked here, it wouldn't be like that. You'd have them here all the time and you'd have to pay them every week, whether they produced anything or not.

Certain prevalent ideas about the appropriateness of different tasks for homework clearly influence employers' strategies for putting out work. The most important factor is undoubtedly the continuity of the sexual division of labor within firms with work performed outside factories. It is no accident that homework, which is widely considered to be a female occupation appropriate particularly for married women, is so commonly used for the stitching of uppers. This phase of production is also dominated by women inside the factories. Indeed, women frequently move from factory employment to homework, and factory owners tend to view *aparadoras* within their firms as potential homeworkers.

Not surprisingly, then, a widespread notion exists that homework in the shoe industry is essentially women's work. Factory owners have a clear image of homework as a secondary activity in the household that is done mainly by married women in conjunction with domestic tasks. This characterization, for some, constitutes the very definition of homework: "Homework . . . is work done by women at home. The women are housewives who have some spare time, or else make the time."

Such ideas underlie a clear distinction made by most factory owners between unregulated homework and the new clandestine workshop production that has been associated with the recent phase of decentralization. While the latter often draws bitter criticism, the former practice is defended both as a traditional and a necessary feature of production. In addition, factory owners point out that homework is a positive good because it helps provide employment for a segment of the population that may otherwise be without work. The assumed economic dependence of women in the household reinforces benevolent attitudes toward unregulated homework. A married woman, even if she does not receive social security benefits through her job, has access to state health services and some other benefits through her employed spouse. Employers note that homeworkers made a conscious decision to sacrifice state benefits and job security in exchange for increased flexibility in their schedules. One factory owner explains: "Women who work at home often aren't interested in receiving social security benefits. They don't have to follow a strict schedule, and so they're perfectly happy to do the work."

Since the restructuring gained momentum, such ideas are becoming gradually less consistent with the actual conditions of homework. First of all, some traditionally male-dominated phases of production—most notably cutting—are being put out by factories, leading many men to join the ranks of homeworkers. Second, some men are assuming traditionally female-dominated activities in response to the opportunities created by the burgeoning demand for outwork. Men do not act as typical homeworkers, however; some become foremen in small workshops of homeworkers under their direction or else distribute piecework to homeworkers in increasingly distant rural locations. One man running a small *aparado* workshop reported that public opinion, initially scornful, no longer condemned his entry into "women's work."

Third, the kinds of women entering homework and their motives for doing so are changing in response to restructuring. Women's inability to find factory jobs often leads them to take up homework earlier, and economic pressures created by the restructur-ing encourage them to regard the activity as more than a supplement to family income. Although we cannot determine to what extent these and other factors combine to alter public perceptions, they highlight the ideological nature of popular views of homework, which stress its "traditional" character.

Popular perceptions of homework contrast strikingly with the actual conditions of this work in the shoe industry. We have detailed information about these conditions from a 1982 survey of homeworkers in the four main shoe-producing towns of Alicante: Elda, Elche, Petrel, and Villena. The survey revealed that homework in the region is rampant. Data were collected on the employment of some 5,000 individuals between the ages of 16 and 60, and 10 percent of those surveyed do some work at home. Among people who work, approximately one in five engages in homework.

More than 90% of 406 homeworkers in the surveyed group are women (for households that held more than one homeworker, the person who dedicated most time to homework was selected for the study). More than 90% of the workers are employed in the shoe industry, with nearly three-fourths specializing in the stitching of uppers. One of the most striking findings is the high proportion of young homeworkers. Individuals between 16 and 29 years old comprise about two-fifths of the total, while the average age is 32 (compared to 39 in the national survey described earlier). Career patterns of homeworkers in the shoe industry appear to be changing as young people encounter greater difficulties in finding jobs in factories.

In fact, the connection between employment trends in firms and the sizable proportion of youths among homeworkers can be traced directly. Young homeworkers do not show a greater tendency to take up homework as a first job. But a significantly higher proportion have *lost* outside jobs and have turned to homework as a replacement. While 60% of homeworkers say they left previous jobs when they married—the traditional pattern in the industry—22% have been affected by factory closures and another 5% were laid off. Events related to the crisis and to the industry's restructuring have had a disproportionate effect on young workers: Of those surveyed between ages 16 and 29, 47% lost jobs because of shut-downs or lay-offs, compared to only 10% of workers between ages 30 and 55 who had to leave previous jobs for the same reasons. About one-fifth of all homeworkers, then, are young workers whose prospects for pursuing alternatives to homework were directly altered by the crisis.

However significant such findings may be, they do not alter the basic fact that the majority of homeworkers—nearly 70%—are married women who describe themselves as "housewives." Most have to juggle household responsibilities with homework and many can and do recruit family members to help. Although homework is for many a fairly stable occupation, homeworkers' earnings consistently fall below amounts prescribed by minimum wage regulations (on this point, see Ybarra 1986). Nevertheless, income from homework is hardly negligible for many households. The average proportion of family income that derives from homework is 39%.

Despite the fact that most homeworkers—more than 70%—work for a single firm, only a tiny percentage enjoy the benefits and protection associated with regular employment. Of those surveyed, 84% report they do not receive any of the employment-associated benefits administered through social security. Only 1% say they are treated and paid by firms "as if they were on-the-books."

These findings should not be interpreted to mean that pressures on firms to provide pay raises and benefits are entirely unsuccessful. Sanchis (1984) noted in his study of homeworkers in Valencia that piecework rates paid to homeworkers often rise in tandem with pay-hikes in the industrywide contract, despite the absence of formal arrangements. Employers I interviewed indicated that they use the official contract rates as a rough measuring stick when setting piecework rates for homeworkers. If the latter complain repeatedly about lower-than-average earnings, an employer will respond by timing one of his own workers on the same job; if she can work at a rate that would yield the industry's minimum wage at an averaged, hourly rate, then the piecework rate remains unchanged. Employers also sometimes pay vacations for homeworkers, particularly if the workers are skilled and the firm is eager not to lose them. In our study, 12% of homeworkers reported that they receive vacation pay, even though they are not registered with social security. In part, these agreements reflect homeworkers' familiarity with the terms of regular employment in the shoe industry, knowledge which they gain both through previous employment in factories and through close association with relatives and friends who also work in the industry. In part, the semiformal arrangements reflect the relatively long-term and stable relationships that develop between homeworkers and particular firms. Many homeworkers in the shoe industry work for factory owners with whom then have dealt for years. In most cases, homeworkers have some frequent, direct contact with a factory owner or an employee of the firm; sometimes they have close relatives who work in the same firm.

If in these respects homework in the shoe industry appears remarkably stable, other similarities to regular employment are even more striking. Perhaps the most significant finding of our survey is that homeworkers tend to devote as much time to their work as do regular employees outside the home. The average workday reported by homeworkers is seven and one-half hours. Nearly two-fifths put in more than eight hours of work a day. It is also striking that young people work the longest hours; 46% of those younger than age 30 work more than 8 hours a day, compared to 29% for workers older than age 30.

The vast majority of homeworkers habitually use machinery and own their own machines. They pay for the electricity used to run the machines as part of their household electrical bill, and they are responsible for necessary maintenance and repairs. For *aparado* work, a machine is essential and can cost as much as two or three times the monthly earnings of a full-time homeworker or one month's pay for a skilled operator in a shoe factory.

About one-half the homeworkers are assisted by other members of the family: women most frequently by their children, and children by their parents. Children are often apprentices and gradually learn to do more skilled tasks until they also become homeworkers. In general, helpers are assigned specific tasks, the most common of which are cutting loose threads (for *aparadoras*) and applying glue (for all tasks in the shoe industry). This is the aspect of homework most severely criticized by union leaders, who say that both the child labor often involved in homework and the substandard and unregulated health conditions that characterize it blatantly violate labor laws. In particular, union leaders point to the potential health hazard of exposure to toxic fumes from glue in spaces that may be inadequately ventilated.

This point helps us recall that the jobs done by homeworkers are essentially *industrial* tasks that are being carried out in a *residential* context. One important implication is that, although the workday of most homeworkers is about as long as that of employees in firms, their work schedules are dramatically different. The majority of workers consistently alternate or combine industrial and domestic tasks, including cleaning, cooking, and childcare. This combination of housework with homework is, in fact, built into the job. Only one-fourth of homeworkers report having a room in the home used exclusively for work; the rest use common rooms, which they must clean daily of waste materials such as scraps of leather, glue, and fragments of thread.

Homeworkers complain most about the lack of social security benefits and legal protection associated with homework, before citing dissatisfaction with the actual conditions of working at home. However, the unregulated status and low pay for homework are closely related to the constraints homeworkers face on the use of their time and the character of their associations with other producers. Because homeworkers are isolated, collective action to demand better conditions from employers is difficult. So are cooperative efforts to improve productivity by forming workshops where workers could divide tasks and share skills.

The greatest obstacle to workers' making these or other improvements is the burden of housekeeping, which is not lessened but is actually increased when industrial work is taken home. The strain of juggling homework, housework, and childcare precludes any initiatives on the part of workers to form associations with other homeworkers or to alter radically in some way a style of production that enables them to accommodate two jobs. This fact has significance both for homeworkers' prospects for improving their welfare and for the industry's potential for adjusting effectively to shifting global markets.

One Homeworkers' View

The conditions described above come to life when we examine the plight of one homeworker. Encarnación lives in Petrel, a small town next to Elda that has long been one of the principal shoe-producing centers of the region. She is 49 years old and has been a homeworker since age 18. Her three daughters also work in the shoe industry—although not as *aparadoras*—and her husband is a relatively skilled assembly-line worker in a local shoe factory. As with most of the homeworkers in the Alicante survey, Encarnación works for only one firm, a small factory that provides her with steady work. The firm pays Encarnación every week, based on the number of pairs of shoes sewn.

Encarnación does not receive social security benefits, nor does she have any guaranteed level of income. Her weekly earnings vary substantially (from about 5,000 to 17,000 pesetas) even when she dedicates the same amount of time to work. She considers a week "good" if she earns 10,000 pesetas and "every good" if she makes 12,000 or more. Having to work on more difficult models will slow her down considerably, which is why her ability to haggle with the factory owner to give her better assignments or to raise the piecework rate by "10 or 20 pesetas" is so important. Different models carry varying rates depending on their degree of difficulty, but the higher rates paid for more complex models rarely compensate the extra time such jobs require.

Although Encarnación considers her situation quite good compared to those of her acquaintances who do homework, what impresses an observer most about her job is how very difficult it is. Stitching shoe uppers is a complex task involving considerable skill. An apprentice usually needs a minimum of three months to learn all the basic operations and may take up to a year before she can work independently. An *aparadora's* work is also physically quite demanding, and most have poor eyesight as a result of their work. Back complaints are also common. Encarnación's close neighbor has given up work as an *aparadora* because of failing eyesight and a chronically swollen arm, the result of hours of leaning against the vibrating machine table. Breathing the fumes from the glue that is used in the *aparado* work is a well-known hazard.

A description of the actual tasks involved in *aparado* work will give some idea of the considerable skill and effort the job demands. During a typical week, Encarnación receives several batches of shoes. Each batch arrives in a large plastic bag containing various pieces cut for a given model and grouped by type and size. A batch may contain anywhere from a few pairs to several dozen, because each represents part of an order from an individual client to the factory (most small and medium factories work only to order rather than producing stocks of particular models). In the same bag, Encarnación also finds a single, sample shoe. She does not get any additional instruction about how to do the job—just the shoe, the cut pieces, and perhaps some extra materials, such as colored thread or bits of foam or elastic.

For each job, then, Encarnación must first decide and plan how and in what order she will do the different parts of the job. Simple models may require perhaps six steps, but more complex styles may have as many as ten pieces or more and involve tricky tasks, such as sewing in padded toes or adornments. In general, the steps of the work follow the same basic pattern. Usually, the pieces of the lining are sewn together first, then the sides of the shoes are joined at the back. Additional pieces are then added to the top of the shoe and the completed upper, looking now like a partially flattened cone, is put together with the lining. Complex models may require numerous intermediate steps of sewing or gluing pieces together. On one afternoon, Encarnación completed only the initial steps for sewing a complicated model and was complaining that she could have nearly completed the work on a simpler model in the same amount of time. Because she was working slowly, she calculated she would make only 7,000 pesetas for that week.

Employers rarely mention this mental work involved in planning and setting up production when they cite the advantages of homework. Yet, as Encarnación's job clearly illustrates, homeworkers routinely assume many burdens that would, in factory production, normally have to be carried out by owners or supervisors, at additional cost to the firms. This tendency to ignore or hide the amount of planning that goes into the job reinforces the popular view of homework in the shoe industry as a relatively unskilled occupation, one that deserves lower pay than factory work.

The difficulties women may encounter in combining homework and housework are also widely underestimated. A typical day for Encarnación is gruelling and somewhat hectic. She rises early and does some housecleaning before beginning work. Her two machines are set up in the narrow, enclosed balcony of her second-floor apartment, so that she does not have to worry about cleaning the workspace daily and can keep an eye on activity in the street. About

12:00, Encarnación begins "to think about what to prepare" for her husband and two of her daughters who come home from their factory jobs for the midday meal. Unlike many Spanish housewives, she does her shopping once a week so that she does not have to interrupt her morning work.

After cooking and serving the midday meal, Encarnación usually spends another hour or two doing housework. Around 4:00 she is ready to begin work again until her husband and daughters come home from work. She then prepares the evening meal; afterward, she works for an hour or two more on jobs that can be done by hand. She usually then does a little more housework before going to bed.

Encarnación has had, at various times, help from family members with homework. She is very lucky, she says, because her husband has been willing to do some of the domestic chores and on rare occasions even helps with the industrial tasks. He helped more often when the three children were younger and Encarnación was taking in more work. Her daughters have at different times all assisted her. She recently bought a second machine from a neighbor so that her youngest daughter, who is 16, could become her "apprentice." But none of her daughters has shown the slightest interest in becoming an *aparadora*. "It's because they see me bent over the machine all day," Encarnación explains. "They come home from school or work and always find me at the machine. They call it slave labor." Encarnación's oldest daughter did become a homeworker, but she works at a different task that pays considerably less then the sewing of uppers but is much less demanding.

Both mother's and daughter's situations illustrate the increasing importance of homework in the context of the industry's restructuring. Encarnación's earnings from homework had to support the family for two months while her husband was on a temporary lay-off and another six months after his firm closed and he was waiting to receive unemployment benefits. Her daughter has sometimes been in the same position because her own husband is a casual factory worker who has been in and out of work. In both cases, having income from homework improves the financial position of the women within the household; neither turns her earnings over to her spouse but instead collects his money and administers household finances "from a single pocket."

The Alicante survey indicates that Encarnación's case is fairly typical of homeworkers in the region. In addition to showing us the conditions surrounding homework in greater detail, her case illustrates the obstacles inherent in homework to improving those conditions or to abandoning the occupation altogether. Encarnación consciously contrasts her work with that of a factory operative. The contrast is clear to her not only because she once worked in a factory but also because her closest family members do so now. Factory work, from her perspective, is in almost all ways preferable to homework. The pay is better, the work is steady, and the hours are both shorter and concentrated rather than stretched throughout the day. The main "advantage" of homework is that it enables one to devote more time and attention to housework and childcare. But what is an advantage for the household is simply more work for the individual.

The isolation surrounding the job makes improving its conditions difficult. Although Encarnación knows several other people who work for the same firm, she rarely sees them and most of the time has no way of knowing whether they, too, are complaining about particular jobs or piecework rates. This did not used to be so common. In the past, more homeworkers went to the firms themselves to pick up work and would meet and socialize with other workers there. But work is more often distributed by van now, in part because homework is more widely used and firms do not want to call attention to the extent to which they employ unregulated labor. While having work delivered saves time for homeworkers, it also intensifies their isolation. As a skilled and probably highly prized worker, Encarnación is able to negotiate informally for higher piecework rates or to declare a personal "strike" if she is assigned too many poorly paid jobs, but the strength of her bargaining position is equal only to the importance of her personal contribution to production.

What about possibilities within the household for increasing productivity and improving conditions? The key element is the homeworker's authority within the household. Encarnación is able to recruit her husband's help only on an irregular basis. She was also unsuccessful in getting her daughters to learn the more skilled tasks and so relieve her from the heaviest and most difficult aspects of the job. Finally, constant juggling of homework with housework already forces Encarnación to follow a strict plan for the use of her time and space. In a sense, she has already perfected the task before her; significant changes would also involve radical changes in her role as a housewife and mother. At the same time, current economic conditions and, particularly, instability in the formal labor market that could threaten the jobs of her husband and daughters, make it unlikely that Encarnación will give up homework. To do so would involve a move toward greater financial dependence on the rest of her family and greater financial uncertainty for the family as a whole.

Conclusion

The analysis of homework provides a model for viewing he evolution of social relations and their effects on production within the informal sector generally. Two aspects of homeworkers' experiences are especially significant and invite comparisons with other informal situations described in previous chapters. One central theme is the role of informal labor—in this case homework—in the career cycle of the individual; another is the effect of the social relations surrounding production on the prospects for dynamic change within the informal sector.

I have shown in this chapter how the trajectories of homeworkers' careers support the stability of this occupation. A large proportion of homeworkers come from groups that tend to dominate the secondary labor market within the formal economy. Homeworkers hold distinctive sets of social expectations regarding employment at the same time that they face real obstacles to progressing steadily toward better jobs in the formal economy. Furthermore, their career patterns tend to mirror closely the evolution of their social roles within the household. Thus, young family members may use homework to begin working at a time when they are still dependent on their families and when, presumably, the substandard conditions and low pay of homework are not viewed as a true reflection of their economic prospects. Women's careers, in contrast, often take them from formal employment to unregulated homework, and this pattern is consistent with the transition to married status and motherhood and the socially-imposed responsibilities that go with either or both roles.

Workers' previous experiences in outside employment can also have a more direct impact on their attitudes toward homework and their prospects for improving its conditions. Male homeworkers, because of their better position in the labor market, will more often have learned special skills through previous employment and may put these to use in homework. Workers may also exploit earlier connections with employers to secure homework assignments, a common pattern in the shoe industry. Finally, the experience of outside employment provides workers with a more precise understanding of the rights that would apply to them as employees in regular jobs, and this knowledge undoubtedly translates into greater pressure placed on employers through informal bargaining to improve the conditions of homework.

The analysis of homework also illuminates ways in which social norms can "regulate" relations of production in the relative absence of state controls. Homework represents an extreme example of informal labor practices in this regard, because the social relations surrounding production are virtually synonymous with those of the family. The different performance of homeworkers often directly reflects the relationships of authority that connect the homeworker with other members of the family. We have seen that homeworkers who are heads-of-household are more likely to recruit other family members' help regularly; homework in this case yields higher earnings and more closely resembles small workshop production, both in its internal operation and in the nature of relationships with clients. Homeworkers as housewives or dependents face formidable obstacles to reordering production in the home, both because of the limited scope of their authority and because of fixed social obligations within the household.

In homework just as in small, semi-informal enterprises, state regulation is never entirely absent, because state-sanctioned practices directly and indirectly influence how, by whom, and under what conditions production is carried out. Yet in both cases, the locus of authority for overseeing relations of production is shifted from the state to sets of norms that derive from and apply to social discourse outside the production process. In homework, the socially-sanctioned authority of a head-of-household translates into authority over the activities of members of the household engaged in productive work. In the small firm trying to break from both hierarchical systems of control and the autocratic control of sweatshop production, social norms of friendship and the implicit authority of peers provide the fundamental underpinning of alternative patterns of organization. Social and cultural patterns do not simply influence the way relations of production are ordered but are also crucial in determining the way unregulated labor and informal enterprises are integrated into the larger economy.

6 The Rise of the Workers' Movement and the Politics of Production

The earlier chapters analyzed entrepreneurs' strategies and the way they have given rise to the process of rapid informalization in Spanish industry. In both Madrid's electronics industry and Alicante's shoe industry, capitalists' concern with cutting labor costs underlay the movement toward productive decentralization and increased use of informal labor. But our understanding of informalization would be incomplete if we were to view it simply as a result of cost-cutting strategies by employers or attribute its outcome only to the varied performance of a new class of informal entrepreneurs. The previous chapter discussed the way social relations surrounding production in the informal sector also help determine the scope for change. This chapter examines the experience of workers and the way their participation in wider political processes molds restructured industry.

The Rise of the Workers' Movement under Franco

The Franco regime based its efforts to control workers on a corporatist philosophy first outlined in the *Fuero de Trabajo* (Labor Charter) of 1938. This document was heavily influenced by the Falangists and was "piously paternalistic" in its tone (Amsden 1972). It called on employers to subtract a "just return" from profits before dedicating the rest of their earnings to increasing financial reserves, building up the means of production, and improving workers' lives. In 1940, the *Ley de Bases de la Organización Sindical* (Law of Syndical Organization) established a state-controlled union, and it was this institution, later referred to as the *sindicato vertical* (vertical union), that became the focus of both the regime's attempts to channel worker protest and the attacks of workers seeking to derail the government and establish *sindicatos de clase* (representative unions).

The national vertical union had branches in each province, in

129

some large cities, and in a few rural areas. Both the national organization and the local branches were divided into "social" sections for labor and "economic" sections for employers. Each of 26 areas of production had *sindicatos* with a similar structure. All national-level officials were appointed by Franco or by his appointees, while middle-level posts were filled through indirect elections. Only the *enlaces* (shop stewards) were directly elected, and until the 1960s they were subject to approval based on their loyalty to the regime. Although vertical union officials did sometimes press the government to make concessions to workers, until 1958 the organization did not participate directly in fixing the terms and conditions of employment in any sector. The Ministry of Labor set standards for each industry, supposedly after reviewing information provided by the various economic and social sections (See Anderson 1970).

The *sindicato vertical* underwent gradual reform from its formation up until its dissolution in 1976. These changes mainly involved the expansion of workers' role in the union, although their relative powerlessness remained a constant feature of the institution. Reforms often came in response to escalating worker protests. Industrial workers had never made complete peace with the Franco regime. Strikes and other forms of protest were already occurring in the industrial north—in Catalonia and the Basque Country—as early as the 1940s. In 1956, a massive strike wave affected not only these regions but also Madrid, Seville, and other major cities (See Ferri, Muixi, and Sanjuan 1978). By the late 1950s, many employers, too, clearly were unhappy with the vertical unions as well as with other features of the paternalistic labor code. The failure of Francoist economic policy during the first two decades of the regime suggested the incompatibility of the corporatist ideology with rapid capitalist growth. Employers sought greater independence from state-controlled institutions, including the *sindicato vertical.* Many favored a system that would allow them to respond at the plant level to growing tensions between management and workers.

The result of pressures by both workers and large capital was the *Ley de Convenios Colectivos* (Law of Collective Contracts) in 1958. In essence, the law established separate systems of collective bargaining in the various sectors under the vertical union. The reform also enhanced the role of the *jurado de empresa* (plant council) and approved plant-level negotiations between employers and workers.

Collective negotiations under the regime were subsequently characterized by a dual bargaining system: The majority of large firms opted for plant-level negotiations, while small firms in highly fragmented industries continued to work through the vertical unions to obtain collective contracts at the provincial level (Amsden 1972).

Knowledge of these institutional arrangements is essential to understanding the dominant strategy of the underground labor movement during the 1960s, which, in turn, shaped the character of organized labor after representative unions were legalized during the transition period. In an initial stage, worker organizing emerged out of a spontaneous movement to form temporary worker committees at the plant level in connection with particular grievances or conflicts. The practice became more common after the strike wave in 1962, and during the following four years *ad hoc* workers' commissions were formed mainly in the industrial zones of Catalonia, the Basque region, and Madrid. The movement at first embraced all pro-labor forces, including the various Catholic organizations that played a crucial role in the earliest phase of the underground movement, the Communist Party (PCE), regional labor groups, and the less active socialist *Unión General de Trabajadores* (UGT). The PCE and its close allies were calling for the formation of a *sindicato obrero unico* (unified workers' union), an idea that had been borrowed in modified form from the anarchist *Confederación Nacional de Trabajo* (CNT), which before the Civil War had favored the formation of a single union organized by branches of production.

To present a direct challenge to the regime's policies toward labor, the PCE proposed a strategy of legally infiltrating the state-controlled vertical union, a tactic that the UGT and some other labor groups opposed. The opportunity to pursue this strategy was provided by the announcement of open elections for worker representatives in 1963, to be held every three years. The PCE alone took part in an intense campaign during the first union elections to place pro-labor candidates in the state-controlled system. Worker-commission candidates were particularly successful in the 1966 union elections, the same year that the first permanent workers' commissions were established, marking the transformation of the movement into a workers' organization (Ariza 1976; see also Monds 1975). By this time, and in part as a result of the success of this tactic, the PCE had also succeeded in gaining a dominant position within the underground workers' movement. Optimism seemed in order; not only did workers now have many pro-labor representatives in leadership positions, but, because of an amendment to the *Fuero de Trabajo* in 1966, they also had a legal, albeit limited, right to strike.

The regime also sensed the growing power of workers, and it responded the following year by initiating a period of intense repression. In November 1967, the Supreme Court declared the *Comisiones Obreras,* or CCOO (Workers' Commissions), an illegal, subversive organization. Union elections for 1969 were suspended, and hundreds of labor leaders were harassed or imprisoned. Between 1968 and 1973, by some estimates, at least 500 labor leaders were imprisoned, and thousands more were removed from union posts and/or dismissed from their jobs. The strategy of open opposition from within the state-run union made it relatively easy for the government to identify and purge the labor leaders.

The intensified repression caused workers to become increasingly politicized and combative after 1967. The number of working hours lost through strikes increased from 1.5 million in 1966 to 8.7 million in 1970 and 14.5 million in 1975. Protests called for political reasons or in solidarity with other workers represented 4% of the total between 1963 and 1967, and this proportion rose to 45.4% of protests between 1967 and 1974. Strikes escalated with particular force after 1973, and labor organizations—including the CCOO and the UGT—began to recover strength (Maravall 1981).

The way in which worker opposition to the regime unfolded before Franco's death has important implications for understanding the labor movement during the transition period and after. First, it is significant that the leaders of CCOO emerged as the most prominent figures of the underground labor movement. Marcelino Camacho, along with scores of other men who would become leaders of CCOO when it finally gained legal recognition, participated in underground grassroots organizing and suffered the consequences of harassment, physical violence, and imprisonment. From the start, the Communist-led union had the advantage, compared to other nascent unions, of greater moral appeal based on its record of underground organizing. In addition, the union already had a dedicated rank-and-file integrated into an organization that was present within individual firms, as well as at the provincial and national levels. Having opposed the main strategy of forming the workers' commissions, the UGT had played a much weaker role in the underground movement. The Socialist leadership in general was less able to influence the movement from its position in exile than was the PCE or the closely related Catholic groups that operated within Spain.

A further significant result of the escalation of worker protests under Franco is that it became increasingly apparent that repression would be unsuccessful in stopping the movement for democratic reform. After the series of events that both discredited the regime and disrupted rightists' schemes to preserve it intact—the murder of Carrero Blanco at the end of 1973, the Anti-Terrorist Law that led to five widely condemned executions in 1975, and King Juan Carlos's actions in support of democratic reform in 1976—liberal and even conservative forces began to mobilize to ensure a smooth transition toward democracy following Franco's death. The left and labor especially continued to play a crucial role as they prodded the interim governments to adopt substantive rather than cosmetic changes and to grant legal status to the opposition parties and unions. The years immediately following Franco's death brought a wave of strikes and other worker protests. The movement's main objectives during this period were to delegitimize the state-controlled union and gain legal recognition for representative unions. Workers also appreciated the necessity of pressing for economic gains in the interim separating one set of institutional controls from another. As our examinations of two cases of worker mobilization during this period will show, the tactics of labor varied in different sectors and regions. The movement was still strongest in Catalonia and the Basque region, but other foci of strong protests emerged, including a long and closely watched strike in the shoe industry in Alicante and strikes by transport, construction, and metalworkers in Madrid.

The intensity of this strike wave and the impetus it gave to the newly forming unions' drive to recruit members raise several questions about the subsequent response of workers to informalization. The same unions that had battled the Franco regime successfully and that, in 1978, claimed the membership of the majority of industrial workers later found themselves to be virtually powerless to reverse a trend that was directly threatening to the union movement. Given the very recent history of outspoken worker protests, what factors explain the relatively weak response to this threat? Why did the massive mobilizations of workers after 1967, and particularly between 1975 and 1977, not produce a stronger commitment to cooperativism, or to other collective strategies, that might have changed workers' response to informalization once the process had gained momentum?

One clear reason for the labor movement's weakness after 1978 is precisely the political context of the protest movement during the mid-1970s. Pressure from strikes remained high throughout the period of mobilization for, and negotiation of, the democratic pacts and decreased substantially after the 1977 elections. To some degree, workers favoring continued confrontation were reined in by the leftist parties and the unions themselves, both of which emphasized the necessity of compromise for ensuring the smooth completion of the transition to democracy and both of which were, moreover, already pursuing their own separate interests. In part, workers were responding to having attained the goals that labor leaders themselves had placed highest on the agenda during the struggles of the previous years: the removal of the *sindicato vertical* and the creation of *sindicatos de clase*. Some analyses have also blamed a "cultural and ideological inheritance of Francoism," which worked against sustaining a more sweeping commitment toward radical social transformation in addition to political change (Maravall 1981).

A further reason for the decline of union strength was the success of the protests in obtaining certain economic objectives. Wages of industrial workers rose rapidly, in more combative sectors continuing to surpass the maximum levels set by the government and, later, by the pacts. To some degree, informalization simply continued a process of bifurcation of the labor force initiated by unevenly distributed wage hikes during the 1960s and 1970s.

The following case studies of the rise of the labor movement in Madrid and Alicante further illuminate these changes and help explain workers' behavior in the posttransition period. The labor movements in Madrid and Alicante have certain broad similarities. Both regions were relatively new to rapid industrial growth and their labor forces were comparatively inexperienced in organizing protests. Yet both regions, for different reasons, played a central role in revitalizing the labor movement—Madrid because of the city's place at the center of national politics, and Alicante because of the remarkable breadth and strength of workers' spontaneous protests. Nevertheless, in these regions as elsewhere in Spain, deunionization and informalization have since proceeded hand in hand. This chapter addresses the questions of how and why these trends occurred.

The Labor Movement in Madrid

Although Madrid had been one of the main Socialist strongholds before the Civil War, the labor movement was never particularly strong there. The region was not, after all, very important industrially until the 1960s. Nor were conditions during the industrial boom especially favorable to the emergence of a unified workers' movement. In the industrial areas that were bastions of worker organizing throughout the Franco period—the mining region of Asturias, Basque shipbuilding centers, and the textile towns of Catalonia—a strong tradition of worker protest was combined with a high degree of concentration of particular industries. In Madrid, industry was widely diversified and plants were spread throughout the city and its periphery.

Nevertheless, Madrid did become an important center for labor protests during the last decade of the Franco regime. According to Maravall (1978), who used press reports to count labor conflicts during the years of clandestine organizing, Madrid experienced the fourth highest number of strikes in Spain between 1963 and 1974, after the Basque Country, Catalonia, and Asturias. Strikes reported in Madrid for this decade accounted for roughly 10% of the total in the country.

Workers in several different industries emerged as the protagonists of national as well as local conflicts. Transport and electronics firms located in the mostly working-class and industrial southern section of the city became hubs of worker organizing and the objects of major strikes. These large firms employed an important portion of the city's metalworkers, who numbered around 200,000 and became highly politically active during this period. The prolonged construction boom in Madrid had also swelled the ranks of the city's proletariat. Many construction workers, who also participated actively in the protests of the 1960s and 1970s, were recent migrants from the south whose political sympathies had already been formed on the left. They populated sprawling southern sections of the city that would become the cradle for the infant labor unions.[1] Finally, the labor movement in Madrid also received support from some white-collar workers, most notably bank employees, who emerged as one of the city's most combative groups.

The resurgence of the labor movement in Madrid was important principally for its role in the creation and consolidation of the Workers' Commissions. The movement was aided by relatively weak repression during its initial stages. The first massive arrests of the Madrid leaders were not made until 1966, following a large demonstration led by an intersectoral Workers' Commission. In Barcelona, in contrast, labor faced serious opposition and experienced greater internal divisions from the start (HOAC 1977; Díaz 1977).

This is not to say that the protest movement had an easy time in Madrid. Grassroots support provided a necessary condition for its success and saved its momentum on more than one occasion. After less than one year in existence, for example, the first Workers' Commissions were ejected by authorities from the community center they had used as a meeting place. Weekly meetings nevertheless continued, first in the Pozo del Tío Raimundo, a poor neighborhood of migrants in southern Madrid, and later in the nearby barrio of Moratalaz. In Madrid, as elsewhere in Spain, local Catholic priests gave crucial support by opening their churches for workers' meetings.

A further important advantage to organizing in Madrid was that the city represented a platform from which to engage in national-level politics. The first provincial-level Workers' Commission was formed in Madrid, and this event directly sparked the formation of similar groups in other regions. In the last year of the organization's tenuous existence as a legal entity, Madrid workers also played a central role. The first judgment questioning the legality of the Workers' Commissions was issued in response to activities of the workers at Standard Eléctrica in Madrid, in January 1967. Madrid leaders reacted by organizing several massive, interindustry demonstrations in the following months. In a worker assembly in Orcasitas, another neighborhood of migrants in the southern section of the city, workers approved a document in April calling for a new labor law. In June 1967, the first national meeting of the Workers' Commissions was held, also in Madrid.

The prominence of Workers' Commissions leaders and their importance for the national movement brought a high price. Both national and local leaders were hit hard by the new wave of repression after 1966. The coordinating committee of the Madrid metalworkers' commission had 60 members in 1967; by 1969, it had two (Maravall 1981). By one estimate, about 1,500 Madrid metalworkers who were union leaders lost their jobs between 1967 and 1970 (Maravall 1978). The strategy adopted by the Workers' Commissions to react to the repression—organizing massive demonstrations demanding the legalization of the union—met increasingly with failure. A document published by the Inter-Industrial Commission in 1969 notes the increasing weakness of mass protests and the widening gap between the activities of the leaders, now operating clandestinely, and the attitudes of the rank-and-file (HOAC 1977, 19):

> Las manifestaciones, concentraciones, huelgas, acciones de caracter general, solo pueden realizarse cuando la protesta que se quiere expresar, los objetivos que se quieren alcanzar han sido hechos suyos por los trabajadores. No son suficientes las octavillas. ES IMPRESCINDIBLE HACER REUNIONES DONDE LOS TRABAJADORES HAGAN SUYA LA CONVOCATORIA. En este sentido, las acciones por "decreto" son peligrosas, ya que los "fracasos" demoralizan.

> Demonstrations, gatherings, strikes, and other actions should only be carried out when workers have adopted the grievances and objectives as their own cause. Pamphlets are not sufficient. IT IS ESSENTIAL TO HOLD MEETINGS AND ASSEMBLIES IN WHICH WORKERS CAN BE MADE TO EMBRACE THE AGENDA. Actions carried out "by decree" are dangerous, because the "failures" serve only to demoralize.

The local Workers' Commissions, as well as the national committees, continued to meet clandestinely, and a number of demonstrations in the 1970s brought massive support, particularly among construction workers. But the momentum of the labor movement in Madrid was not regained until after 1975 and in the midst of the transition period. When it did reemerge with force, the issues that united workers were strikingly different. During the period of clandestine organizing, strikes in Madrid were very often politically motivated. Protests called in solidarity with other workers, for example, outnumbered strikes over wages and did so by a greater margin than in either Asturias or Catalonia (Maravall 1978). In the mid-1970s, despite the tense political climate surrounding the debate over the transition, it was the issue of wages that galvanized worker support for the strikes. Labor leaders found themselves cast in a markedly different role in this second round of protests. Entirely unprepared for the strength of the strike movement, they found their organizations inadequate to control it and witnessed the strikes from the political sidelines.

Conflict began brewing toward the end of 1975, when the government announced that the wage ceilings already in effect would be prolonged through all of 1976. Once again, the main protagonists of the protests were Madrid metalworkers. Contract renewals were pending in some 70 Madrid firms, including the largest and traditionally the most conflictive. Labor organizations had been gearing up for the expected contract negotiations by studying wage scales across Spain and in similar industries elsewhere in Europe to show that wages were unacceptably low in Madrid industry. A high inflation rate over the previous two years had eaten further into real wages. By the time the government announced that it would continue the freeze, the issue of wages had become very volatile.

Signs of the impending crisis were clear by mid-December 1975, when a number of large firms in Getafe, in the heart of Madrid's southern industrial zone, joined in a day of protest. The catalyst of a wider conflict proved to be a strike by Madrid subway workers begun on January 5. In the same week, Standard Eléctrica workers began a work stoppage for four to six hours each day to demand contract negotiations for metalworkers. By the time the subway strike ended on January 9, strikes and lock-outs were affecting virtually all the major transport and electronics firms in the southern industrial zone. Metalworkers were joined the following week by construction workers, public employees, and bank workers. The feverish strike activity lasted until February, and in the more conflictive centers such as Standard Eléctrica it had gone on for two months. At the height of the conflict, strikes and lock-outs affects between 200,000 and 300,000 workers (Santos, Arija, and Crespo 1976).

The strike did not take place under the direction of any particular labor organization. Labor leaders, in fact, found themselves in a peculiarly disadvantaged position for leading the protest movement. In some sectors—and this was the case among metalworkers—leaders sympathetic to the workers' grievances had infiltrated the established union hierarchy and attempted from this vantage point to help direct the protest. Their actions, however, were viewed with skepticism by many of the rank-and-file who saw their support as an attempt to coopt the movement. The official union representatives of the metalworkers were ultimately ignored as bargaining agents both when leaders met with government officials and once conflicts were temporarily resolved at the plant level. A leader of the strike at Standard observed, "The *verticalistas* were totally overwhelmed, they found themselves joining the bandwagon because they couldn't do otherwise. They had to save face." (Santos, Arija, and Crespo 1976, 128).

In other sectors, the clear nonrepresentativeness of the official unions helped lend legitimacy to parallel organizations that negotiated on behalf of the sector. In construction, for example, an Advisory Committee was established that became the de facto negotiating agent for construction workers and secured a favorable contract, the most positive achievement of the strike movement. In contrast, metalworkers returned to work having abandoned almost all their original demands—both economic and political—in exchange for certain basic guarantees, including, for example, a promise of no reprisals and the readmission of workers who had been laid off.

In evaluating the impact of the labor movement's history in Madrid on the process of productive decentralization that character- ized the next decade, one must consider several features of the earlier worker protests. The first and perhaps most important is that conflict was concentrated in Madrid's large firms. This was true both of the clandestine phase of organizing, which focused on the formation of pro-labor plant councils, and the strikes of the transition period, which were led by workers in large firms. As a result, despite the magnitude of these conflicts, a substantial proportion of the work force participated only indirectly in the struggles.

Second, organizing labor did not emerge from the transition period with a strong positive image among Madrid workers. The role of *Comisiones Obreras* in underground organizing did provide the union with a moral claim to leadership in the labor movement, and it undoubtedly helped lay the groundwork for later protests. But the intervening years of harsh repression, combined with a very different political climate in the mid-1970s, transformed that role into a very different one. In 1967, effectively the end of the first stage of the emergence of the Workers' Commissions as an organization, leaders had to cajole the rank-and-file to embrace the tenets of the protest movement; in 1976, workers acted independently and spontaneously to organize a massive strike movement, and many labor leaders were found advocating compromise. Ultimately, the results of the strikes were quite mixed, with the greatest disappointment for workers occurring in the industry that had provided the most volatile setting for protest. If the protests of the mid-1970s left out many workers in the Madrid area, many others who participated actively must have come away with their enthusiasm for mass protests and/or the new unions altered by the experience. Alfonso Peña, the leader of the Standard strike, attributes the evolution of workers' interests to the peculiar political conjuncture (Santos, Arija, and Crespo 1976, 113–14):

> In my opinion, economic concerns—mainly low salaries—were the main cause of the strike, although there were also some political causes. In Standard, the real cause was the contract . . . . We thought it was going to be a good contract, but first they froze our salaries again and again and then, with the speech of Villar Mir,[2] it became quite clear what the government's attitude was going to be . . . . That's when there was a qualitative leap from working toward a contract for one firm to working against the official policy toward labor. We went from local negotiations to broader political issues because the situation required it.

The large firms rode out the struggle so successfully that it is difficult to justify a view of this wave of protests as a serious threat to management control over the production process. The movement did represent a threat insofar as it made clear workers' determination to take advantage of the political change to secure significant increases in wages. A third salient feature of the strikes during 1975 and 1976 was the dominance of economic concerns among workers. To be sure, the distinction between economic and political goals is somewhat misleading; by demanding wage hikes, workers were also making the clear political statement that they would not accept a transition that did not contemplate radically different treatment for workers (even though the unions did later sign pacts limiting gains to workers). Yet the protests of the transition period were political mainly because of the context in which they took place; workers themselves were not necessarily *politicized* either before or after these events. Antonio López, who helped lead striking workers at Casa, a large motor company in southern Madrid, was sharply critical of the role played by leaders of the vertical syndicate, including many of those who had arrived at their posts as candidates of *Comisiones Obreras* (Santos, Arija, and Crespo 1976, 131–47):

> Excessive attempts to legalize negotiations during the strike had the effect of blocking the most representative outlets for negotiation of leadership by workers. It's one thing to negotiate the end of the strike by exploiting legal channels; it's another to try to direct the strike from a legal position that is severely limited . . . the tactics of certain groups, like the CC.OO., were inappropriate in that regard . . . . I think the strike had a good start, a lot of strength, an impressive duration . . . . But the end of the conflict was not convincing to me, and it wasn't convincing to the vast majority of workers. My opinion is that the vanguard was overwhelmed and so tried to put the breaks on. The effect of this is that . . . although I think we struck a great blow, the working class feels bitter toward the leadership.

Understanding the recent history of the labor movement in Madrid makes reconciling the magnitude of past worker protests in the area with the experiences and perspective of workers one now encounters in small industry easier. Workers who were not disillusioned after active participation in the movement were often relatively untouched by the strike waves. Of the worker-entrepreneurs I interviewed in the auxiliary branches of the electronics industry, most had worked formerly in small or medium firms where they did not participate directly either in the earlier stages of organizing or in the strikes of the mid-1970s. And because most were in their thirties and forties, half or more of their adult working lives had been experienced after Franco's death. Many do not belong to the generation which fought the underground battles nor even to that which forged the transition. Some who did participate in the movement when they were in their twenties now find themselves made more conservative, or at least more cautious, by the burdens of property ownership and family responsibilities.

The cooperative movement in Madrid was also too weak to provide an alternative source of inspiration for workers responding to lay-offs and productive decentralization. The experience of the

Mondragón cooperatives, the robust network of worker-owned enterprises in the Basque region, is quite exceptional in the history of cooperatives in Spain.[3] After the Civil War, scant institutional support combined with slow economic growth to provide an unwelcoming climate for new cooperative ventures. Of 58 cooperatives founded in Madrid between 1944 and 1960, only seven survived. The political and economic climate improved in the 1960s, when Mondragón's experiment began to show signs of success and when the first national association of cooperatives started to operate. But cooperativism in Madrid could not draw strength from tight social networks or a sense of solidarity based on a distinct regional identity. Only 212 cooperatives were operating in 1979, and most of these had been founded after 1975, prompted not by a movement in favor of alternative systems of production but by the crisis in regular industrial employment. The distribution of firms by sector bears this out: in 1981, metalwork and construction, two industries hit hard by the crisis, accounted for 39% of Madrid cooperatives and more than 40% of cooperative members (Vara 1985).

The lack of a strong cooperativist movement, or of some other source of strength for workers facing dislocation or unemployment after 1975, was not only a logical outcome of the legacy of labor relations under Franco but also one that the particular type of labor movement that emerged was unable to change. On its face, productive decentralization may have looked similar to trends in the rest of Europe a decade earlier. But the most important participants, the workers themselves, faced the experience with a very different, and far more developed, sense of their own limitations, and a profound, learned distrust of many of their own leaders.

The Assembly Movement in Alicante's Shoe Industry

Superficially at least, the workers' movement in the shoe industry in Alicante is strikingly different from that in Madrid. The movement, which eventually spread beyond the Vinalopó Valley to other shoe-producing regions, was strongly rooted in a commitment to worker democracy. Unlike some workers' movements emerging elsewhere in Spain during the same period, the so-called Assembly Movement in the shoe industry encompassed not only salary issues and demands for worker representations but also workers' concerns about the conditions and organization of production. The sheer scope of participation in the movement—it culminated in a 17-day strike that paralyzed the sector—suggest that these same workers, 10 years later, would not submit easily to the poor conditions and low pay of informal jobs. However, a closer look shows that the movement displayed some of the same problems observed in Madrid and that its outcome had a similarly damaging effect on workers' confidence in organized labor.

One puzzle surrounding the resurgence of labor organizing in Alicante toward the end of the Franco regime is the degree to which it was connected with the region's history of fairly active worker protests before the Civil War. The emerging proletariat of Alicante was already highly combative during the first decades of this century, with conflicts centered in the textile industry in Alcoy and in the shoe and alpargata industries in Elda and Elche. [4] The two leading shoe-producing towns had worker movements with somewhat different political orientations. The labor movement in Elche began with a nine-month strike by *alpargata* workers in 1903. That strike gave impetus to a strong Socialist movement in the area, and Elche remained a stronghold of Socialist workers throughout the early part of the century. Under the Second Republic, Elche workers became progressively more radical. A strike of *alpargata* workers in 1934 touched off a general strike in the city, after workers refused an unfavorable settlement decreed by the government.

In the upper Vinalopó Valley, the adjacent towns of Elda and Petrel have a strong anarchist tradition that also dates from the early part of the century. Before 1923, the anarchist-led CNT was the dominant labor organization in Elda. That union led a successful two-week strike for an eight-hour workday in 1919. Declared illegal under the dictatorship of Primo de Rivera, the CNT virtually disappeared during the 1920s, and its decline clearly benefitted the traditionally weaker Socialist Party. Nevertheless, anarchist sympathies in the region remained strong, a fact that was reflected in the series of sharp conflicts that took place in the 1930s. Particularly important was a one-month strike by some 8,000 shoe industry workers in 1930, when the CNT again prevailed over moderate Socialist leaders advocating compromise and a quick settlement. [5] The protests and strikes of the 1930s were closely related to the broader revolutionary movement being led by the CNT against the government of the Second Republic. Elda was the only city in Alicante where this movement had consistent support; however, a general strike in Elda in 1934 was accompanied by the increasingly radical positions of workers in other, Socialist-dominated centers of production (Forner 1982).

The Civil War and its aftermath of repression ended this phase of worker activism. As occurred all over Spain, the anarchist movement never regained strength in the region, even after the resurgence of worker organizing in the final years under Franco. Current labor leaders disassociate their own motives and actions from the anarchist and socialist movements of the past. They emphasize that there was little or no continuity between the two phases of labor organizing and deny that they were influenced by an older generation of worker activists—who were imprisoned, killed, or simply silenced after the Civil War.

Nevertheless, it seems likely that the prewar events *indirectly* affected younger workers' attitudes and influenced the character of the movement that would emerge several decades later. Particularly in Elda, certain characteristics of the more recent labor movement— for example, an emphasis on grassroots democracy and an aversion to formal political parties—suggest some continuity with anarchist-inspired notions. Labor leaders seem to agree when they note the "natural combativeness" of people in the area. Some also point out that successful past strikes were sometimes cited to boost worker morale during the strikes of 1976 and 1977; in Elche, according to one union leader, workers exhorted each other to persevere by recalling the strike of 1903: "We told each other that if our grandfathers had held out for nine months, we could certainly keep up the strike for at least that long." Still, evidence for continuity in the labor movement before and after Franco remains very thin.

As in other Spanish regions, the movement in the early 1960s took the form of worker assemblies and committees formed extemporaneously and in response to particular problems. The first interindustry commissions were formed toward the end of the 1960s, led particularly by workers in the textile industry but also with the active participation of workers in construction and footwear. In each of these three industries, which formed the focus of worker mobilization in Alicante, organizers adopted a different mix of strategies. In the large textile firms of Alcoy and Crevillente, workers formed committees that operated parallel to the vertical union. In construction, which was concentrated in Alicante and Elche, labor leaders schemed to infiltrate the official union; Justo Linde, who later joined the national committee of the CCOO, was elected head of the "workers' section" of the vertical union in construction. In the shoe industry, both these strategies were followed, with the result that the local and provincial vertical organizations were unevenly penetrated by pro-labor candidates.

The range of strategies followed reflected the variety of groups and political ideologies represented in the workers' movement at this stage. The movement encompassed numerous groups with varying political outlooks. The two most important during this period were the Catholic organization *Hermandades Obreras de Acción Católica* (HOAC), the cradle of many of the movement's leaders, and the PCE, here as elsewhere the main force behind the formation of the interindustry Workers' Commissions. Neither group ever came to dominate the movement and activists consequently did not unite behind a single strategy to combat the authority of the *sindicato vertical*. However, the two favored strategies—attempting to delegitimize the state-controlled union by forming representative workers' committees outside its channels and infiltrating the union with pro-labor candidates—on the whole proved to be compatible. It was not unusual for individuals to advocate both positions and to hold elected posts in the vertical union while organizing outside it.

After 1967, however, the movement focused increasingly on the goal of breaking apart the *sindicato vertical* and replacing it with representative unions. This posture became quite fixed after the wave of repression in the late 1960s succeeded in removing most outspoken leaders from office and banning them from future candidacy. José Leal, then the secretary general for the shoe industry in Elda, recalls being expelled from the *sindicato vertical*:

> They expelled me because we were mobilizing. There was a lot of street fighting [in Elda] and a number of injuries. [In 1968,] we celebrated May 1st and they took seven *compañeros* and beat them severely. That same day they took me to City Hall and placed me under arrest, and after that they wouldn't let me enter the *sindicato* building, even to collect my things.

Although many workers sympathetic to the movement again found posts in the vertical union when elections were renewed in the 1970s, the provincial-level workers' council continued to be presided over by men viewed as the puppets of employers. By this time, in any case, workers had clearly shifted their energies toward directly challenging the authority of the *sindicato vertical* and aiding the movement to destabilize the regime.

A concerted effort to organize workers clandestinely in the industry laid the groundwork for the emergence of broad support for such a confrontation. In the early 1970s, an important step was taken toward consolidating the various trends within the underground movement. In response to a government announcement that it would "restructure" the shoe industry through support for large, modernizing firms, workers formed "restructuring groups" of five or six workers each to study the proposal and consider possible actions in opposition to it. Although the plan was subsequently scrapped, workers preserved the groups as the backbone of an underground structure that encompassed all the groups within the movement—the HOAC, the PCE, the Valencian nationalists, and a variety of smaller groups—and existed in virtually all the main centers of production in the region.

The structure of "cells" permitted workers to communicate effectively and share information about struggles in different firms and towns; for example, when workers initiated one of the industry's first big strikes at Facasa, a large auxiliary firm in Elche, groups in Elda and Petrel met to publicize and discuss the events. Labor leaders describing this period speak of meeting clandestinely "at night, in the mountains, in country houses around Elche, in convents, cemeteries, train stations, in the most unimaginable places." Participants used false names and several activists circulated an underground newssheet about the industry. An important outcome of this phase or organizing was that a core group of emerging leaders came to know each other and to be known by workers generally. The men most active in the clandestine movement were also the future leaders of the protests during the transition; Batiste Pérez and José Leal, for example, both from Elda, helped lead the movement at both stages. The ranks also included men who would become important local figures in *Comisiones Obreras,* such as Tito Plaza. The differences in the leaders' political loyalties and inclinations were at that time still overshadowed by their common goals of undermining the vertical union and establishing *sindicatos de clase.*

The clandestine movement also had some immediate and tangible results. In Elda, for example, leaders organized a clandestine office to provide workers with free legal advice. The labor lawyer García Miralles (who would later become President of the Cortes of the Valencian government) spent several days a week in Elda during 1975 and 1976 helping workers to take their disputes beyond the biased settlement proceedings in the vertical union to the labor courts. In addition to providing workers with a new avenue for pursuing their claims against employers, the office serves as an informal meeting hall and cultural center for workers. According the Batiste Pérez, a local leader who was instrumental in establishing and running the office, it quickly acquired some 1,500 paying members, yet was never discovered and shut down by authorities, a fact that was in itself a considerable victory for workers.

If these activities helped prepare for large-scale protest, the political hiatus following Franco's death created the perfect conditions for it to occur. With the approach of contract negotiations in 1976, the goal of establishing truly representative worker organizations became more urgent. Workers wanted to push the interim governments into making more than the nominal reforms of the vertical union that had already been announced. At the same time, workers understood that regardless of whether representative unions were legalized soon, the negotiations during the transition period would provide the starting point for future rounds of bargaining. If the vertical union was permitted to handle negotiations for yet another year, gains to workers would be minimal, and the official salaries in the shoe industry would remain far behind those in other Spanish industries. Economic and political considerations thus blended in producing an urgent call to action.

Attacks on the vertical union drew strength in February 1976 from the failure of the official union to represent workers' interests effectively in contract negotiations. In Elda, workers held a series of demonstrations in front of the vertical union office and presented the union with a petition in support of demands drafted by workers. To discredit the *sindicato vertical,* the workers asked permission to use its offices to hold assemblies; when they were refused, the protesters organized demonstrations outside the offices. Marches through the town and worker assemblies in the main public square became increasingly common. Although initially only a handful of activists participated, the actions quickly drew wide support, often uniting several thousand workers. In Elche, the protest movement was also rapidly gaining force. On February 19, some 2,000 workers (according to possible low official estimates) attended a demonstration there. At an assembly held later in a local church, workers decided to elect a commission to negotiate directly with employers. Workers also agreed that, if employers refused to negotiate with the representative group, they would strike the following week.

Events came to a head during the next week in both Elche and Elda. On Monday, February 23, an estimated 60% of firms in Elche were affected by a one-hour sit-down strike, following the refusal of employers to negotiate with the workers' committee. Workers continued the sit-down strike for the next three days, with the participation on the second day of between 5,000 and 8,000 workers.[6] Although this strike ended without securing the desired recognition for the workers' representatives, it galvanized support for the protest movement. Organized, monitored, and officially ended by democratic vote in worker assemblies, the strike rehearsed a format that would emerge again in stronger mobilizations the following year. Even more important was the effect the strike had on hardening workers' resolve and preparing them for confrontation with employers. The strike signified a rupture with the ideology of paternalism that had pervaded labor relations in the shoe factories. Workers stood for three full days in front of their machines with arms folded, resisting the coercion and threats of factory owners and foremen trying to force them back to work. Gaspar Agulló, a leader of the strike movement that was to take place a year later, stresses the importance of the sit-down strike of 1976 in strengthening workers' resolve:

> I had just started to work in a factory in Elche at the time. I had been working on a trial basis for a couple of months and had just been put on the books 15 days before the strike. That strike was crucial because it brought the conflict into the heart of the firm. The employers had never been confronted with anything like it. In the firm where I worked, the owners and the foremen put the assembly line into operation and started to work the machines themselves . . . . We had to stand there, at our machines, with

work being pushed at us down the line and the machines running, and the owners yelling at us, telling us "Okay, that's enough, now let's get some work done." It was difficult to resist, but we *did* resist, and this was fundamental to everything that followed. It made us finally realize that we had real bargaining power.

In Elda, during the same week, events had also taken a dramatic turn. The continuing large public demonstrations and worker assemblies prompted an unprecedented show of force by the national police, who occupied the town and enforced a ban on all gatherings. On February 25, a 20-year-old boy was shot and killed by the soldiers, who claimed that he and several other youths had attacked them with stones. But local residents who witnessed the shooting quickly spread word that the boys had been unarmed and passive, and that the one boy killed had been shot to death as he lay wounded in the street. As with the strike in Elche, this event marked a turning point for the workers' movement in Elda, because it sparked the support of the entire community. The funeral for the dead youth prompted a spontaneous strike and a large demonstration, as people left work and filed past the coffin for four hours on the following day.

Although the vertical union negotiated and signed the 1976 contract, little doubt remained that some form of direct representation for workers would be necessary to contain worker protests the following year. The government's dissolution of the vertical union in March 1976 created a void that the democratic unions, not yet legally established, could not fill. Workers continued to use their own methods of organizing to prepare for the next round of negotiations, selecting about 500 representatives from individual firms in Elda, Elche, and other towns.

Several features of this phase of the movement merit comment. One striking characteristic is the degree to which the movement was self-directed rather than led by particular political parties or unions. In both Elda and Elche, a strong independent line within the movement prevented any particular political line's dominance and encouraged an air of caution, if not skepticism, about the emerging central unions with links to the political parties. Indeed, workers made a point of their independence from organized groups. In Elda and Petrel, workers voted to create an independent union called the *Frente Obrero Unido,* or FOU (United Workers' Front), described by one leader as "a movement to unite wills . . . a movement started *not* to create a permanent union, but because of the suspicion we had that the unions themselves would be born domesticated. [The FOU] came into being as a place to 'park' the workers until we could see clearly." The organization had "no membership cards, no officials, no elections. Someone with charisma would simply talk and other people would listen. The FOU had no offices. We met under an olive tree. We began with 20 people and ended up with 5,000 or 10,000 meeting in the open country." The organization was so self-consciously distanced from any ideological position that even its name had been selected at random. Workers had simply written suggested names on slips of paper and selected one from a hat: "*Frente Obrero Unido* came out. But it could have been anything."

Related to this attitude was a strong emphasis on worker democracy within the unions. Leaders had to submit all decisions to worker assemblies, and at these gatherings, all workers had the right to speak and vote. Faith in the assembly movement and distrust of other forms of organizing reflected workers' euphoria about the promise of democracy and their complete rejection of the authoritarian regime. Holding assemblies also proved to be an efficient way to unite workers. As one leader explained, one advantage of this style of organizing was that it eliminated common sources of divisiveness:

> No one could take an order if it wasn't given in the assembly. As for rumors—rumors always break apart mass movements—people knew that anything was a lie that hadn't been said . . . in the stadium, and discussed there and agreed upon. Everything else was rumor and treated as rumor, even if it was true. The only truth was what was said in the assemblies.

The ambitious platform drawn up in the first months of 1977 illustrated the sincerity of workers' commitment to democracy. Leaders sent out questionnaires through representatives in firms to solicit workers' demands for the upcoming negotiations and limited their own role merely to compiling the results. The finished platform included, among other points, demands for a 45% salary increase, quarterly revisions of the wage scale, 30-day vacations, expanded benefits for sickness, social security payments for homeworkers, and the creation of child-care centers in large firms and in neighborhoods with high concentrations of small factories. Some leaders were aware of the danger that such a platform would create unrealistic expectations, but the commitment to purely representative methods prevented them from limiting its content.

Although the government legalized the central unions in April 1977, the Assembly Movement was already in a strong enough position to stake the claim that it alone should represent workers in contract negotiations. Even local employers appeared to be on the verge of recognizing the Assembly Movement as a bargaining partner. In May 1977, employers met with worker representatives for the first time. The site agreed on for the meeting in and of itself represented a moral victory to workers. Movement leaders recall with relish watching some of the most influential businessmen in the industry slosh up the steep, muddy streets of La Tafalera, the poor, gypsy neighborhood in Elda where the meeting took place.

The threat of an imminent strike planned by labor leaders led employers to agree to meet with worker representatives in Madrid on August 22, 1977. But leaders in Elche had already called for a strike beginning the same day, and they could not be persuaded to change their plans by workers from Elda and other towns, where the strike was not set to begin for another two days and was contingent on the results of the Madrid meeting. Employers arrived at the meeting on August 22 shaken by the news that an estimated 80% of firms in Elche were already out on strike. To the astonishment of the workers' committee, the employers agreed to recognize the Assembly Movement and to schedule negotiations with its representatives in Valencia. They also agreed to take on reprisals against workers during the negotiations, to allow assemblies in firms, and to permit the absence of worker representatives for two hours each day to attend assemblies. The site chosen for negotiations again represented a concession to workers, who had proposed that bargaining take place in Alicante rather than Madrid so that they could confer more easily with workers in assemblies throughout the region. The workers' committee returned to Alicante with the surprising good news that, for the moment, the strike was unnecessary; employers had conceded nearly all their original demands.

However, events in Elche took an unexpected turn on the same afternoon. About 8,000 striking workers who had assembled in the soccer stadium voted to send pickets out to the firms that remained open. At a large firm only a block away, police attacked pickets outside the firm, and the clash resulted in a number of injuries, including that of a youth struck in the eye by a rubber bullet.[7] Workers in the stadium learned of the violence within minutes and voted to continue the strike despite the news brought by representatives returning from Madrid. The following day, about 3,000 workers gathered in the stadium at Elda and voted to strike in solidarity with Elche workers, also despite the favorable result of negotiations in Madrid.

Once the strike was officially underway, workers began feverish preparations to ensure its success. The enthusiasm and solidarity displayed by workers surprised even Assembly Movement leaders. "They ran over us. *They* organized *us*," one leader comments. Within a few days, workers established both free and partially subsidized food stores for striking workers and began a massive drive to collect contributions for a strike fund. In all the shoe-producing towns in the area, workers held assemblies in the stadiums twice each day. Attendance reached as high as 15,000 to 20,000 people in Elche and 12,000 to 15,000 in Elda, by some counts even higher. The atmosphere was euphoric, and participants I interviewed remember their joy in observing that democracy had not only at last arrived but that it appeared to function as well as, or better than, they had ever hoped. Batiste Pérez Verdú recounted:

> Some aspects of the Assembly Movement would be wonderful to relive. One lived intensely during those days. They were beautiful days . . . . . After the strike started, people began to take up collections, to distribute food, to form contact groups, to write and distribute a newsletter. An information service was organized and worked splendidly. Delegates were elected everywhere . . . . In the morning, there would be assemblies outside the factory gates, and from there people would go to the stadiums to hear whatever message there was. After lunch it was once more to the factory gates and later again to the stadiums—and this went on, every day . . . . A complete system of self-governance had been set up . . . . While it lasted, it was something extraordinary, a sort of fabulous, 10-day demonstration of how well people are capable of organizing themselves.

The scope of the strike was indeed impressive. Movement spokesmen estimated on the second day that 47,500 workers in the province were out on strike, including workers from small factories. Only the most marginal workshops were exempt, and many of these also began to close as the larger firms halted work orders. Representatives from the Assembly Movement travelled to other shoe-producing regions and were successful in extending the strike to the Baleares, Castellón, La Rioja, and Zaragoza. Workers in these areas also sent representatives to an 18-member negotiating committee selected to meet with employers.

Despite the strength and unity of the strike, considerable obstacles remained to the resolution of the crisis. Employers agreed to begin negotiations but then quickly changed their position and refused to negotiate further until the strike ended. Workers proposed a limited round of negotiations on only some points of the contract before ending the strike. Resumed briefly, bargaining again stalled, and the only path to a settlement appeared to be one dictated by the government.

Workers' response to this situation was unequivocally to continue the strike in the hopes of forcing employers to the negotiating table. But the unity of support for this posture was ruptured by the leadership of *Comisiones Obreras*. The role of the central unions in the Assembly Movement had been somewhat ambiguous from the start. The UGT had opposed the Assembly Movement (after initially endorsing it) as well as the strike, arguing that only the central unions, and not independent worker movements, should represent workers at the bargaining table. Because the UGT had not played a significant role in underground organizing in the area, it had few followers and little to lose from openly taking such a position. The remaining unions enthusiastically endorsed the Assembly Movement and its goals, although they also clearly shared the UGT's interest in establishing the central unions as the sole legitimate representatives of workers. Support for the strike was in part forced on the unions, because so many of their militants were already participating actively in the Assembly Movement. The position was also motivated by a desire to attract more members. Throughout the strike, the CCOO actively recruited new members, setting up tables at worker assemblies and thrusting CCOO leaders into the limelight. Current local leaders of the CCOO still attribute the superior strength of the union in the shoe industry to the membership drive mounted during the 1977 strike.

Comisiones Obreras also had a larger hidden agenda that was served by their participation in the strike. It was by now clear that the objective of a single workers' union was not possible and that the CCOO would have to create a more traditional trade union structure to compete on a national scale with the UGT. At the same time, widespread fears that its ties to the PCE made the union a dangerous partner in national social and economic pacts were hurting its efforts to influence the direction of policy under the transition. It was widely perceived that intransigence on the part of the union could damage the chances for a strong showing by the Communist Party in the first elections, scheduled for 1977. The national leaders of the CCOO had much to gain if they could deliver a solution to the conflict in Alicante. Pressed by the leadership of the PCE, they accordingly began to push hard for an end to the strike, first proposing that the workers themselves request a settlement dictated by the government and then, after such a settlement was issued, advocating quick acceptance of its terms and a return to work. Justo Linde, then a member of the CCOO national committee, explains that the organization

> couldn't afford the luxury of going against the very government that was bringing in democracy . . . . The national secretariat decided to release a statement showing that we were reasonable, that we weren't against democracy. The statement asked the *compañeros* to end the strike. It said that we had failed and explained a little about why we had failed . . . [T]he whole [Communist] Party got involved with this.

CCOO officials I interviewed criticized other leaders of the Assembly Movement for naively believing that workers had a choice of accepting or rejecting what was legally a definitive settlement. But many workers felt deceived by the union's self-serving strategy. The members of the negotiating committee witnessed the maneuvering of the union leadership at close range, but it was also made visible to strikers themselves. In a morning assembly in Elche, workers voted overwhelmingly (8,014-to-2,500) to continue the strike in defiance of the government decree-settlement. On the afternoon of the same day, national leaders of the CCOO, overriding the wishes of many local CCOO leaders, took the microphone to insist that workers had no other option but to accept the settlement. After hours of heated debate, interrupted by announcements that other towns were voting to go back to work, workers in Elche voted by holding up matches in the twilight to give up the strike. Torn CCOO membership cards littered the stadium grass as the assembly broke up.

As with the 1976 strike movement in Madrid, the Alicante Assembly Movement derived its strength from grassroots organizing rather than from union support. The emerging unions, in fact, had strong reasons to favor labor peace during this period. Somewhat surprisingly, given its strength, the Assembly Movement succumbed rather quickly to pressures to back the central unions' more moderate approach. Although representatives from individual firms continued to meet for several months after the strike, the national unions rapidly gained strength and represented workers in new contract negotiations six months later. Eventually, Assembly Movement leaders also joined the unions. The CCOO continued to be the strongest union in the industry because it had at least initially backed the movement and had used it as a vehicle for recruitment of members. In Elda, however, most prominent leaders and their followers instead joined the *Unión Social de Obreros* (USO), which they judged then to be the only politically independent union.[8]

Suggesting that workers lost ground immediately as a result of the break-up of the Assembly Movement is misleading. In fact, negotiations carried out six months after the strike resulted in a contract that was extremely favorable to workers and secured some of the benefits demanded during the 1977 strike. But the ambiguous role of the central unions during the transition period undoubtedly helps explain the relative docility of workers after 1978. None of the three largest unions came out with its reputation unblemished by the events of 1976 to 1978. The UGT had not even supported the Assembly Movement and had openly criticized it as undemocratic. Not surprisingly, many workers and some of the most prominent leaders of the movement still avoid association with the CCOO because of its efforts to end the strike. Even the USO occasioned a certain amount of bitterness among workers and prompted an exodus of members when rumors of its close ties to the UCD began to surface. One union official who was "just another militant" during the Assembly Movement attributes his and many other workers' current pessimism about the labor movement to the frustrations they experienced with the ending to the strike:

Afterwards, I asked myself what it had all been for, all those nights without sleep, the trips to Murcia to collect money for the strike fund when I didn't have any money myself . . . What good did it do? It's made me become very passive, for better or for worse . . . . I think that this has happened to 90% [of the workers]. They became disillusioned in that era. We lost the illusion that we were self-sufficient enough to govern.

Symbolizing the disaffection of workers are the subsequent career histories of many Assembly Movement leaders. Some of the most outspoken leaders have now abandoned union involvement. Gaspar Agulló, a member of the negotiating committee and a young, outspoken leader from Elche, lost his job when his firm closed soon after the strike and took a job in a clandestine firm where there was "nothing to do but grit your teeth" and put up with the poor pay and conditions. He later worked as a clerk in the public library in Elche and recently reentered politics as a municipal delegate for the CCOO. Batiste Pérez, a member of the negotiating committee representing Elda and Petrel and a mastermind of underground organizing, became a leader in the USO but left when he discovered its ties to the UCD. He worked in the factory where he had been employed for 33 years (since age eight) until it closed in 1986; he is no longer active in union politics. José Leal, a leader in both the Assembly Movement and the USO, also left union work. He tried working with the UGT after leaving the USO but finally abandoned it too because of the union's unwillingness to bypass strictly institutionalized channels to mobilize workers against the trend of false closures. He lost his job when the factory in which he worked also closed. The president of the Assembly Movement, Roque Miralles, surprised his followers by helping to form a right-wing faction of the USO and then later by becoming a factory owner and commercial agent—relying heavily on informal labor, according to some. Although these men sometimes differ in their opinions of the events surrounding the 1977 strike, most share what is probably a widespread view that nothing short of the unprecedented unity displayed by workers during the Assembly Movement will forward their interests substantially and recover some of the ground lost in recent years. At the same time, they believe that recent trends and the altered political situation make the emergence of a mass movement less likely to occur.

We should note that the relatively rapid demise of worker

strength in the industry was also due in part to the fulfillment of economic goals that clearly motivated some workers to participate in the Assembly Movement. The platform included such demands as improved terms and conditions for homeworkers, child-care centers, a shorter work day, and other objectives indicating workers' desire to influence directly the organization and conditions surrounding production in the factories. However, the most widely shared objective of workers participating in the strike was obtaining a significant increase in the official wage rate. Other important economic issues surfaced in demands for more vacation days, payment during military service, and the distribution of bonuses. For those workers concerned mainly with preserving economic gains, the later willingness to accept informal jobs was not always inconsistent; short-term economic incentives for workers to accept unregulated work are sometimes considerable (see Chapter 4).

Informalization was not simply a response to the Assembly Movement. The number of plant closings did escalate considerably in the immediate wake of the strike. But according to labor leaders, the first several years after the strike was one of relatively steady and solid gains for workers. Employers also deny that escaping confrontations with workers was a principal motive for decentralization. In fact, the epidemic of false bankruptcies and the more dramatic phase of restructuring did not occur until after 1979. The Assembly Movement did, however, have an important indirect effect on employers' strategies in subsequent years. Substantial salary raises obtained by workers clearly prompted employers to begin to look for ways to use more informal labor and to increase productivity (mainly through intensifying labor) in established firms. Finally, the Assembly Movement marked an official break on both sides from perpetuating the myths of paternalism and worker loyalty that had pervaded the industry during the Franco years.

Conclusion

The history of workers' struggles in Madrid and Alicante illustrates the differences between the strike wave in Spain in the mid-1970s and that of the late 1960s in Italy. Although both movements preceded a phase of accelerated decentralization and informalization in industry, their relationship to these trends and their effect on workers' response to them were very different. The eruption of worker protest in Spain followed 40 years of repression and of depressed wages for workers. A huge backlog of economic demands exploded, at the same time that the dismantling of the institutions of the regime created a void in workers' representation both within particular industries and at the national level. The independent and spontaneous movements that arose, such as the Assembly Movement in the shoe industry, sometimes suggested a desire on the part of workers not only to make strong economic gains and establish basic worker rights but also substantially and permanently to alter the balance of power between workers and employers. But in general, the objectives were reformative; the contrast between the labor movement's methods and those of the emerging liberal institutions made them appear radical.

The fact that the protests of the mid-1970s took place in the context of the political transition meant that workers could claim a moral victory for these struggles even though the tangible results, as demonstrated by the Madrid strikes, were often disappointing. Workers who participated actively in the protests at this time correctly perceived themselves to be at the forefront of the movement toward democracy. There is little doubt that pressures "from below" pushed the liberal reform movement further than many of its leaders had originally intended to take it. The leaders of the Assembly Movement I interviewed, despite being embittered by the direction of political trends following the 1977 strike, were extremely proud to have participated in an authentic mass movement that had marked a turning point of the transition.

But moral victory or no, the worker movement did run into a wall at the end of the transition period. The debate over whether this was due to stonewalling by the unions or to the dissolving of grassroots support for mass mobilizations can be resolved in favor of an interpretation that combines both factors. The unions opted for conformity to the newly transformed institutional order, whose structure crystallized divisiveness and competition among the main labor organizations. In part precisely because of this turn of events, and in part because the return of democracy and specific economic gains fulfilled the aspirations of some participants in the movement, support for and faith in the strategy of mass actions faded.

The resurgence of the labor movement contributed little to

fomenting a cooperativist tradition or other collective movements that might have generated new strategies for organizing production along novel lines. The emphasis was on altering the terms and conditions of existing relations of production rather than on rethinking the fundamental basis for them. In both the shoe and the electronics industries, cooperativism arrived late, as a *response* to decentralization and informalization rather than as a continuation of an earlier public commitment to worker control or profit-sharing. The Madrid strikes focused on the plight of workers in large firms, not on support for alternative ventures. In Alicante, although the protests perhaps did more to awaken workers' opposition to the system of production, this realization did not in and of itself generate a commitment to collective action or to innovative approaches to production. It inspired highly individual strategies to obtain the "best deal" possible under difficult conditions.

Finally, the unions' usurpation of the direction of the workers' movement was a removal of power from workers at the local level and an attempt to repress the importance of local differences in guiding union policies. This shift undoubtedly affected the ability of workers to form local alliances as one possible response to informalization and its effects. The next chapter analyzes local and national political responses of industrial restructuring and explores the contribution of organized labor to policymaking in both these spheres.

PART IV

7 National Pacts and Local Alliances: The Political Response to Informalization

The social relations of informal production must be placed in the broader context of political change at the local and national levels. Not only are workers' and entrepreneurs' attitudes molded by their participation in, and perceptions of, such processes, but certain institutional supports for small and informal industry are necessary if the emerging informal sector is to evolve beyond a subordinate position. We have seen that in Madrid's electronics industry the presence of some conditions favorable to such an outcome have proved insufficient as long as certain institutional and political obstacles remain. Similarly, the government's policy toward restructuring in the shoe industry has contributed mainly to accelerating a regressive pattern of informalization. In neither case did local alliances prove capable of transcending the political constraints on effective policymaking that exist at the national level.

How can the state encourage innovative change in highly fragmented industries? Particularly where the state's industrial planning apparatus is configured to promote a different type of industrial growth, how can the state intervene to facilitate experimental production techniques in small, scattered firms, many of which may be operating on the borderline of illegality? Proponents of "flexible specialization" have not directly addressed such questions. In central Italy, local support for informal sector firms was made possible by the peculiar role of the Italian Communist Party in uniting the interests of small employers, workers, and local officials. We cannot expect similar conditions to prevail in Spain. Yet without such a context, how can the state create an appropriate climate for decentralized growth?

The limitations of local and sectoral industrial planning must be understood within the context of national tripartite bargaining in

163

democratic Spain. As with some other European countries which relied on a system of national agreements to provide stability and the basis for postwar economic growth, Spain turned to "neo-corporatist" arrangements after Franco's death to guarantee the smooth completion of the transition to democracy and provide the political basis for economic stabilization in response to the crisis (see Schmitter 1979). Five national pacts were signed between 1977 and 1984.[1] The apparent orderliness and functionality of the pacts have disguised some serious problems. To begin with, the degree of participation by bargaining agents in actual policymaking has not expanded significantly under the system of tripartite bargaining. This became painfully obvious under the Socialists when the unions—first the CCOO and eventually also the socialist UGT—backed away from further negotiations. The arrangement itself has also generated some new problems for the state. By focusing public attention on the largely symbolic process of tripartite bargaining and compromise, the state drains force from more substantive policy initiatives; by entering into national pacts and participating in an advisory capacity at the national level, business and labor organizations undermine their own legitimacy as well as their own ability to promote alternative measures.[2] These shortcomings are clear in the political response to informal sector growth and the evolution of industrial policy.

National Pacts and Employment Issues

The Spanish government's response to the informal sector has been one of extreme ambivalence. Creating jobs in the unregulated sector is seen as favorable to the state because it mitigates the political tensions resulting from the high rate of official unemployment. The tranquility with which Spanish workers have responded to consistently high rates of unemployment in the posttransition period is indeed remarkable.[3] At the same time, the state recognizes that the growth of the informal sector poses a threat, however indirect, to its authority. Actual losses of revenue because of evasion of taxes and social security are undoubtedly a concern, but the more important damage to the government of widespread evasion is to its image as manager of the nation's economy. Although informal employment may help diffuse political opposition in the short run, it also increases the potential for political opposition, particularly because the new employment in the informal sector does not go to the credit of government efforts to create jobs. Both these concerns—the state's ability to plan for economic recovery and its capacity to create jobs—have been at the center of political debate in democratic Spain.

The state faces three policy options vis-a-vis the informal sector, and none of these is entirely satisfactory (Moltó 1982). A first option is to attack the problem head-on with a public commitment to wipe out the informal sector. The government has indeed engaged in some rhetoric supportive of such a policy and has taken certain steps in this direction, for example, by increasing the number and scope of inspections and introducing stronger penalties for fiscal fraud. However, this position is one that has not been enthusiastically embraced, nor is it likely to be. The high rate of unemployment leaves the government open to the charge that it is not only failing to stimulate the economy but is actually destroying existing employment. Trying to halt the growth of the informal sector without first controlling unemployment runs counter to the state's own interests in preserving political peace. Support for this option has been resisted even by the unions. Given their recent difficulties in attracting and holding members, the unions, like the government, do not want to be cast in the unpopular role of putting people out of work. An active campaign to denounce irregular practices would succeed only in alienating that portion of the labor force that is in greatest need of being organized.[4]

A second alternative and a more realistic possibility is simply to ignore the phenomenon and proceed with economic planning as if the informal sector did not exist. Curiously, the political costs of this position derive more from the posture of private industry than from that of labor. While business may reap considerable benefits from the existence of a large unregulated sector, its official position is different, for obvious reasons. Business leaders have consistently asserted that the informal sector is harmful and presents established firms with unfair competition; they have sought to use this complaint to strengthen their demands for greater flexibility in the labor code applied to the formal sector.[5] Although the government shares this goal, it must preserve an independent position that neither concedes too much to business interests nor condones widespread tax evasion.

A third alternative for the state would be to encourage the

legalization of clandestine firms and the registration of "self-employed" workers. This position has the advantage of improving official employment statistics at the same time that it appears more politically responsible. Its major difficulty, however, is that the methods proposed to achieve *formalization* of the informal economy entail changes in the labor code that are highly controversial. The unions have a high political stake in the defense of existing state controls on the labor market. Not only do these ensure the existence of a core of stable jobs on which union strength may continue to depend, but in the face of the erosion of union prestige (resulting in part from the unions' past participation in pacts with the government), the defense of existing norms becomes the lowest common denominator of unity in organized labor.

The supreme irony of the transition to democracy in Spain is that the burden has fallen on the new democratic governments to dismantle a labor code that contains some features highly beneficial to workers. The former regime offered workers stability in exchange for labor peace; a series of laws protected workers from firing and guaranteed them severance pay beyond certain levels. Business leaders were already chafing at these and other restrictions in the 1950s. Despite the liberalizing economic reform movement led by Opus Dei from within the government after 1958, the protective labor code continued to represent a way of buying labor peace until Franco's death.

Producers' eagerness for reforms intensified enormously as a direct result of the economic downturn in the 1970s. The challenges to firms in the previous decade were how to expand the work force without incurring substantially greater costs and risks; whether to pay the required indemnity to be rid of an unproductive or intractable worker; and how to reconcile demand for temporary or seasonal workers with employees' rights to stable jobs and severance pay. After the mid-1970s, the most salient problem became how to *reduce the labor force* without aggravating firms' economic problems. The alternative to reducing the work force in many cases was to close, an option neither satisfactory to the state nor positive for the economy as a whole.

From the perspective of employers, a good part of the problem focused on the requirement that they pay indemnities to workers laid off for "good reason." Business leaders and recent governments have pushed for two kinds of reforms that would allow firms to avoid or at least minimize the costs of indemnification to workers. One is to facilitate use of temporary contracts. When these end, firms are under no obligation either to rehire a worker or to award him severance pay. Another is to alter the procedures and limit the costs to firms of firing workers.

Successive governments in the post-Franco period have consistently pursued making these and related changes in the labor code to make it more flexible. In 1977, temporary contracts were introduced for certain categories of workers in all industries. The UCD government further widened the scope of legal temporary hiring and, in addition, established social security deductions for firms hiring registered unemployed workers who were no longer receiving state benefits. At this stage, government spokesmen rarely, if ever, mentioned these measures in connection with policy responses to the growth of the informal sector. This phenomenon did not become the focus of widespread national attention until after 1980 or 1981, in large part because informal sector growth by then was much more marked than it had been in the late 1970s.

Ironically, the Socialist government, with its broad majority, found itself in the strongest position politically to escalate the process of easing restrictions and lowering costs to employers. A first set of measures further widened the possibilities for temporary hiring and increased particularly the potential benefits of this practice to new firms. Limits were removed on the percentage of the work force firms might hire under temporary contracts. A second set of measures announced in April 1985 included the introduction of subsidies of 50% of the social security costs for hiring workers younger than age 24, broadening tax benefits for hiring new workers, and other, more general measures designed to enhance flexibility, such as streamlining legal procedures for the formation of new firms. Other, similar reforms have followed these changes.[6] In 1988, the Socialists proposed a more sweeping Youth Employment Plan that would introduce more flexible guidelines and special subsidies for hiring young workers.

In contrast to earlier governments, the Socialists have made an explicit connection between such measures and the state's policy to assist in the legalization of the underground economy. Government spokesmen have also waged a rhetorical battle to establish the view that official unemployment rates are artificially high (because so many Spaniards are employed informally and presumably go undetected in standard employment surveys).[7] The government's often whimsical interpretation of its own survey data has drawn so much attention and criticism that public discussion about the informal sector is increasingly removed from the context of actual policy debates. Yet disagreements about the size and significance of the phenomenon continue to reflect wider conflicts about the terms and scope of state regulation of the labor market.

Whether changes in the labor code will, in fact, significantly affect firms' and individuals' incentives to use or participate in informal labor is unclear. Small, informal firms and self-employed workers are the least likely to learn about new programs that reduce the economic risks of hiring. Moreover, there is no guarantee that if the programs enacted were made more sweeping, employers would automatically respond by converting unregulated jobs to legally declared employment. Even when they are reduced, the costs of maintaining a regular employee are greater than those of using casual labor. The psychological implications of both situations are different; the more specific and complex the reforms, the less likely they are to alter employers' fundamental fears of problems they associate with managing a regulated labor force. Legalization creates a labor force capable of appealing to the state and susceptible to union organizing.

Indeed, the fact that the unemployment rate has fallen only slowly in the midst of the economic boom of the late 1980s implies that employers are not ready to forget the lessons learned during the economic crisis. Equating economic expansion with swelling employment rolls is now not something to be accepted but a danger to be protected against. Mere reform of the labor code does not necessarily compensate for the benefits to employers of using unregulated labor.

If anything, the political focus on labor code reform has shifted attention from measures which would address more directly the problems of newly restructured industry. The situation reflects more broadly the difficulties of the system of neocorporatist national bargaining. Aware of their weakness, the national leadership of unions and business associations have made a stand on a narrow range of employment issues. (The unions, for example, cited their vociferous opposition to a more flexible labor code as one of the main reasons for organizing a general strike in December 1988.) Actual influence in policymaking by either set of corporate groups has been slight, and the symbolic importance of certain positions—for example, those for and against making the labor market more flexible—has been magnified.

Industrial Reconversion

Industrial policy, too, has been shaped by the system of pactmaking without admitting much direct influence by nongovernment interest groups. One result is that industrial policy has remained highly centralized. A policy approach which seems appropriate for state-directed heavy industry has been poorly adapted to meet the needs of decentralized manufacturing.

The most immediate goal of industrial planners in Spain's new democratic governments was how to withdraw state support from costly and increasingly uncompetitive industries. This was to be achieved under the rubric of an industrial reconversion program that was introduced in 1981 under the Suárez UCD government. Spanish steel and shipbuilding, both of which had been hard hit by international competition from lower-cost producers, posed the greatest financial burdens. It was also certain that these industries would be forced to cut back production as a condition of Spain's entry into the EEC.

Industrial reconversion was extended to other sectors and was suggested as a tool for guiding the process of spontaneous restructuring that was already underway in light manufacturing industries. The Socialists made the reconversion program the centerpiece of a general program designed to improve the competitiveness of Spanish industry. To stress the positive benefits of the program, the Socialists created a special fund to support workers who were unemployed through reconversion. They also started a subsidiary program to provide tax subsidies and other benefits to firms which were established in designated Zones of Urgent Reindustrialization. The evolution of the reconversion program varied according to government priorities and the nature of political pressures in each case. The program originally included eight industries. Others were added later, and some industries and subsectors from the original list were passed to other assistance programs and out of reconversion.

The complexity of this panorama and its continuing changes make it impossible to describe the program in detail here. However, a close look at some of its features will help to illuminate the limitations of industrial planning in sectors that have undergone spontaneous restructuring.

First, it should be noted that industrial reconversion was directed mainly toward public rather than private industry. Industries in which public funding is greater than private investment consistently received the majority of funds and increased their share steadily to around 80% in 1985 (Fernandez 1985). In private industry, reconversion affected mainly large firms, even in the textile and shoe industries and in others where small firms predominate. The public image of industrial reconversion remained stubbornly unchanged: it was that it was a political program designed to curtail public investment in troubled heavy industries and to save selected private firms whose failure would entail high social and political costs. Most of the attention of the public and the press focused on the loss of jobs due to reconversion. Greatest in steel and shipbuilding, the lay-offs triggered massive worker protests and even violent clashes with the police, especially in the hard-hit northern steel plants and shipyards in Guipuzcoa, Asturias, and Galicia.

Another characteristic of industrial reconversion is that it entailed relatively little participation of business and labor organizations. Although these groups were invited to join tripartite commissions to discuss how reconversion should be implemented in individual cases, they were permitted to do so only if they approved initially to go ahead with reconversion in the affected industry. As the largest union opposed to reconversion, the CCOO had to choose in each case between opposing the plan from the outside or signing mini-pacts in order to have some input into its implementation. Even the UGT, which in general supported reconversion, had more influence on the program through informal rather than formal channels. The leading business association, the Confederación Española de Organizaciones Empresariales (CEOE), was skeptical about the potential benefits of reconversion and also had little effective input (Fernandez 1985).

The industrial reconversion program did not offer most sectors a coherent program of assistance. Small firms in particular missed out on the benefits of reconversion and were forced either to close or to pursue some other restructuring tactics, such as decentralization and expanded use of informal labor. Spontaneous restructuring thus continued to take place in some industries that possessed formal reconversion plans. Neither employers nor workers were able to exert strong pressures on the government to adapt the reconversion program to the needs of newly forming, small firms.

The failure of industrial planning to control and guide restructuring is apparent in both the electronics and shoe industries. In the electronics industry, only the large firms benefited to any degree from state assistance under the reconversion program. One subsector of the industry—electronic component production—was brought under industrial reconversion in March 1982. Only about one-third of the 28 firms that applied to receive benefits, which ranged from access to official credit to subsidies for fixed-capital investments and research, were accepted into the program. In its 1983 report on the industrial reconversion program, the government noted that the benefits destined for those firms accepted for assistance had been only partially distributed. Medium and small firms complained that they were not receiving sufficient financial support for research and expansion, while larger firms had not been able to apply assistance through the program to needed cutbacks in personnel (Ministry of Industry 1983a). While the inability to aid larger firms was clearly embarrassing to the government, the program's failure to supply support to small firms was in fact more significant; the eight largest firms in the subsector accounted for well in excess of one-half the value of production, but about 80% of the firms were of small or medium size, with fewer than 100 workers (Ministry of Industry 1983b). The government's report concluded that the results of the reconversion program for electronic components had been "quite unsatisfactory," and that it was "probably a strategic error to have treated the electronics components sector with a reconversion program" rather than to have taken steps to assist the industry as a whole and thus strengthen demand for electronics components (Ministry of Industry 1983a).

The other assistance brought to the electronics industry through the industrial reconversion program was aid for the restructuring of the Standard Group, comprised of Standard Eléctrica, S.A.; Citesa, S.A.; and Marconi Española, S.A. These firms received low-interest loans, along with social security and tax benefits, in exchange for promises that the firms would invest in research and capital improvements, and create employment through diversification and growth. Although officials were satisfied with the firms' compliance with these terms, it soon became apparent that the measures had not altered the need to reduce employment in the large concerns. Rather then stimulating growth and employment, support for the Standard Group conformed all too well to the record of the reconversion program in other areas where it functioned to aid declining firms while reducing employment (Ministry of Industry 1983a).

Such policies hardly seemed appropriate to an industry that was in fact rapidly expanding, particularly in a few subsectors. In its 1983 report on industrial reconversion, the government made clear its decision to shift the burden of fomenting growth to the national plan for the electronics industry that was then being drafted. In 1984, the government approved the *Plan Electrónico e Informático Nacional* (PEIN) with the objectives of stimulating demand and production, promoting exports, and encouraging technological development. Unlike the reconversion program, the plan consisted of a series of measures designed to aid the industry as a whole rather than particular firms. The projected measures included direct stimulation to domestic demand through government-sponsored projects, subsidies for investment by both national and foreign producers, broad assistance to export efforts (e.g., through support for international fairs), and financial support for research and development.

The introduction of these broad-based programs hardly solved the problem of how to reach the panoply of small- and medium-sized producers. The government offices through which the various measures would be implemented were very new or were already dedicated to other functions. For their part, small producers continued to be puzzled and often misinformed about the availability of support. They did not have an employers' association to help disseminate and verify information about the programs. A final shortcoming was the difficulty of measuring the impact of the plan's various features—a problem that was not shared to the same degree in the reconversion program (De Oyarzábel 1984).

Indirectly, the reconversion program fed another, separate government initiative to promote growth in the electronics industry. Encouraged by national leaders, the Madrid regional government utilized the greater part of its funds for Zones of Urgent

Reindustrialization to create a high technology industrial park at Tres Cantos, a site north of Madrid. The centerpiece of the park would be an American Telephone and Telegraph (AT&T) computer chip plant that was lured to Madrid by a generous package of subsidies, including some reindustrialization funds. In exchange for AT&T's pledge to invest $52 million in the plant, the company was promised about $82 million in direct subsidies, roughly $66 million in official credit, an additional $13 million from a local partner, the Spanish company *Telefónica*, the use of 160 hectares at Tres Cantos, and sizable tax credits (Estevan and Soto 1987).

The peculiar quality of this deal is that neither the regional nor the national government was able to spell out just how the presence of the AT&T plant can support a surge in related industry in the area. As a consultant's report to the regional government pointed out, there is very little to lure other chip-makers to Madrid other than comparable packages of tax breaks and subsidies. Further, the expected backward linkages of the AT&T plant are not especially promising. AT&T's style of production has been highly vertically integrated in the past, and there is little to indicate that it will aggressively seek out Spanish suppliers, with whom the firm would have to share its know-how. In any case, it seems likely that the presence of the plant will have little direct impact on the plight of the small and medium producers and subcontractors that now make up the most innovative and vulnerable segments of the local electronics industry (Estevan and Soto 1987).

A similar evolution of industrial policy is also apparent in the shoe industry. The failure of reconversion in this sector is noteworthy because it had strong support from both the business association and the unions. The first step was the creation of a Tripartite Commission under the UCD government to make specific recommendations of the content of the reconversion plan for the sector. There were some disagreements about the best way to aid the industry. The unions tended to favor strong technical assistance and credit programs, while business advocated a moratorium on social security payments and expenditures to improve the general reputation of Spanish shoes in important export markets. In principle, however, the two sides agreed that a reconversion program should be created to provide the industry with direct assistance.

The plan never received strong backing from the government.

The UCD gave in reluctantly to pressures to incorporate footwear in the reconversion program.[8] The May 1982 bill provided for certain broad forms of assistance to the industry without specifying the administrative channels through which such programs would be implemented. It also promised direct financial help and a moratorium on social security payments to firms, which qualified to participate in reconversion. But this part of the bill contained a catch-22: Only those firms that had paid their complete social security debts through March 1981 could qualify. The restriction excluded not just most small firms but most large businesses as well. Another problem was that even under reconversion businesses would be required to pay indemnities to workers being laid off; closing firms and reopening streamlined enterprises entailed far fewer costs. The employers' association and the unions were also critical of the program because it eliminated their participation following the dissolution of the Tripartite Commission. The result of these shortcomings was that in a sector with more than 1,800 firms, 195 applied for the program before the deadline had passed, and only 34 of these were accepted.

The government soon recognized the serious flaws of a program which would give preferential treatment to a handful of mostly larger firms while ignoring the needs of the vast majority of producers. Under the Socialists, the Ministry of Industry phased out the shoe industry's reconversion program altogether, continuing to assist only those firms that had already been accepted into the program and replacing it in the future with a series of measures designed to assist the industry as a whole. Such measures include stepped-up technical assistance administered through the *Instituto Nacional Español del Calzado* (INESCOP), a technical organization already established and centered in Alicante; access to inexpensive, long-term credit; direct financial and management assistance to groups of producers interested in establishing associations to make purchases or export collectively; and various other programs to help improve quality in the industry, including the introduction of a mandatory labelling system that is supposed to permit detection of informal subcontracting. Interestingly, the government's position after 1982 was that the shoe industry had already undergone its own process of restructuring and that there was no need for the government to support "dying" firms by keeping them out of the fray.[9]

One problem with phasing out the reconversion program was

that, as with the National Plan adopted for the electronics industry, the group of measures introduced in the shoe industry did not have the prominence and unified appeal of the reconversion program. Few factory owners are fully informed about the new programs. When they do have such information, they tend to regard the new forms of assistance as simply revised versions of programs that have been only marginally useful in the past. It is fair to say that the *failure* of reconversion attracted more attention than the policies which replaced it. Moreover, its failure is used to illustrate the futility of relying on the government and the implied necessity of proceeding with what employers refer to as the *reconversión salvaje* (untamed or wild reconversion; see Chapter 4).

Moreover, in the shoe industry as in the electronics industry, the programs designed to supplement or replace reconversion also suffer from the absence of truly representative employers' associations through which to disseminate information. Existing organizations tend to attract large firms, while small and medium firms participate marginally, if at all. Entrepreneurs interviewed admit their own tendency to regard the existing association as "just another bureaucracy" to which they must pay dues but through which they do not expect to achieve very much. Government officials bemoan the absence of "true intermediaries" as a major obstacle in implementing the state's programs in such a fragmented industry.

This example implies that the effectiveness of policies toward the informal sector in industry has been limited by the structure of centralized policymaking and mainly symbolic tripartite negotiating around policy issues in democratic Spain. Productive decentralization has acted to weaken representative organizations at the national level, at the same time that it has made it more difficult for state agencies to reach producers through local-level intermediaries. There is evidently a lag in the state's response to this relatively new trend in industrial growth; policies designed for a different purpose are adapted to new ends, and disconnected measures are pieced together to form a policy which as a result lacks coherence. Under these circumstances, the burden of dealing with the informal sector tends to shift to the local level.

Local Politics and the Informal Sector

One of the most important factors contributing to the outcome of informalization of central Italy was the strength of local alliances. The emergence of supportive policies toward small firms in some regions helped to create the conditions for some small, informal firms to prosper. It is no accident that the areas of central Italy where informal sector growth is found to have contributed most to industrial development are dominated by the Communist Party. A convergence of political sympathies among labor activists, small proprietors, and local government officials in Emilia Romagna, for example, created conditions favorable to the emergence of associations among small producers and collective enterprises capable of solving artisans' management and production problems:

> The founders of many of the innovative metalworking firms . . . were Communists or Socialists expelled from the large factories for political reasons; and often they have remained loyal to the leftist parties. . . . This loyalty contributes to the Left's preeminence in regional politics and is in turn reinforced by the extensive aid that town and regional agencies under the Left's control give to small employers: Towns, for example, often construct industrial parks in which tens or even hundreds of artisans can rent space. . . . For their part, the region advises small firms on market strategy and the use of technology. The success of agricultural and industrial producers' cooperatives, owing in some measure to the government's willingness to place orders with local artisans determined to defend their independence against large firms, has popularized the idea of collectively owned enterprise while drawing the state and the labor movement still closer together (Sabel 1982, 229).

The situation in Spain is quite different, not only because the Spanish Communist Party does not play an analogous role in any region, but more generally because the tradition of local or regional autonomy in policymaking is substantially weaker. Like other important policy areas, industrial planning was highly centralized under Franco. Although nearly all the autonomous regional governments now offer assistance programs to small and medium firms, ranging from credit for research and capital improvements to subsidies on social security payments for particular classes of workers, most of these programs were put in place only in 1984. The regional governments have to overcome organizational shortcomings and the difficulties of disseminating information about the programs, and they must also overcome the skepticism instilled in many producers by past dealings with the central government.

The problems of the regional governments are similar but more acutely felt at the municipal level. Town governments were also strictly subordinate to the central state under the authoritarian regime. In fact, Franco's tenure was characterized by the nearly complete absence of local-level planning despite decades of extremely rapid urban growth (see Celada, López, and Parra 1985). It is significant that one important demand of leftist and reformers during the transition period was the authorization of local governments to draft their own urban plans. Yet the municipalities under the new democracy found themselves still financially quite weak, and they are now dependent on the regional governments for funding and approval of local plans. Decentralization of industry significantly intensified pressures at the municipal level to provide costly infrastructure and regulate a burgeoning market in real estate and construction for industry, often in areas not appropriately zoned. Perhaps more than the regions, municipal governments also faced the obvious threat that efforts to crack down on unregulated practices or raise taxes on local producers would be rewarded with the flight of industry to other, more welcoming districts.

Two main geographical patterns were created through productive decentralization in Spanish industry, and each brought a different set of problems to local municipalities. First, decentralization of urban-based industries gave rise to an outer ring of small, often informal workshops around the largest cities. This trend placed a growing burden on the small municipalities, most of which had inadequate existing infrastructure for industry and a poor tax base. A second pattern of growth was the expansion of informal industry in rural areas, usually as a direct result of decentralizing strategies of larger firms. The latter began increasingly to transfer piecework by truck or van to workshops or homeworkers in small towns and villages. The landscape in this case would often appear deceptively unchanged. Small municipalities with large numbers of outworkers would not confront new clusters of industrial firms in need of support and services. Instead, the role of local officials was restricted to desultory attempts to curb the most blatant excesses of exploitative outwork, without causing employers to take their work elsewhere. In both the peripheral-urban and rural settings, the basis for local-level policy initiatives to assist new industrial subcontractors or outworkers was very weak. Several examples will make this point clearer.

In Madrid, as we saw in Chapter 3, rapid decentralization of leading industries prompted the growth of a new outer ring of industrial workshops. The small firms were clustered in and around small municipalities on the city's periphery. Many of the areas that were created by private developers for industrial expansion were on land that was still zoned for agricultural uses. Under these circumstances, town governments could not collect the full complement of taxes from local firms and could not even issue all firms operating licenses. Official plans for the areas could not be redrawn to incorporate existing industrial enclaves because these were improperly zoned. The regional government became responsible for overseeing local planning and controlling the distribution of zoning rights. The situation of the small town of Paracuellos del Jarama, 17 kilometers northeast of Madrid, was not unusual: by 1985, about 300 industrial firms near the town were "squatting" on agriculturally zoned land, and the mayor had been unsuccessful in getting the plots rezoned or proposed improvements for the area approved.[10]

The semilegal status of many of the small workshops outside Madrid would not be so troublesome if it did not create obstacles to their continued growth. One problem is the inadequacy of local infrastructure and services. The roads of some industrial areas are little more than muddy tracks. Postal services and waste collection are unreliable, and the water supply is often inadequate to meet industrial needs. Another problem for some firms is that their status compounds the difficulties in obtaining creditors or wooing clients; both like to visit firms to assess their productive capacity or potential. In conducting the research on electronics subcontractors reported in Chapter 3, I was struck by the efforts of many small producers to ward off such visits. One firm producing integrated circuits was particularly careful to disguise its location on the side of a steep embankment in an illegal industrial subdivision.

When local administrators try to force support for local policy initiatives, the results are not always encouraging. Arganda del Rey is a Communist-led municipality outside Madrid where local officials tried to develop a plan for an industrial park for cooperatives. The plan was blocked because of the regional government's control of funds and the reluctance of Socialist regional leaders to give special assistance to a Communist municipality. Small firms already established in the area were unenthusiastic about efforts to create the industrial park before improving services to existing firms. Roughly one-half of the firms in the area were founded in the 1980s, and about one-fourth still did not have operating licenses in 1985. Entrepreneurs' contacts with local officials centered mainly around tax collection and conflicts over the provision of services. Without either institutional or grassroots support, the municipality clearly had little chance of establishing a new and independent local plan for industry.[11]

The possibilities for developing local support for industrial subcontractors are often more remote in rural areas. Consider the response of local governments in Alicante to the rapid growth of the informal sector in the shoe industry. For a brief period in the early 1980s, officials in the largest shoe-producing towns were drawn into an agreement with the regional government, the unions, and the main business association to conduct inspections of local establishments in order to force "underground" workshops to obtain operating permits and place their workers on the books. In spite of impressive results in the first two such campaigns, the coalition supporting the effort dissolved.[12] Local governments feared that one consequence of forcing small firms and outworkers to "emerge" would be for producers simply to shift work to other, more tolerant municipalities. A further concern was that investigating unregulated employment would mean invading the private homes of constituents, because decentralized work in the shoe industry can be done in attics, garages, rural cottages—virtually anywhere in the rural-urban matrix where electricity can be installed. Finally, because production is so spatially diffuse, little pressure exists to upgrade local services in new or existing industrial zones. Local officials were able to abandon efforts to contain informal sector growth without offering any replacement for this policy.

The disarray of local-level planning may eventually be corrected by the increasing intervention of the regional governments. Not surprisingly, regional planning in response to decentralization has been most effective in those areas with a strong movement for autonomy from the central government. Catalonia and the Basque region have developed their own reconversion plans for key industries concentrated in these regions. Other regional governments are beginning to experiment with policies geared toward specific industries and conditions. But most such efforts have been limited to helping to implement national policies that require some degree of subordination to the central government. The high-technology park outside Madrid is a clear example of what can happen when regional interests are compromised for the sake of national political priorities; high-profile agreements with multinationals take precedence over the plight of new small firms, hurt by their anonymity and their own lack of political organization. With pressures from the national government on one side, and the slippery alliances of the new local politics on the other, regional initiatives to support decentralized industry clearly have a difficult road ahead.

Conclusion

The limited efficacy of Spain's version of neocorporatism is apparent in the political responses to industrial decentralization. As we have seen, the efforts to adjust nation-level policies to the new needs of industry proved disappointing. Alternative measures at the same time operated with either little institutional backing, on the one hand, or little grassroots support, on the other. Productive decentralization exacerbated these problems by fragmenting the constituency of corporate groups to the point where national-level policies of any kind became difficult to administer effectively in industries that had undergone spontaneous restructuring.

The emphasis on national-level tripartite agreements in the post-Franco period has also influenced the formation and evolution of political alliances at the local level. When they apply pressure to recast state policies at all, unions and business associations tend to address national-level debates. But a weak leadership is able to press energetically for only a narrow set of demands. Again, productive decentralization further weakens corporate groups. It is not surprising to find that employers' associations in large-scale industry have been able to exert far more influence in policymaking than their counterparts in highly decentralized sectors. Similarly, national union leadership is much more attentive to workers' interests where membership is greatest: in the large firms. The other potential partners in local alliances, the regional or municipal governments, meanwhile face severe fiscal constraints and enjoy limited power.

These findings should not be interpreted to mean that further change toward political decentralization is not possible. The new autonomous regional governments can be expected to become stronger. The poor showing of the Socialists in the 1987 municipal elections suggests, too, that local governments may gain strength in opposing the state's initiatives or proposing alternatives. Along with greater political decentralization would come the opportunity for more effective local responses to problems created by productive decentralization and informal sector growth, especially in highly geographically concentrated industries.

Yet the state may continue to try to tailor specific sectoral or local policies while still preserving the principle of centralized, top-down economic planning. This, at least, has been the Spanish government's response to pressures to devise more effective industrial policies. Actions to shore up the state's authority may coexist with rhetoric about the promise of decentralized patterns of industrial growth and the empowerment of small firms. For example, the new Socialist orthodoxy speaks of the need to nurture a vibrant "tissue" or "network" of industrial producers and users of new technologies. But the proposed remedies for Spain's relative technological backwardness harken back to the days when development economists recommended achieving "modernization" by attracting multi-nationals and sponsoring "transfers of technology." The omniscient state selects and invites in the right mix of international capital, and domestic producers profit by association.[13]

A critique of highly centralized industrial planning does not imply an endorsement of deregulation as an appropriate response to informalization in industry. One influential view of the informal sector is that it represents the collective efforts of "natural" entrepreneurs who are frustrated by the demands of state regulations; lifting the burden of these controls is all that is needed to stimulate development (De Soto 1987). But as both the Italian and Spanish cases show, not only is active intervention by the state—finely tuned to regional and sectoral conditions—an important precondition to dynamic restructuring, but deregulation in and of itself does not automatically alter entrepreneurs' employment strategies.

The truly interesting twist is that regardless of whether national leaders approve, some degree of political decentralization may be necessary to preserve the economic foundation of strong states.

Traditional state-led steps to promote export-oriented industrialization run into a new set of obstacles in a climate of rapidly restructuring, decentralized industry. The selective support of large-scale and foreign-assisted ventures gives life to the visible part of the industrial structure and leaves the care and tending of the subterranean roots to hazard. It remains to be seen whether the state will heed warnings that large-scale pet projects may die on the vine without greater attention to the new, still tangled mass of small ventures and would-be innovators. New contradictions, and new tensions, between corporate group leadership and the interests of rank-and-file members, between national and local priorities, and between political action and rhetoric, will drive this process of negotiating the new regulatory context for industrial development.

8 Some Reflections on the Informal Sector and Capitalist Development

It has become commonplace in Spain to refer to the informal sector as *el tercer mundo en casa*—pockets of Third World conditions in an otherwise highly industrialized and fairly advanced economy. This way of talking about the problem reveals certain prevalent assumptions in Spain about the regressive character of informalization and its negative effects on labor. The analogy of *tercermundismo* also draws support from much of the broader literature on the informal sector, which equates it with backward economic practices.

Approaches that adopt this view range from descriptions of the informal sector as a petty capitalist or noncapitalist mode of production, to characterizations of labor conditions in the informal sector as resembling those of early capitalism. Numerous resemblances between modern informal labor and protoindustrial labor seem to provide ample support for such views. Modern industrial homework recalls the putting-out systems common in European manufacturing of the eighteenth and early nineteenth centuries, and conditions in many modern sweatshops appear to be analogous to those of the early factories, in which capitalists and foremen used their unchallenged authority to impose long work days and continual speed-ups.

Although on the surface there is nothing wrong with such comparisons, nor with casually drawn analogies of modern informal-sector workers to nineteenth-century outworkers and factory hands, the historical parallels become more problematic the more closely they are scrutinized. Facile comparisons clearly do not take into account the immense complexity of the historical record itself, with the inconclusive findings it has generated about the transformation of industrial putting-out systems and the role of small workshop production in the rise of capitalism. Likening modern casual labor to

183

early or precapitalist labor also presents a one-dimensional view of relations of production in the informal sector under advanced capitalism. To equate present-day casual labor with nineteenth-century labor is to underestimate the influence of the rise of strong states and of ideas about work that derive from the experience of Fordist production. It is, in short, to ignore the importance of the contexts in which apparently similar forms of labor are embedded.

A search for the roots of informal labor in pre- or protocapitalist modes of production treads on very uncertain ground. As Marx himself noted, and as subsequent authors on the rise of capitalism tend to agree, the putting-out systems of early capitalism—which bear perhaps the closest superficial resemblance to present-day industrial outwork—were fully capitalist in the sense that they were produced by, and did not precede, the rise of "classic" capitalist relations of production in the nascent factory system. The skilled artisan-homeworker of the eighteenth century bore little resemblance to the industrial outworker of the nineteenth century, who not only labored under substantially worse conditions and without the protection associated with earlier crafts but also came from a quite different stratum of the population. E.P. Thompson warns of the error of attributing the appalling conditions surrounding outwork to its roots in an earlier, precapitalist era:

> [The conditions of outwork] can somehow be segregated in our minds from the true improving impulse of the Industrial Revolution—they belong to an "older," pre-industrial order, whereas the authentic features of the new capitalist order may be seen where there are steam, factory operatives, and meat-eating engineers. But the numbers employed in the outwork industries multiplied enormously between 1780–1830; and very often *steam and the factory were the multipliers*. . . . Indeed, we may say that large-scale sweated outwork was as intrinsic to this revolution as was factory production and steam (Thompson 1964, 261, emphasis in the original).

Accounts of the rise of a purely capitalist "domestic industry" also reveal the existence of segmentation in the labor market dating from this early stage of capitalist growth. Although we are right to think of nineteenth-century factory labor as relatively unregulated compared with its modern counterpart, historians point out that the degree of regulation and control over working conditions in the factories very soon surpassed that which existed for industrial outwork, the casual labor of the docks and building trades, and the "dishonorable," or illegal, labor markets that comprised a portion of all manufacturing industries. Toward the end of the nineteenth century, the casually-employed poor were so numerous that Victorian England recognized their plight as one of the gravest problems of the day, albeit one that was expected to be solved through further economic growth and moral reform of the pauper class.[1]

Without sharing the same ideological viewpoint and vision of progress, Marx also expected the disappearance, not of poverty, but of the casual and decentralized occupations of the poor. Curiously, while Marx noted the expansion of these sectors of seemingly backward, but in fact entirely "modern," forms of unprotected labor in the wake of the introduction of restrictions on the length of the working day in mid-nineteenth-century England, he also predicted that increasing regulation of the labor process would ultimately lead to the replacement of such occupations with jobs in the mechanized and centralized factory system. This change would take place because capitalists would respond to increased regulation with greater concentration of production and more rapid introduction of machinery to compensate for declining rates of surplus-labor extraction. Marx thus echoes classical economists in their prediction of the "triumph" of more effective and more rational forms of production over others that were based on simple exploitation:

> England is at present experiencing . . . the conversion of manufacture, of handicrafts, and of domestic work into the factory system, after each of these forms of production, totally changed and and disorganized under the influence of modern industry, has long ago reproduced, and even overdone, all the horrors of the factory system, without participating in any of the social progress it contains (Marx [1987] 1967, 474).

While Marx held this view, he also provided clues to some mechanisms that might contribute to the stability and even growth of the casual occupations. He observed first that "capital, so soon as it finds itself subject to legal control at one point, compensates itself all the more recklessly at other points," thus giving rise to "the wildest excesses" of exploitation outside the productive circles subject to control

(Marx [1867] 1967, 424, 490). Marx also noted that the newly passed regulations of factory and, especially, small workshop labor were only desultorily enforced,, leaving ample room for the continuation of exploitative practices in the small firms that could postpone the pressure for introducing machinery and accelerating the process of deskilling. But these countervailing pressures were evidently assumed to be only temporary barriers to the eventual spread of mature capitalist relations to the fringe regions of the industrial labor market.

If the persistence of casual labor and dualism represents something of a contradiction of "classical" theories of industrialization, including modified views that portray early capitalism as relatively homogeneous, a still more serious challenge is presented by evidence of the persistent dynamism of small workshop manufacturing. In some highly adaptive, modernizing sectors and regions within the emerging industrialized economies, small-scale production rather than large-scale, mechanized production created and responded to expanding demand. The resilience of some sectors that failed to pass through a centralizing, modernizing phase suggests to some authors that the model of classic industrialization, based on the experience of England and, in part, the United States, is in fact inaccurate, both as a description of industrialization in either of these cases and as a model of modernization in manufacturing elsewhere:

> Silks in Lyon; ribbons, hardware and specialty steel in neighboring Saint-Etienne; edge-tools, cutlery and specialty steels in Solingen, Remscheid and Sheffield; calicoes in Alsace; woolens in Roubaix; cottons in Pawtucket, Rhode Island; textiles of all kinds in Philadelphia—the history of all these industries challenges the classical view of economic progress. Small firms in these "industrial districts" . . . often developed or exploited new technologies without becoming larger; large firms that employed sophisticated and expensive technology from the start did not concentrate on the production of standardized goods. The long-term technological dynamism of both flies in the face of the notion that craft production must be either a traditional or subordinate form of economic activity. It suggests instead that there was a craft alternative to mass production as a model of technological advance (Sabel and Zeitlin 1985, 142).

Together, recent reinterpretations of the structure of both the labor market and industry in early capitalism present a much more complex picture than is assumed in references to the "backward" nature of the labor processes produced through decentralization. Perhaps the more serious criticism of such views is that they shift attention from the most important determining factor in both the emergence and persistence of modern informal labor: its juxtaposition to a large, state-regulated sector in which Fordism is held to be the central organizing principle. The result of this juxtaposition is that relations of production in the informal sector *are* qualitatively different from the earlier forms of casual labor they seem to resemble. State-regulated labor processes serve as precedents for negotiations over employment terms and conditions in the informal sector. This influence is often not indirect, but is promoted by individuals, including employers, who have direct experience in production in the formal sector. The same is true of ideas about the way production should be organized and the growth of the firm pursued. In a situation in which highly formal and centralized relations of production are considered the norm, and in which contingent factors do not facilitate the emergence of alternative ways of viewing production, workers and entrepreneurs alike will continue to emulate established techniques and systems for ordering work.

The existence of Fordism as the reigning paradigm for industrial development also influences informal and decentralized industry by reinforcing state policies that support large industry (including large capital engaging in decentralizing strategies) while choosing to ignore, or to seek to eliminate through growth, the burgeoning sector of small-scale and partially unregulated industrial enterprises. In this sense, popular understandings of employment in the informal sector resemble attitudes toward pauperism in Victorian England: observers at all points on the political spectrum deplore the disadvantaged status of the entrepreneurs and the substandard conditions of many of the workers, but they expect economic development ultimately to do away with the problem. In their view, the state's role should be to promote development in a "classic" sense, either through deregulation of the economy or through the elimination of dependent ties to advanced capitalist countries.

Historical comparisons help us to understand dualism in the modern economy precisely because they illuminate the failure of classical theories to recognize the centrality of casual labor and workshop production to capitalist industrialization. This error cautions against the assumption that current informal forms of production merely respond to the dynamics of large-scale capitalist industry and are thus "marginal" to the process of development. New historical interpretations of the rise of capitalism also instruct us by emphasizing the power of particular and sometimes highly localized social and political conditions to shape the process of industrialization. The discovery of a wider array of historical patterns of industrial growth, none of them determined by the imperatives of technological progress, parallels our observation of a broad range of experiences of industrialization in the modern economy molded by varying political and social conditions.

The variability of decentralized patterns of growth has been the theme of much of our discussion of restructuring in Spanish industry. On one level, social patterns and shared experiences have ordered production. In the shoe industry, the fact that a large proportion of industrial outwork is done by women workers in the home has had a direct bearing on the dynamics of growth in the industry, because it limited the contributions that outworkers can make to innovative changes. In Madrid's electronics industry, groups of skilled workers bound by friendship and shared experiences in factory employment were better able to improve their position within the industrial structure and contribute directly to product design. In both sectors, the regional context of restructuring also affected its direction. Salient class divisions in the small shoe-producing communities stifled new forms of cooperation. In Madrid, the legacy of worker mobilization in large-scale firms and around broad-based issues added little impetus to a drive for collective ventures among skilled workers.

On another level, the success of efforts at "bottom-up" industrial restructuring continues to depend on the wider political environment in which they take place. A spontaneous movement by workers to experiment in small firms with new types of organization must be answered by institutional support; this missing element in Madrid's electronics industry has left many small new firms doubting their capacity to emulate the success of other experimental enterprises. By the same token, government efforts to give broad support for a modernizing brand of spontaneous restructuring may fail if the political structure provides little room for local-level alliances that would translate state assistance into viable and effective forms. Thus in the Spanish shoe industry, the government's recent attempts to assist small producers have had little impact in changing the profile or prospects of the industry. And locally based attempts to help decentralized industry in Madrid have faltered because of a dearth of resources and lack of autonomy at the local level.

The two cases represent two alternatives with different sets of implications for semiperipheral industry. In the electronics industry, the industrial structure has begun to approximate a system of multiple, interconnected layers of independent producers of high-quality goods. A diagram of such an emerging system of flexible specialization would resemble an intricate web that would link even the smallest firms with a widely varied array of other enterprises. In the shoe industry, by contrast, firms that do outwork have remained highly dependent on larger producers for orders and design specifications. A simplified diagram of this system of informal sector subcontracting would show a downward-pointing branch, with homeworkers and small workshops each connected to a single client or intermediary (see Capecchi 1989).

The contrast between the two systems is highlighted when we imagine the consequences of another global shake-up similar to the one experienced in the 1970s. In a system of informal sector subcontracting, firms at the top of the production ladder would respond to restricted demand by cutting back on work orders to subcontractors. The latter would bear the brunt of the crisis, while the industry as a whole would be no better positioned to introduce changes to alter its position in the market. In the flexibly specialized system heralded by Piore and Sabel, firms respond to unsettling market shifts by recasting production to anticipate, rather than react to, trends in consumer and producer goods markets.

The contrast between the two scenarios highlights the high stakes that semiperipheral states have in monitoring the outcome of productive decentralization. The dilemma becomes how to adopt effective measures to aid the emergence of flexible specialization without surrendering the prerogatives of highly centralized states. In earlier periods of rapid industrialization, the semiperiphery's strong states intervened heavily and directly in the economy to foment growth. Productive decentralization and informalization of industry change the ground rules for such intervention. At the national level, the trends create conditions that might be viewed as signs of instability by investors, both foreign and domestic: high (even if artificially high) unemployment rates, seen as a sign of potential political instability, and the introduction of uncertainty about the availability and cost of goods and services provided by informal producers. At the local and regional level, the twin trends introduce new problems that cannot be solved except through alliance-building and nontraditional types of state intervention.

Productive decentralization and informalization may thereby create an opening for *political* decentralization on two levels. First, fragmentation of the production process generates opportunities for control over production to shift toward skilled workers and worker-entrepreneurs—an opening that might or might not be seized by workers. Second, productive decentralization sets in motion changes that cannot be effectively responded to by a politically centralized state. In Spain, note how local changes created by productive decentralization reinforce demands for increased local autonomy in urban management and industrial policymaking. By the same token, productive decentralization creates an opening for new, local-level alliances to emerge among groups increasingly dissatisfied with the lack of effective policymaking at the national level and with their own inability to influence national-level decisionmaking.

These trends together indicate that although growth of the informal sector may reinforce political stability in the short run, it creates greater uncertainty about long-term political processes. In Spain, flux and uncertainty are rooted in the very nature of the neocorporatist "solution" to the problems of the transition. And changes set in motion by productive decentralization could significantly alter the terms of political bargaining. One important change would be the emergence of stronger and more independent local initiatives that would effectively shift the primary focus of tripartite bargaining from the national to the regional level. A second potential source of change is the possibility of political activism among groups not represented in current bargaining arrangements.[2] Particularly unsettling would be the mobilization of workers or small-scale entrepreneurs who are engaged in unregulated activities.[3]

The potential for such scenarios suggests an inherent incompatibility between the persistence of strong states in semiperipheral countries and the ability of the latter to respond effectively to changing international economic conditions. In suggesting such a connection, we join scholars who have searched for consistent links between the nature of the state and shifts toward successive stages of industrial development in the past. One school looked for connections between the rise of bureaucratic-authoritarian states and the creation and transformation of import-substituting industrialization.[4] Others posited a link between the intervention of strong stages and their ability to propel a shift from import-substituting industrialization to export-led growth.[5] Critics of these approaches have noted that the patterns of industrial growth identified are not nearly so universal as proponents claim; nor do regime changes consistently denote shifts in the style of state interventions or coincide with similar economic transformations.[6]

We do not want to perpetuate the shortcomings of earlier attempts to link particular styles of state control with different stages of industrialization. Without predicting either the precise relationship of different *regimes* with patters of industrial growth, and without suggesting that state *policies* can alone determine the direction of industrial growth, we can nevertheless point to the clear connection that emerges in our discussion between the presence of *strong states* in the semiperiphery and the difficulties these countries encounter in propelling a shift toward a different style—a new phase, if you like—of export-led industrialization. The existence of strong, centralized states poses an obstacle to a move toward flexible specialization in manufacturing industry that would be better suited to more competitive, more crowded, and continually fluctuating world markets. Whereas earlier studies suggested that strong states were needed, either to orchestrate large-scale investments required to "deepen" import-substituting industrialization or to implement consistent policies supportive of industrialization for export, our hypothesis suggests that political decentralization is needed if effective institutional support is to emerge for the newly decentralized systems of production leading the push toward the more flexible, more dynamic pattern of export-oriented growth.

As productive decentralization proceeds, in other words, semiperipheral states might be forced to concede some of the power they garnered in the initial push toward industrial growth. I am not making overly ambitious claims about the ties of this process to democratization. Rather than as a loss of power, we should understand "political decentralization" as a shift in the locus of the alliances underpinning capitalist industrialization. The challenges of sustaining export-led growth make this shift a possible, but not a necessary, accompaniment to spontaneous restructuring of industry.

The transformation of the informal sector into a catalyst for the creation of flexible, specialized, and highly competitive industry depends, then, on the convergence of a remarkably varied set of social and political conditions. None of the favorable factors identified—including political decentralization itself—is alone a sufficient condition for the transformation of the informal sector into a locus of dynamic growth. Neither naive optimism nor reflexive cynicism is an appropriate reaction to this phenomenon.

The attitudes and behavior of small groups of people in particular towns and regions, as well as the actions of seemingly marginal social actors, have a deep and decisive impact on the way national industries are poised to respond to international change. In Spain, as elsewhere, dependent development responds to no quiet logic, but instead unfolds through the noisy interventions of men and women who battle imaginatively against some constraints and succumb reluctantly to others. As history teaches, the new patterns of capitalist industrialization will claim some victims, but they will defeat no one.

Notes

Introduction

1. Debate about the scope and significance to the economy of recent industrial restructuring (see Gordon 1985; Bluestone and Harrison 1982) is intricately linked to analysis of the political underpinnings of this shift. Politics here is broadly defined. Sabel (1987) calls attention specifically to the transformation of the regulatory structure of industry, both now and in past periods of rapid industrial change, and emphasizes the embeddedness of distinctive regional economies in regulatory frameworks that are constructed through conflict. Lipietz speaks of a "regime of accumulation" supported by a "body of interiorized rules and social processes . . . called the *mode of regulation*" (1986, 19). In his view, the regime of accumulation in the immediate postwar decades focused on mass consumption and is now, together with the mode of regulation, undergoing a profound transformation that also implies a change in the relationship between "core" and "peripheral" countries.

2. The most prominent work in recent Marxist literature on deskilling and worker alienation in modern capitalism is by Braverman (1974). For an analysis of Smithian notions about technological change and the division of labor, see Piore (1980b).

3. Excellent critiques of both modernization theory and Marxist approaches to development are by now numerous. Gereffi (1983, Part I) outlines succinctly the problems in both perspectives as they relate specifically to Third World industrialization. Roseberry (1983) gives a detailed analysis of debates in the Marxist literature about the role of noncapitalist enclaves; on this subject, see also Chapter 8 herein.

4. Lewis's view of rural economies as holding areas for surplus labor (Lewis 1959) fits neatly into a long tradition of dualist notions in social theory. Perlman traced this thread in social thinking from Durkheim to contemporary treatments of the urban poor as a "marginal" population (Perlman 1976). For a more recent critique of Lewis's model and

193

subsequent, related theories of industrial labor absorption, see Portes and Benton (1984).

5. The most outspoken proponent of this interpretation of dependency is Frank (1969). For a critique of this and other prominent versions of dependency theory, see Booth (1985).

6. On the critique of marginality theory, see Perlman (1976). Case studies illustrating the interconnections between informal and formal labor include those by Birbeck (1979), Bromley (1978), Lomnitz (1978), and Tokman (1978). For a summary of relevant case studies from Latin America, see Portes and Benton (1984).

7. The term *informal sector* was first used by Keith Hart (1973) in an article on the economic strategies of urban migrants in Ghana. The term was picked up in development circles and much of the early research focused on the Third World. For a review of early debates on the role of the informal sector in development, see Moser (1978); and for a critique of the preservation of dualist notions in this literature, see Peattie (1980). Portes (1983) argued persuasively that the informal sector should be defined by the relative lack of state regulation, because this distinction accounted for employers' incentives in creating and preserving informal labor and also for the close ties between formal and informal firms. Portes emphasized the functionality of informal labor, which both lessens costs and risks to employers and also exerts a generalized downward pressure on wages by helping to provide goods and services to workers at lower cost (see Portes and Walton [1981], Chapter 3).

8. An excellent presentation of this view of dualism that is also sensitive to its shortcomings is given by Piore (1980a, 1980b). See also Edwards, Reich, and Gordon (1975).

9. See Sabel (1982); and Chapter 1 herein. The conditions necessary for this scenario to occur will be discussed in later chapters. See also the Conclusion in Portes, Castells, and Benton (1989). The promise of dynamic restructuring seemed to be supported by impressive records of employment growth in small firms in the advanced economies (Sengenberger and Loveman 1987).

10. Piore and Sabel (1984) discuss these systemwide trends in detail and analyze their implications for shifts in production styles in the advanced economies. While the crisis of the 1970s increased pressure on employers to rely on cheaper and less conflictive industrial outworkers, increasing market differentiation continues to favor the production of

shorter series and the use of general-purpose rather than specialized machinery. See especially Sabel (1982), Chapter 5. In the next chapter, I relate this observation to an understanding of the challenges facing export-oriented, newly industrializing countries.

11. The wide range of experiences of industrial restructuring has become even more evident since this study was begun. A group of comparative studies (Portes, Castells, and Benton 1989) from both advanced and developing countries included cases in which informalization simply reinforced existing tendencies toward the exploitation of certain vulnerable social groups, and examples of genuine revitalization of industrial growth led by newly generated small firms that offered conditions that were, if anything, more beneficial to workers. Individual studies sensitive to the possibilities for widely different outcomes of restructuring, even for different actors within the same industry, have also appeared. For example, Christopherson and Storper, in analyzing productive decentralization in the motion picture industry in the United States, suggest that new forms of flexible production are not incompatible with new sources of social inequality (Christopherson and Storper 1987; Storper and Christopherson 1985). Waldinger (1985), in a different example, notes the uneven impact of restructuring in the New York apparel industry on immigrant workers and worker-entrepreneurs.

Chapter 1

1. See Wolf (1982), Worsley (1984), and especially Mintz (1977).

2. Excellent examples include the studies by Trouillot (1982), Roseberry (1983), and Verdery (1983).

3. These views have been eloquently put forth by historians and anthropologists writing about other settings. E.P. Thompson (1964, 1967) has stressed the importance of workers' experiences in industrialization in forming their perceptions of class, while Gutman (1972) and others have examined the influence of cultural patterns and beliefs on the organization of production. This attention to the interpenetration of culture and relations of production is addressed only obliquely in some influential accounts of the evolution of capitalist control in the workplace (see especially Braverman 1974 and R. Edwards 1979). But as other authors have pointed out, worker autonomy (stemming from the continued need for worker skills) has remained an important element of shop-floor organization even in the

most mechanized and best controlled environments (see Burawoy, 1985 and Offe, 1985).

4. Unconsciously echoing "official" interpretations of Spanish history and culture, many scholars writing during the Franco regime gave the impression that little change in Spanish society was worthy of chronicling. In anthropology, the emphasis on homogeneity and stability was closely related to its rural bias. Pitt-River's (1954) formulations about the socially integrating functions of the values of honor and shame, patron-client relations, and village customs such as nicknaming were echoed in similar rural community studies in other regions of Spain undertaken over the next decades (e.g., Kenny 1960; Freeman 1970; Brandes 1975). An implicit and sometimes explicit critique of this perspective prompted both historical and ethnographic studies of rural change (e.g., Hansen 1977; Greenwood 1976; Aceves 1971; and Behar 1986) and greater attention to hidden conflicts (Gilmore 1980; Collier 1987; Kaplan 1977; Mintz 1982; and Martinez-Alier 1971). But these works continued to focus mainly on rural society, despite the extremely rapid urbanization taking place in Spain and the political and social transformations this implied (Kenny and Knipmeyer 1983; see also the discussion of urbanization in Chapter 2 herein). A notable exception is McDonogh's research on the evolution of elite culture in Catalonia (McDonogh, 1986).

5. The OECD (1979) identifies 10 countries as NICs, mainly because of their record as exporters to OECD markets: Hong Kong, Taiwan, South Korea, Singapore, Mexico, Brazil, Spain, Yugoslavia, Greece, and Portugal. Edwards (1979) agrees but excludes Greece. Balassa (1981) uses two criteria—per capita income and manufacturing as a share of GDP—to produce a list that includes all the above countries as well as Argentina, Chile, Israel, Uruguay, Turkey, Hungary, Bulgaria, and Rumania. Other definitions are offered by the British Foreign and Commonwealth Office and various development agencies (see Turner and McMullen 1982).

6. See, for example, Arrighi 1985a. For further discussion of the definition of semiperipheral states and the inclusion of Spain in this category, see Arrighi 1985b and Wallerstein 1985.

7. On this shortcoming of dependency theory, see Browett (1985) and Booth (1985).

8. In a prominent version of this view (Balassa 1981), developing countries proceed through two stages of import substitution before

replacing this "inward-oriented" policy with a set of "outward-oriented" measures designed to simulate exports of manufactures.. Countries that get stuck in the initial inward-oriented stages falter, while outward-oriented nations progress.

9. Authors such as Amsden (1985), Wade (1983), and Castells (1984) have argued that the state has played a central role in promoting industrial growth in the East Asian NICs, and Evans (1979) has traced the state's participation in the alliances with national and international capital that underpinned Brazilian industrial development. The views of these authors need to be distinguished, however, from claims that a simple switch to outward-oriented policies will accomplish such growth (see note 4.) The fundamental flaw in the latter approach is that it adopts an excessively narrow view of politics and overestimates the state's autonomy in both designing and implementing its policies. This shortcoming is implicitly recognized by proponents of state-led, export-led development when they enumerate the many other conditions that must accompany outward-oriented policies in order for them to be effective (e.,g., see Bradford 1982).

10. For a general discussion of the issues raised in the literature on the informal sector in developing countries, refer to the Introduction herein. For a compendium of recent works on the phenomenon, see Portes, Castells, and Benton (eds.) 1989.

11. Portes and Walton (1981) and Portes and Benton (1984) emphasize the structural stability of the informal sector in developing economies. Piore (1980a, 1980b) and Berger (1980) trace the economic and political functions of dualism as a permanent feature of advanced economies.

Chapter 2

1. Castillo (1983) gives the figure as 56.8%; I have not come across any official statistics to confirm this figure.

2. The implicit goal of this study was to demonstrate that the official unemployment rate (then higher than 20%) was artificially high. On the controversy surrounding government efforts to quantify the informal sector, see Parra (1988), and the discussion of government strategies in Chapter 7 herein. Note that two reports summarizing the results of the 1985 survey were prepared based on two slightly different analyses of the data. All the figures cited here are from the second

report, which was published by the Ministry of Economy in 1988 (Muro, et al. 1988).

3. See Chapter 3, note 1.

4. McDonogh's (1986) study of the nineteenth-century Catalan elite discusses the social basis for strong group solidarity among leading industrialists. Solé (1987) traces the long history of corporatist arrangements in the Catalan textile industry. There is no guarantee, of course, that the Catalan setting will actually favor the emergence of flexible specialization in industry. Despite some evidence of the formation of new networks of microenterprises on the outskirts of Barcelona (Costa and Trullen 1987), most studies of informalization and its effects have emphasized the degradation of labor in new putting-out systems in industry. See Solé (1987) and especially Recio and Miguélez (1988b). The findings to date are by no means conclusive; it is significant that most of the studies in this region have focused on the textile industry, where homework is widespread and the reliance on sweatshop arrangements is more predictable, and not on the more complex mix of small-scale industrial ventures that cluster on the outskirts of Barcelona.

   In the Basque region, the example of the Mondragón cooperatives continues to attract much of the attention given to alternative plans for industrial growth. The first cooperative in this group was formed in 1956, and the complex now includes 130 cooperatives and employs 19,000 worker-owners. The group has outperformed the rest of the Basque economy, even in recession years. It is built around an unusual, and perhaps unique, social nexus that tightly ties worker-producers. They are also bound institutionally by the cooperatives' widely ranging ventures, which include a bank that extends credit for new cooperatives. Although the success of Mondragón has been loudly acclaimed, and even romanticized by some, little evidence exists that the experiment will be, or can be, reproduced in other parts of Spain. See Gutiérrez and Whyte (1982) and Greenwood (1986).

5. Gilmore (1980) provides a detailed ethnographic account of the workings of the casual labor market in agriculture. See García de Blas and Ruesga (1988) for an overview of the informal sector in Andalucia.

Chapter 3

1. Dragados, the country's largest construction firm, reduced its workforce by 46% between 1977 and 1982. Other large firms showed similar

patterns of decline (see Comunidad de Madrid 1984). A second indication of change is the recent, rapid rise in the number of self-employed workers in construction, from 113,800 in 1980 to 142,800 in 1984, an increase of 25.5%, while during the same period, the number of employees in construction firms decreased by 30.9%. The practice of hiring casual and nominally self-employed labor through independent intermediaries (called *pistoleros*) is widely known (see e.g., DOPESA 1977; Comunidad de Madrid 1984). In July 1983, I interviewed several employers and workers in the Madrid construction industry who confirmed accounts of growing fragmentation in the industry and the increasingly widespread hiring of casual workers.

2. I am indebted to Antonio Estevan for advising me in planning field research in the electronics industry and for allowing me access to the detailed records of his own research. The results of his study of small and medium firms in the Madrid electronics industry are presented in a report prepared for the Madrid regional government (Estevan 1984). I draw extensively on this report in describing the history of Madrid's electronics industry in the second section of this chapter (see also Estevan 1986).

3. The three medium-sized firms are atypical of the auxiliary industry. One is a nonprofit enterprise that employs 120 handicapped people to do assembly work. The other two are the largest firms in their respective subfields: a 130-worker firm producing printed circuits and a metalworking firm with 75 workers, which was founded in the 1940s.

Chapter 4

1. In 1980, three-fourths of the firms dedicated to exports of shoes were located in just three towns: Elda, Elche, and Petrel. Five towns in Castellón accounted for about the same proportion of the ceramic tile industry's exporting firms. Valencia and three surrounding towns held 44% of furniture exporters. More than one-half of firms exporting blankets and related textile products were concentrated in Onteniente, Bocarente, Alcoy, and Albaida; and about two-thirds of all toys for export were made in Ibi and Denia (Mas, Mafé, and Rico 1982, 132–47).

2. For a good introduction to the transformation of Spanish rural society during this period, see Aceves and Douglas (1976).

3. The progress of the industry was, in fact, not quite so smooth as the figures indicate. Further restrictions on imports of shoes to the United

States caused the industry's first crisis between 1969 and 1970. In February 1973, a drastic devaluation of the U. S. dollar also had disastrous effects on demand, and this coincided with a speculative trend in raw materials for shoes. Thus, although net exports did not decline until 1979, the industry was already showing signs of extreme vulnerability to fluctuations in the international market, but particularly in American demand. This weakness was not completely offset by increased sales to France and Germany between 1974 and 1976. See Méndez (1985).

4. For 1976 figures, see A. Edwards (1979). Rates of increase in the value of imports of shoes to OECD countries from leading NICs between 1965 and 1973 are as follows: for Taiwan, 7,591%; Spain, 2,634%; Portugal, 1,947%; Mexico, 1,916%; South Korea, 2,634%; Brazil, 2,517%. These six countries, ranked in the order listed, accounted for 34% of all imports of footwear to OECD countries in 1973 (OECD Foreign Trade Statistics, Series C).

5. The same employer recounted how he had struck a bargain with a worker who had "cheated" when the scientific method was being introduced by working at a rate much slower than normal. Having established a low fixed rate, the worker would then consistently produce well above the set rate and earn high premiums. When the employer realized this, he negotiated an arrangement whereby the worker would receive a higher fixed wage than normal but would also have to work overtime, without compensation, if he failed to produce a fixed daily quota.

6. In the record performance year of 1984, the high U. S. dollar helped to fuel a surge in the value of exports by 40.6%. Gains fell to 13.1% in 1985, and for the first time in this decade, exports registered a decline (5%) in 1986. In 1987, a modest climb of 1.6% reflected the falling share of exports to the United States, which decreased from 41% of total exports in 1986 to 34% in 1987. At the same time, imports rose dramatically, suggesting that Spanish producers were being squeezed at both high and low ends of the market even on the domestic front.

7. For example, the head of the employers' association for the shoe industry in Elche, Pedro Méndez Reyes, writes that the recuperation of exports in the 1980s was the result of "a frenetic attempt by employers to adapt the character of the product to the exigencies of the market, often operating on the margins of strict legality" (Méndez 1985). Méndez and other officials of the employers association were candid in

interviews about the crucial role of the informal sector in maintaining exports.

8. The Inspector General of the provincial office of the Ministry of Labor informed me that the three factories had all received visits from inspectors in 1981 and had been fined for having workers not on the books: Seven such workers were found in the first factory described, six in the second, and 26 in the third. The inspection office does not continue to monitor sanctioned firms and thus has no way of knowing whether the workers were ever actually put on the books. My visits to these and other previously inspected firms suggested that clandestine practices often simply continue without change after the fines have been paid.

9. Nearly all the towns in the province of Alicante hold annual *fiestas* that reenact the victory of the Christians over the Moors during the *Reconquista*. Groups of costumed Moors and Christians may be sponsored by individuals, and this is one more highly visible way for entrepreneurs to display their wealth. Several informants remarked on the lavish costumes that had been paid for by certain "insolvent" employers during the town *fiestas*.

Chapter 5

1. Pesce (1987) has emphasized the importance of social roles and gender in the Italian case, and Truelove (1989) makes gender the key to her analysis of productive decentralization in the Colombian garment industry.

2. For example, a study by Frey (1975) of homework in Italy suggested that low-status, low-paying outwork by women has played a central role in Italian export industries and their success in the 1970s. See also Pesce (1987).

3. This comment is not intended as harsh criticism of the excellent studies that have laid the groundwork for current research on women in industry. See, for example, Fernandez-Kelly (1983a, 1983b) on women in Mexican border industrialization; Ong (1983, 1985) on the employment of young women in Asian industry; and Prates (1985) and Benería and Roldán (1987) on outwork done by women in Latin American industry. An example of the type of comparative analysis that I suggest here is a recent work by Fernandez-Kelly (1989) contrasting the plight of Hispanic women who work as industrial homeworkers in Southern California and Florida.

4. The survey was administered in separate phases spaced several months apart. The first phase was conducted between February 24 and March 23, 1983; the second, from May 20 to June 23, 1983; and the third, from October 7 to November 15, 1983. Close similarities in all three phases suggest that this approach did not produce significant distortions. For example, the percentage of homeworkers detected was nearly identical in the three phases. Nevertheless, the method has the major disadvantage that the possible impact of short-term economic changes or seasonal shifts in the activities of homeworkers cannot be evaluated. Combining the results of the separate phases presented the best method of analysis because it improved the statistical significance of the data related specifically to homeworkers. A second note of caution about the survey concerns the system of sampling. The sample was stratified by region and size of population center, and households were selected by a system of random routing. Widely dispersed rural populations were underrepresented, so that certain results of the survey must be viewed with caution. A complete analysis of the survey is contained in my report published by the Ministry of Economy (Benton 1986).

5. This number excludes households with professionals who work at home. The educational and income profiles of these individuals and their families suggest that homework in such cases represents mainly a complement to jobs held outside the home. I also chose to exclude artists, mainly because the distinction between remunerated artistic work and hobbies was too difficult to make in most cases.

6. Complete tables for the national study, as well as for the Alicante survey discussed in a later section of this chapter, can be found in Benton (1986). For gender, age, and household status, the complete figures are as follows:

Gender	Number	Percentage
Male homeworkers	116	24.9%
Female homeworkers	349	75.1%
(Incomplete information in two cases.)		
Age		
15 years or younger	4	.9%
From 16 to 29 years	128	27.9%
From 30 to 54 years	253	55.1%
55 years or older	74	16.1%
(Incomplete information in eight cases.)		
Household status		

Heads of household	90	19.5%
Housewives	259	56.0%
Sons or daughters	92	20.0%
Other household members	21	4.5%

(Incomplete information in five cases.)

7. The actual number of homeworkers about whom we have information from the survey is larger than the number of households included, because 13% of the households hold two homeworkers and another 3% have three or more family members working at home. (The total number of homeworkers detected in the survey equals 560.)

8. As part of a 1982 government study of the informal sector in the shoe industry 42 semistructured interviews were recorded. This quote and others in this section are from the transcribed interviews with employers.

Chapter 6

1. An excellent analysis of the political orientation of Madrid workers in migrant communities in the southern section of the city can be found in Castells (1983), Part 5.

2. Villar Mir was the government minister who, in a November 1975 speech, announced prolongation of the wage freeze. The speech was instrumental in fomenting support for worker protests.

3. See Chapter 2, note 4 above.

4. Elda and Petrel are adjacent towns; my description of political trends and events in Elda applies to both towns.

5. The cause of the strike was a complaint by homeworkers—specifically, by *aparadoras*—that employers were overcharging them for the thread used in their work. The homeworkers initiated the strike and were joined by other workers in solidarity. Although the Socialists advocated compromise and attempted to end the strike after negotiating a plan to reduce the cost of thread to workers, the more radical CNT prevailed and maintained the strike long enough to obtain both a promise from employers to provide thread without charge to homeworkers and a slight increase in wages. The episode represented a significant victory for the CNT (Forner 1982, 188). Viewed in retrospect, the strike highlights the politically marginalized position of homeworkers in the industry today. Although they participated in the Assembly Movement

described in this chapter, the improvement of conditions of homeworkers was not among the central issues discussed in negotiations.

6. The vertical union estimated that 56 firms with 5,200 workers observed strikes; according to the workers' committee, 110 firms were closed and 8,000 workers went on strike. See *La Verdad*, February 25, 1976.

7. The encounter took on such great importance because the firm, La Zapatilla, employed a prominent official of the vertical union, who was widely considered a puppet of employers. Workers suspected that he had been in close touch with employers negotiating in Madrid and that they had instructed him to prevent workers at La Zapatilla from joining the strike.

8. In the 1978 union elections, the USO gained about 7% of the delegates and emerged a solid third behind CCOO. and the UGT. Nationally, the USO made a much weaker showing, gaining 3.7% of all delegates and coming in fifth behind the two major unions and the two strongest regional unions (Beneyto and Picó 1982, 128–29).

Chapter 7

1. The Moncloa Pacts were signed in October 1977. The following year, no agreement was reached and the UCD government unilaterally imposed ceilings for wage hikes at between 11% and 14%. In July 1979, the UGT and the CEOE signed the *Acuerdo Básico Interconfederal* without participation of the government. This pattern was repeated in the *Acuerdo Marco Interconfederal*, which was prolonged into 1981. In June 1981, the government, the CEOE, the UGT, and the CCOO signed the *Acuerdo Nacional sobre Empleo* (ANE). In 1983, the unions and the CEOE also arrived at an agreement to limit salary increases. The 1984 *Acuerdo Económico y Social* (AES) was signed by the government, the small business association, the Confederación Española de Pequeñas y Medianas Empresas (CEPYME), the CEOE, and the UGT, with the CCOO dissenting and refusing to sign. See Schmitter (1984) on the role of pacts in other transitions to democracy.

2. I am indebted to Lynne Wozniak for her observation of these and many other points regarding the pacts and their relationship to industrial planning in numerous discussions. See Wozniak (1990). For a more positive assessment of the role of neocorporatist politics in Spain's political transition and its economic recovery, see Pérez Díaz (1984, 1985).

3. The number of working days lost because of strikes and other types of labor conflicts has been decreasing. In 1985, 52% fewer days were lost in strikes than in 1980. In industry, days lost through strikes decreased by 67% during the same period. The decline was not steady, however. Strike days decreases through 1982 and increased again through 1984 before declining sharply. (These figures, from the Ministry of Labor, do not include strike statistics for Catalonia.) In general, levels of conflict in the 1980s are far below what they were in the 1960s and 1970s. Protests outside the workplace have also wanted. For example, the neighborhood-based urban protests of the last decade of the Franco regime have lost much of their strength despite soaring unemployment and persisting housing problems in the neighborhoods involved. For an interesting account of the neighborhood movement in Spain before and during the transition period, see Castells (1983), Part 5.

4. Sanchis describes, for example, an attempt by Comisiones Obreras to force firms in a small town in Castellón to take on additional workers by threatening to denounce their use of unregistered homeworkers. When employers responded to these threats by actually decreasing work given to homeworkers without hiring new factory workers, the unions were blamed for having driven away one of the main sources of income in the town. The recounting of these events reinforced antiunion sentiments in other areas (Sanchis 1984).

5. For example, the president of the CEOE, José María Cuevas, complained in September 1985 of the government's failure to introduce measures in compliance with the 1984 pact, the AES, which called for, among other changes, conforming Spanish labor legislation to that of the rest of the EEC. Cuevas added that entry into the Common Market would threaten Spanish business: "With our fiscal and labor policies, the only way to become competitive is by starting new firms that can qualify for public assistance or by entering into the world of the underground economy." El País, September 11, 1985.

6. On the Socialists' commitment to making the labor code more flexible, see Almunia (1983, 1984).

7. In November 1984, the Socialist Minister of Labor, Joaquín Almunia, stated that it was "necessary to try to accept the underground economy because it reflects the inadequacy of the laws." He characterized unregulated employment as a "lesser evil" and explained that the approach of the government would be to facilitate the legalization of clandestine enterprises "through the reduction of social security payments" and other, similar measures. El País, November 3, 1984. In

the same year, the government initiated a national survey on "living and working conditions in Spain," the implicit goal of which was to arrive at a measure of the informal sector. As a participant-observer on the original study team, I was very aware of pressures to produce statistical "proof" that a significant percentage of the officially unemployed population was, in fact, working informally. The results of the study did not clearly support this claim, as a second in-depth analysis of the data showed (Muro, et al. 1988). The government, however, relied on a preliminary analysis of the results to announce publicly that it had "discovered" 1,600,000 new "workers" in the economy and that the real unemployment rate was not 21.5% but only 15.9%. (Most of the "extra" workers turned out to be, on closer analysis, persons who were working so few hours, or so intermittently, that they could not be counted as "employed" by any official measures; other data from the study were very useful in describing the profile of workers in the informal sector, although this goal was never a priority.) This focus on appropriate measures of the informal sector deflected attention from more substantive debates about the government's policies toward changes in the labor code and industrial restructuring (see Parra 1988).

8. In fact, the bill to implement a reconversion program in the shoe industry was introduced by the Communist Party and was originally opposed by the UCD. The threatened dissent of a faction of UCD delegates from the Valencian region forced the government to issue the decree-law creating reconversion in the sector.

9. Interview on February 4, 1985, with Luis Escauriaza, then Director of the *Instituto de la Pequeña y Mediana Empresa Industrial* (Institute of Small and Medium Industrial Firms, or IMPI) under the Socialists.

10. Interview with the mayor of Paracuellos del Jarama, May 1985. See also the study by Celada, López, and Parra (1985).

11. These observations are based on interviews with town officials and local entrepreneurs conducted in April and May, 1985. The figures derive from a survey conducted for the regional government by the municipality in 1985.

12. In May 1984, the provincial labor office reported that as a direct result of the campaign, 168 firms (equal to roughly one-fifth of the total number of legally registered firms in the area) had been legalized in the two zones affected; 1,386 workers (equal to about 7% of the officially reported labor force for the industry in those areas) had been brought

on the books. *La Verdad,* May 31, 1984; and interview with Luis Feced Navarro, inspector general for the Province of Alicante, July 1985.

13. A study of new technologies in Spain that was funded and highly praised by the Socialist government emphasized the importance of nurturing innovation among small producers but actually reinforced the government's commitment to large-scale ventures by recommending that Spain step-up efforts to "capture" foreign technology, in part by courting multinationals. See Castells et al. 1986, especially 331–34.

Chapter 8

1. See especially Stedman-Jones (1984).

2. An example of the impact such groups could exert in local and even national politics is offered by the neighborhood movement of the 1960s and early 1970s. Urban working-class residents, particularly in Madrid but also in Barcelona and some of Spain's smaller cities, formed neighborhood associations to represent their demands for better housing, improvements in infrastructure, and official recognition of areas of illegal *chabolas,* the self-constructed houses of migrants and other working-class families that covered massive areas of Spain's largest cities. This movement was successful in obtaining many of its demands, and greater activism of particular neighborhoods was rewarded with greater benefits secured from both local and national governments (Castells 1983). Although the activism of these groups has since subsided, the possibility remains that they—or others who perceive that they are being left out of deliberation over the distribution of benefits under the democratic government—would begin to organize grassroots movements that would bypass established forms of representation.

3. For a cogent discussion of these and other sources of instability in neocorporatist politics, see Schmitter (1981) and especially Sabel (1981). Linz (1981) also notes the discontinuities in the weak role of corporate groups during the Franco regime and their expected strength in bargaining in the new democracy.

4. O'Donnell's work on bureaucratic-authoritarian states was especially influential (O'Donnell 1978). In a less systematic fashion, Poulantzas's work (1976) framed the debate about the relationship between authoritarianism and economic change in southern Europe.

5. I refer mainly to Balassa (1981), although this view is echoed in many accounts of the rise of export-led growth, including some works, like

those of Amsden (1985), which are clearly not sympathetic to all of Balassa's views.

6. Two very intelligent critiques of the linking of regime changes and economic shifts in Europe are provided by Kurth (1979) and Serra (1979).

Bibliography

Aceves, Joseph. 1971. *Social change in a Spanish village*. London: Schenkman Press.

Aceves, Joseph and William Douglas, eds. 1976. *The changing faces of rural Spain*. Cambridge, Mass.: Schenkman.

Almunia Amann, Joaquín. 1983. El mercado de trabajo español: Ante la crisis económica actual. *Boletín de Estudios Económicos* 38 (119):11–22.

———. 1984. Medidas de política de empleo (1984). *Economistas* 11:114–16.

Amsden, Alice H. 1985. The state and Taiwan's economic development. In Peter Evans, Dietrich Rueschemeyer, and Theda Skocpol, eds. *Bringing the State Back In*, 78–106. Cambridge: Cambridge University Press.

Amsden, John. 1972. *Collective bargaining and class conflict in Spain*. London: LSE Monograph.

Anderson, Charles W. 1970. *The political economy of modern Spain: Policy-making in an authoritarian system*. Madison, Milwaukee, and London: University of Wisconsin Press.

Ariza, Julián. 1976. *Comisiones Obreras*. Barcelona: Editorial Avance.

Arrighi, Giovanni. 1985a. Fascism to democratic socialism: Logic and limits of a transition. In Giovanni Arrighi, ed. *Semiperipheral development: The politics of Southern Europe in the twentieth century*, 243–79. Beverly Hills, London, and New Delhi: Sage.

———, ed. 1985b. *Semiperipheral development: The politics of Southern Europe in the twentieth century*. Beverly Hills, London, and New Delhi: Sage.

Bagnasco, Arnaldo. 1977. *Tre Italie: La problematica territoriale dello svilupo italiano*. Bologna: Il Mulino.

Balassa, Bela. 1981. *The newly industrializing countries in the world economy*. New York: Permamon Press.

Banco de Bilbao. 1984. *Informe económico.* Madrid.

Behar, Ruth. 1986. *Santa María del Monte: The presence of the past in a Spanish village.* Princeton, N.J.: Princeton University Press.

Benería, Lourdes and Martha Roldán. 1987. *The crossroads of class and gender: Industrial homework, subcontracting, and household dynamics in Mexico City.* Chicago: University of Chicago Press.

Beneyto, Pere and Josep Picó. 1982. *Los sindicatos en el País Valenciano (1975–1981).* Valencia: Intituto de Alfonso el Magnánimo.

Benton, Lauren, 1986. *El trabajo a domicilio en España.* Madrid: Ministerio de Economía y Hacienda.

Berger, Suzanne. 1980. The traditional sector in France and Italy. In Suzanne Berger and Michael Piore, eds. *Dualism and Discontinuity in industrial societies,* 88–131. Cambridge: Cambridge University Press.

———, ed. 1981. *Organizing interest in Western Europe: Pluralism, corporatism, and the transformation of politics.* Cambridge: Cambridge University Press.

——— and Michael Piore. 1980. *Dualism and discontinuity in industrial societies.* Cambridge: Cambridge University Press.

Bernabé Maestre, José María. 1976. *La industria del calzado en el Valle del Vinalopó.* Valencia: Universidad de Valencia.

Bier, Alice Gail. 1980. *Crecimiento urbano y participación vecinal.* Madrid: Centro de Investigaciones Sociológicas.

Birbeck, Chris. 1979. Garbage, industry, and the "vultures" of Cali, Colombia. In Ray Bromley and Chris Gerry, eds. *Casual work and poverty in third world cities,* 161–84. New York: Wiley.

Bluestone, Barry and Bennet Harrison. 1982. *The deindustrialization of America: Plant closings, community abandonment, and the dismantling of basic industry.* New York: Basic Books.

Booth, David. 1985. Marxism and development sociology: interpreting the impasse. *World Development* 13 (7):761–87.

Bradford, Colin I., Jr. 1982. The rise of the NICs as exporters on a global scale. In Lewis Turner and Neil McMullen, eds. *The newly industrializing countries: Trade and adjustment,* 7–24. London: George Allen & Unwin.

Brandes, Stanley. 1975. *Migration, kinship and community: Tradition and transition in a Spanish village.* New York: Academic Press.

Braverman, Harry. 1974. *Labor and monopoly capitalism: The degradation of work in the twentieth century.* New York: Monthly Review Press.

Bromley, Ray. 1978. Organization, regulation and exploitation in the so-called urban informal sector: The street traders of Cali, Colombia. *World Development* 6 (9/10):1161–71.

Bromley, Ray and Chris Gerry, eds. 1979. *Casual work and poverty in Third World cities.* New York: John Wiley.

Browett, John. 1985. The newly industrializing countries and radical theories of development. *World Development* 13 (7):789–803.

Bru Parra, Segundo. 1982. La economía del País Valenciano. *Información Comercial Española* 586:9–19.

Brusco, Sebatino. 1982. The Emilian model: Productive decentralization and social integration. *Cambridge Journal of Economics* 6:167–84.

Burawoy, Michael. 1985. *The politics of production.* London: Verso.

Capecchi, Vitorio. 1989. The informal economy and the development of flexible specialization in Emilia Romagna. In Portes, Castells, and Benton, eds. *The informal economy,* 189–15. Baltimore, Md.: Johns Hopkins University Press.

Casals Couturier, Muriel and José María Vidal Villa. 1985. La economía subterranea en Sabadell. *Papeles de Economía Española* (22):395–402.

Castells, Manuel. 1983. *The city and the grassroots.* Berkeley and Los Angeles: University of California Press.

———. 1984. *The shek dip mei syndrome: Public housing and economic development in Hong Kong.* Hong Kong: University of Hong Kong.

——— et al. 1986. *El desafío tecnológico: España y las nuevas tecnologías.* Madrid: Alianza.

Castillo, Juan José. 1983. Trabajo y sindicatos. *Leviatan* (13):19–28.

Celada, Francisco, Francisco López Groh, and Tomás Parra. 1985. *Efectos espaciales de los prosesos de reorganización del sistema productivo en Madrid.* Madrid: Comunidad de Madrid.

Christopherson, Susan and Michael Storper. 1987. Flexible specialization and new forms of labor segmentation. University of California at Los Angeles, Department of Geography. Mimeo.

Collier, David, ed. 1979. *The new authoritarianism in Latin America.* Princeton, N.J.: Princeton University Press.

Collier, George. 1987. *Socialists of rural Andalusia: Unacknowledged revolutionaries of the Second Republic.* Stanford, Calif.: Stanford University Press.

Comunidad de Madrid. 1984. *La influencia de la crisis económica sobre el territorio.* Madrid: Consejería de Ordenación del Territorio, Medio Ambiente y Vivienda.

Conselleria D'Industria, Comerç I Turisme de la Generalitat Valenciana. 1984. *Planeamiento para la reestructuración del sector del juguete, vols. I and II.* Valencia: Generalitat Valenciana.

Costa Campi, Teresa and Joan Trullen Thomas. 1987. Decentrement productif et diffusion industrielle. Paper presented at the International Symposium on New Trends in Industrialization, Tunis, December.

De Oyarzábel, Miguel. 1984. Políticas de promoción industrial: El Plan Electrónico e Informático Nacional. *Economistas* 11:82–84.

De Soto, Hernando. 1987. *El otro sendero.* Buenos Aires: Sudamericana.

Díaz, José Antonio. 1977. *Luchas internas en Comisiones Obreras: Barcelona, 1964–1970.* Barcelona: Bruguera, 1977.

DOPESA. 1977. *Los trabajadores de la construcción frente a la crisis.* Barcelona: DOPESA.

Edwards, Anthony. 1979. *The new industrial countries and their impact on Western manufacturing.* London: The Economist Intelligence Unit, Ltd.

Edwards, Richard. 1979. *Contested terrain: The transformation of the workplace in the twentieth century.* New York: Basic Books.

————, M. Reich, and D. Gordon, eds. 1975. *Labor market segmentation.* Lexington, Mass.: D.C. Heath.

Estevan, Antonio. 1984. *Relaciones interindustriales entre un grupo de PYMES tecnologicamente cualificadas en la Comunidad de Madrid.* Madrid: Comunidad de Madrid.

————. 1986. *La industria electrónica en la comunidad de Madrid.* Madrid: Comunidad de Madrid.

————. 1988. *Estrategia de localización del terciario avanzado en la comunidad de Madrid.* Madrid: Comunidad de Madrid.

———— and Paul Soto. 1987. *Actuaciones de promoción industrial y tecnología en torno a la factoría de AT&T en Madrid.* Madrid: Comunidad de Madrid.

Evans, Peter. 1979. *Dependent development: The alliance of multinational, state and local capital in Brazil.* Princeton, N.J.: Princeton University Press.

Fernandez Castro, Joaquín. 1985. Una aproximación sociológica a la reconversión industrial. *Papeles de Economía Española* 22:403–24.

Fernandez-Kelly, Maria Patricia. 1983. Mexican border industrialization, female labor force participation and migration. In June Nash and Maria Patricia Fernandez-Kelly, eds. *Women, men, and the international division of labor,* 205–23. Albany, N.Y.: SUNY Press.

————. 1983. *For we are sold, I and my people* Albany, N.Y.: SUNY Press.

———— and Anna García. 1989. Informalization at the core: Hispanic women, homework and the advanced capitalist state. In Alejandro Portes, Manuel Castells and Lauren Benton, *The informal economy,* 247–64. Baltimore, Md.: Johns Hopkins University Press.

Ferri, Llibert, Jorki Muixi, and Eduardo Sanjuan. 1978. *Las huelgas contra Franco.* Barcelona: Editorial Planeta.

Forner Muñoz, Salvador. 1982. *Industrialización y movimiento obrero: Alicante 1923–1936.* Valencia: Institución Alfonso el Magnánimo.

Fortuna, Juan Carlos and Susana Prates. 1989. Informal sector versus informalized labor relations in Uruguay. In Alejandro Portes, Manuel Castells, and Lauren Benton, eds. *The informal economy,* 78–94. Baltimore, Md.: Johns Hopkins University Press.

Frank, Andre Gunder. 1969. *Capitalism and underdevelopment in Latin America.* New York: Monthly Review press.

Freeman, Susan Tax. 1970. *Neighbors: The social contract in a Castilian hamlet.* Chicago: University of Chicago Press.

Frey, Luigi. 1975. *Lavoro a domicilio e decentramiento dell'attivita produttiva nei settori tessile e dell'abbigliamento in Italia.* Milan: Franco Editore.

García de Blas, Antonio and Santos Ruesga Benito. 1982. La economía irregular en el mercado de trabajo. *Información Comercial Española* (July):91–102.

————. 1988. El trabajo no observado en Andalucía. In Enric Sanchis and

Jose Miñana, eds. *La otra economía: Trabajo negro y sector informal,* 305–40. Valencia: Edicions Alfons el Magnànim.

Gereffi, Gary. 1983. *The pharmaceutical industry and dependency in the Third World.* Princeton, N.J.: Princeton University Press.

Gilmore, David. 1980. *The people of the plain: Class and community in lower Andalusia.* New York: Columbia University Press.

Gaomez Perezagua, Rafael. 1982. Estructura empresarial y economia oculta. *Información Comercial Española* (587):109–17.

Gordon, David. 1985. Globalization or decay? Alternative perspectives on recent transformations in the world economy. Paper presented at the conference Three Worlds of Labor Economics, Department of Economics, University of Utah, Salt Lake City.

Grasa, Jorge and Julia Carricajo. 1985. Avance del estudio sobre descentralización productiva. Madrid: Comisiones Obreras. Mimeo.

Greenwood, Davydd. 1976. *Unrewarding wealth.* New York: Cambridge University Press.

———. 1986. Labor-managed systems and the *Second Industrial Divide:* The Fagor group of Mondragón. Paper presented at the Annual Meetings of the American Anthropological Association, Philadelphia.

Gutiérrez Johnson, Ana and William Foote Whyte. 1982. The Mondragón system of worker production cooperatives. In Frank Lindenfeld and Joyce Rothschild-Whitt, eds. *Workplace democracy and social change,* 177–97. Boston: Porter Sargent.

Gutman, Herbert. 1972. *Work, culture and society in industrializing America.* New York: Vintage Books.

Hansen, Edward C. 1977. *Rural Catalonia under the Franco regime.* Cambridge: Cambridge University Press.

Hart, Keith. 1973. Informal income opportunities and urban employment in Ghana. *Journal of Modern African Studies* 11:61–89.

HOAC. 1977. *CC.OO. en sus documentos: 1958–1976.* Madrid: HOAC.

Kaplan, Temma. 1977. *Anarchists of Andalusia: 1868–1903.* Princeton, N.J.: Princeton University Press.

Kenny, Michael. 1960. *A Spanish tapestry: Town and country in Castille.* London: Cohen and West.

Kenny, Michael and Mary C. Knipmeyer. 1983. Urban research in Spain: Retrospect and prospect. In Michael Kenny and D.I. Kertzer, eds. *Urban life in Mediterranean Europe*, 25–52. Urbana, Ill.: University of Illinois Press.

Kurth, James R. 1979. Industrial change and political change: A European perspective. In David Collier, ed. *The new authoritarianism in Latin America*, 319–62. Princeton, N.J.: Princeton University Press.

Lafuente Félez, Alberto. 1980. Una medición de la economía oculta en España. *Boletín de Estudios Económicos de Deuste*, 111.

Lange, Peter. 1985. Semiperiphery and core in the European context: Reflections on the postwar Italian experience. In Giovanni Arrighi, ed., *Semiperipheral development: The politics of Southern Europe in the twentieth century*, 179–219. Beverly Hills, London, and New Delhi: Sage.

Lewis, W. Arthur. 1959. *The theory of economic growth*. London: George Allen & Unwin.

Lieberman, Sima. 1982. *The contemporary Spanish economy*. London: George Allen & Unwin.

Lim, Linda. 1983. Capitalism, imperialism, and patriarchy: The dilemma of Third-World women workers in multi-national factories. In June Nash and Maria Patricia Fernandez-Kelly, eds. *Women, men, and the international division of labor*, 70–91. Albany, N.Y.: SUNY Press.

Linz, Juan. 1981. A century of politics and interest in Spain. In Suzanne Berger, ed. *Organizing interests in Western Europe: Pluralism, corporatism, and the transformation of politics*, 365–415. Cambridge: Cambridge University Press.

Lipietz, Alain. 1986. New tendencies in the international division of labor: Regimes of accumulation and modes of regulation. In A.J. Scott and M. Storper, *Production, work, territory: The geographical anatomy of industrial capitalism*, 16–39. Boston: George Allen & Unwin.

Lomnitz, Larisa. 1978. Mechanisms of articulation between shantytown settlers and the urban system. *Urban Anthropology* 7 (2):185–205.

Maravall, José María. 1978. *Dictadura y disentimiento político*. Madrid: Ediciones Alfaguara.

———. 1981. *La politica de la transición: 1975–1980*. Madrid: Taurus.

Martínez-Alier, Juan. 1971. *Labourers and landowners in southern Spain.* Totowa, N.J.: Rowman and Littlefield.

Marx, Karl. [1867] 1967. *Capital, vol. I.* New York: International Publishers.

Mas, Francisco, Joaquín Mafé, and Antonio Rico. 1982. Exportación industrial valenciano. *Información Comercial Española* (June) 132–47.

McDonogh, Gary. 1986. *Good families of Barcelona: A social history of power in the industrial era.* Princeton, N.J.: Princeton University Press.

Méndez Reyes, Pedro. 1982. Calzado. In A. Rico et al., eds. *L'Economía del País Valenciá: Estratégies sectorials, vol. II,* 325–50. Valencia: Instituió Alfons el Magnànim.

———. 1985. Repercursiones para los exportadores del ingreso en la C.E.E. El caso del calzado. Sociedad de Estudios Internacionales. Mimeo.

Migúelez Lobo, Faustino. 1982. Economía sumergida y transformaciones socio-laborales. *Boletín de Estudios Económicos* 117:439–60.

Ministry of Industry. 1983a. *Libro blanco de la reindustrialización.* Madrid: Ministry of Industry.

———. 1983b. *Plan de la industria electrónica.* Madrid: Ministry of Industry.

Mintz, Jerome. 1982. *The anarchists of Casas Viejas.* Chicago and London: University of Chicago Press.

Mintz, Sidney. 1977. The so-called world system: Local initiative and local response. *Dialectical Anthropology.* 2(4):253–270.

Moltó Calvo, M.A. 1980. La economía irregular. Una primera aproximación. *Revista Española de Economía* 3.

———. 1982. Incidencia de la economía oculta en la política económica. *Boletín de Estudios Económicos* 117.

Monds, Jean. 1975. Syndicalism and revolution in Spain: The Workers Commissions. *Radical America* 9 (2):49–77.

Moser, Caroline. 1978. Informal sector or petty commodity production: Dualism or dependence in urban development? *World Development* 6 (9/10):1041–63.

Muro, Juan et al. 1988. *Análisis de las condiciones de vida y trabajo en España.* Madrid: Ministerio de Economía y Hacienda.

Nash, June and Maria Patricia Fernandez-Kelly, eds. 1983. *Women, men, and the international division of labor.* Albany, N.Y.: SUNY Press.

O'Donnel, Guillermo. 1978. Reflections on the patterns of change in the bureaucratic-authoritarian state. *Latin American Research Review* 13:3–38.

OECD. 1979. *The impact of the newly industrializing countries on production and trade in manufactures*. Paris: OECD.

Offe, Claus. 1985. *Disorganized capitalism: Contemporary transformations of work and politics*. Cambridge, Mass.: MIT Press.

Ong, Aihwa. 1983. Global industries and Malay peasants in peninsular Malaysia. In June Nash and Patricia Fernandez-Kelly, eds. *Women, men, and the international division of labor*, 426–39. N.Y.: SUNY Press.

————. 1985. The production of subjects in high-technology industries. Paper presented at the 84th Meetings of the American Anthropological Association, Washington, D.C.

Orgiles, César. 1982. Industrial auxiliar del calzado. In A. Rico et al., eds. *L'Economía del País Valenciá: Estratégies sectorials Vol. II*, 351–56. Valencia: Instituió Alfons el Magnànim.

Parra Baño. 1988. Pretextos de empleo. In Enric Sanchis and Jose Miñana, eds. *La otra economía: Trabajo negro y sector informal*, 369–402. Valencia: Edicions Alfons el Magnànim.

Peattie, Lisa R. 1980. Anthropological perspectives on the concepts of dualism, the informal sector, and marginality in developing urban economies. *International Regional Science Review* 5:1–31.

Pérez Díaz, Victor. 1984. Política económica y pactos sociales en la España de la transición: La doble cara del neocorporatismo. In Juan Linz and E. García de Enterría, eds. *España: Un presente para un futuro, vol. I*, 21–55. Madrid: Instituto de Estudios Económicos.

————. 1985. Gobernabilidad y mesogobiernos: Autonomías regionales y neocorporatismo en España. *Papeles de Economía Española* 21:2–39.

Perlman, Janice. 1976. *The myth of marginality*. Berkeley: University of California Press.

Pesce, Adele. 1987. Trajectoires de femmes dans la famille ouvrière. *Annales de Vaucresson* 1 (26):149–67.

Picó Lopez, Josep. 1976. *Empresario e industrialización*. Madrid: Editorial Tecnos.

Pitt-Rivers, Julian. 1954. *The people of the Sierra.* London: Weidenfeld and Nicolson.

Piore, Michael J. 1980a. Dualism as a response to flux and uncertainty. In Suzanne Berger and Michael Piore, *Dualism and discontinuity in industrial societies,* 23–54. Cambridge: Cambridge University Press.

Piore, Michael J. 1980b. The technological foundations of dualism and discontinuity. In Suzanne Berger and Michael Piore. *Dualism and discontinuity in industrial societies,* 55–82. Cambridge: Cambridge University Press.

Piore, Michael J. and Charles F. Sabel. 1984. *The second industrial divide.* New York: Basic Books.

Portes, Alejandro. 1983. The informal sector: Definitions, controversy, and relation to national development. *Review* 7 (1):151–74.

——— and Lauren Benton. 1984. Industrial development and labor absorption: A reinterpretation. *Population and Development Review* 10 (4):589–611.

——— and John Walton. 1981. *Labor, class, and the international system.* New York and London: Academic Press.

———, Manuel Castells, and Lauren Benton, eds. 1989. *The informal economy: Studies in advanced and developing countries.* Baltimore, Md.: Johns Hopkins University Press.

Poulantzas, Nicos. 1976. *The crisis of the dictatorships: Portugal, Greece, Spain.* London: NLB.

Prates, Susana. 1985. *Trabajo femenino e incorporación de tecnología: El 'putting-out system' en la industria del cuero en Uruguay.* Montevideo, Urguay: CIESU.

Recio, Albert and Fausto Miguélez. 1988. Economía sumergida y organización productiva en Cataluña. In Enric Sanchis and Jose Miñana, eds. *La otra economía: Trabajo negro y sector informal,* 341–68. Valencia: Edicions Alfons el Magnànim.

Roseberry, William. 1983. *Coffee and capitalism in the Venezuelan Andes.* Latin American Monographs No. 59. Austin: University of Texas.

Ruesga Benito, Santos. 1984. Economía oculta y mercado de trabajo. *Información Comercial Española* (607):55–61.

Saba, A. 1981. *La industria subterránea. Un nuevo modelo de desarrollo.* Valencia: Institut Alfons el Magnànim.

Sabel, Charles F. 1981. The internal politics of trade unions. In Suzanne Berger, ed. *Organizing interests in Western Europe: Pluralism, corporatism, and the transformation of politics,* 209–44. Cambridge: Cambridge University Press.

————. 1982. *Work and politics.* Cambridge: Cambridge University Press.

————. 1987. The reemergence of regional economies. Massachusetts Institute of Technology. Mimeo.

———— and Jonathan Zeitlin. 1985. Historical alternatives to mass production: Politics, markets, and technology in nineteenth-century industrialization. *Past and Present* 108:133–76.

Sanchis, Enric. 1984. *El trabajo a domicilio en el País Valenciano.* Madrid: Ministerio de Cultura, Instituto de la Mujer.

Sanchis, Enric and Jose Miñana, eds. 1988. *La otra economía: Trabajo negro y sector informal.* Valencia: Edicions Alfons el Magnànim.

Santos, Felix, José Manuel Arija, and Seguismundo Crespo. 1976. *Trabajadores en huelga: Madrid enero '76.* Madrid: Editorial Popular.

Schmitter, Philippe. 1979. Still the century of corporatism? In Philippe Schmitter and G. Lehmbruck, eds. *Trends toward corporatist intermediation,* 7–52. Beverly Hills: Sage.

————. 1981. Interest intermediation and regime governability in contemporary Western Europe and North America. In Suzanne Berger, ed. *Organizing interests in Western Europe: Pluralism, corporatism, and the transformation of politics,* 285–327. Cambridge:Cambridge University Press.

————. 1984. Patti e transizioni: Mezzi non-democratici a fini democratici? *Revista Italiana di Scienza Politica* 14:363–82.

Sengenberger, Werner and Gary Loveman. 1987. *Smaller units of employment: A synthesis report on industrial reorganization in industrialized countries.* Geneva: Institute for Labor Studies.

Serra, Jossé. 1979. Three mistaken theses regarding the connection between industrialization and authoriarian regimes. In David Collier, ed. *the new authoritarianism in Latin America,* 99–163. Princeton, N.J.: Princeton University Press.

Solé, Carlota. 1987. El sistema asociativo empresarial en el sector textil español. In Carlota Solé, ed. *Corporatismo y diferenciación regional*, 211–49. Madrid: Ministerio de Trabajo y Seguridad Social.

Stedman Jones, Gareth. 1984. *Outcast London*. New York: Pantheon Books.

Storper, Michael and Susan Christopherson. 1985. *The changing organization and location of the U.S. motion picture industry*. Los Angeles: UCLA School of Urban Planning. Research monograph #127.

Thompson, E.P. 1964. *The making of the English working class*. New York: Pantheon Books.

————. 1967. Time, work discipline, and industrial capitalism. *Past and Present* 38:56–97.

Tokman, Victor. 1978. Competition between the informal and formal sectors in retailing: The case of Santiago. *World Development* 6 (9/10):1187–89.

Trigo Portela, Joaquín and M. Carmen Vázquez Arango. 1983. Opciones y criterios de política económica para la emerción de la economía irregular y un intento de fundamentación. Paper presented at the Jornadas de Estudio sobre Economía Sumergida, Madrid.

Trouillot, Michel-Rolph. 1982. Motion in the system: Coffee, color and slavery in eighteenth-century Saint-Dominque. *Review* 5:331–88.

Truelove, Cynthia. 1989. *Factories in the fields of plenty: Gender, agrarian transformation, and industrial restructuring in the southwestern regional economy of Colombia*. Doctoral dissertation, Department of Sociology, Johns Hopkins University, Baltimore, Md.

Turner, Lewis and Neil McMullen, eds. 1982. *The newly industrializing countries: Trade and adjustment*. London: George Allen & Unwin.

Vara Miranda, Jesús. 1985. *Análisis de las cooperatives de trabajo asociado en Madrid*. Madrid: Ministerio de Trabajo y Seguridad Social.

Vázquez Arango, Carmen and Joaquín Trigo Portela. 1982. Las vías de transformación de la economía formal en irregular. *Información Comercial Española* 587:81–89.

Verdery, Katherine. 1983. *Transylvanian villagers: Three centuries of political, economic and ethnic change*. Berkeley, Los Angeles, and London: University of California Press.

Wade, Robert. 1983. South Korea's agricultural development: The myth of the passive state. *Pacific Viewpoint* 24 (1):11–28.

Wallerstein, Immanuel. 1985. The relevance of the concept of the semiperiphery to Southern Europe. Pp. 31–39 in Giovanni Arrighi, ed. *Semiperipheral development: The politics of Southern Europe in the twentieth century*, 31–39. Beverly Hills, London, and New Delhi: Sage.

Wolf, Eric. 1982. *Europe and the people without history*. Berkeley, Los Angeles, and London: University of California Press.

Worsley, Peter. 1984a. *The three worlds: Culture and world development*. Chicago: University of Chicago Press.

Wozniak, Lynne. 1990. *Economic orthodoxy and industrial protest*. Doctoral dissertation. Department of Government, Cornell University.

Wright, Alison. 1977. *The Spanish economy 1959–1976*. London and Basingstoke: MacMillan Press.

Ybarra, Josep-Antoni. 1982. La reestructuración de la industria del calzado español: Aspectos laborales y territoriales. *Boletín de Estudios Económicos* (117):483–503.

———— and José Antonio Manteca. 1986. Sector calzado: Presente y futuro. Alicante: University of Alicante. Mimeo.

Index